Praise for *Little Big Man*

Wonderful. An addictive book! Stanley J. Browne could have died many times. Thankfully he lived to tell the tale of his remarkable life.

All the darkness and light can be found in this line 'My locks hang like curtains on a window to a lost soul.'

—Lemn Sissay, author of *My Name is Why*

A haunting and important book written by an indomitable spirit. There is so much life, and suffering, and love in these pages that no reader with a heart could not fail to be moved.

—Katy Massey, author of *Are We Home Yet?*

Little
Big
Man

A story of survival, redemption
and belonging

Stanley J. Browne

JACARANDA

This edition first published in Great Britain 2022
Jacaranda Books Art Music Ltd
27 Old Gloucester Street,
London WC1N 3AX
www.jacarandabooksartmusic.co.uk

Most names have been changed and dialogue and events have been recreated.

A CIP catalogue record for this book is available from the British Library

ISBN: 9781913090869
eISBN: 9781913090876

Cover Design: Rodney Dive
Typeset by: Kamillah Brandes

For my mother, Joy
(Joy: a feeling of great pleasure and happiness)

And my son, Malakai
(Hebrew: meaning 'my messenger')

To my Mother,

It's hard to put into words the overwhelming feelings that can still flow through me all these years later. It took a lot of courage to acknowledge the pain, struggles, and sheer trauma myself and siblings faced coping with your mental illness. Yet, there is a special place that lives on inside of me and continues to shine the light on the abundance of love you gave to us before the clouds set in. Those memories may have become faded, but they are never forgotten. Some say the definition of a good mother, is a mother who always puts her children first. You always put us first, until you were incapable of controlling the demons that plagued you. Still, in the mist and fog, you never forgot us and showed up wherever we were taken, refusing to leave your kids behind no matter what state of mind you were in.

Yes, I remember. You were and are still my hero.

Looking back, I guess I never really did quite get over my first true love. A Mother, a Mummy, a Nana. Your children and your grandchildren miss you. You were gone way too soon even before you passed.

Writing this memoir is my homage to you. To acknowledge your journey, to tell your story, our story. A chance for us all to heal and to help others who may have travelled the same path or suffered a similar fate to ours, by sharing our truth. I have not forgotten you and refuse to leave you behind.

Thank you for being my mummy.

A letter to the reader

I first started writing this memoir in 2005. Due to life's ups and downs, work and family, I dipped in and out of it over the years, but for the most part, it remained on the shelf in my computer. I printed a hard copy at the time for my ex-neighbours Karen and Tim to proofread, both journalists working for major newspaper companies, who gave me invaluable feedback encouraging me to finish my book. I always knew that day would come when I could finally get down to the nuts and bolts and do just that.

I picked it back up again in 2019 whilst on a three-month theatre tour around the UK. The tour ended in December of that year, and I found myself putting a proposal together for the book during the first lockdown early in 2020. The timing could not have been more perfect for me to seize this opportunity to finish what I had started all those years ago. If I'm honest, I guess part of my procrastination was I didn't feel quite ready to share my inner most story with the world just yet. The fear of being critiqued by exposing myself was uncomfortable, but to lay bare my soul in this way needed a different type of courage all together.

To help me to find that courage, I read autobiographies back-to-back. They became my staple over the years and kept burning the fire of my desire to write it all down. I was moved, touched, and inspired by their bravery to bare all unapologetically.

For some, my story may be a little hard to digest. Growing

up with a schizophrenic mother was traumatising, and there were times, after I decided to finish the memoir, when it was a struggle to revisit the memories of that trauma and get though the day. So why would I choose to share such pain and anguish? Why would I choose to bare my soul to the world? The answer to that is; I am not alone. I am not alone with my story. I know others have shared the same or similar fates. Through sharing my story, I hope to be of service in some way by reaching out to help those who have suffered or are suffering to overcome and heal from the wreckage of their pasts. If you can relate to what I have shared, then you are not alone. I send you a huge, warm hug for surviving your past as I and countless of others have done. For those who have never had any of the experiences I have shared, I bow to your humanity and courage for keeping an open mind and thank you for taking the time to read this memoir.

Prologue

I am a Soldier. I am dressed in green military fatigues and a gold dog tag swings from my neck. I have an audience, held captive within the four walls of this theatre, and I tell them. I tell them everything. This proud, accomplished General has worked his way up through the ranks. Whatever was needed, I did it. Whatever it took to be seen, to be feared, to be recognised, I acted on it. I had no boundaries, when it came to war.

I am 40 years old. I still don't know how I've made it to this age. From a young boy I've known nothing but battles. The scars are largely hidden now, but I'm well versed in disaster. I've run headlong into adventure. I've been lost over and over, enslaved by my past, but somehow I've always found freedom. Worst of all are the tales I can tell of my fellow men. I've watched those cannibals, grasping at survival, turn inward to eat each other.

I lower my head slowly and look across the auditorium. All I can hear now is the faint white noise of the air-con. I hold out my forearms in surrender. I am playing the part well. It's the part I've rehearsed all my life. Othello is about to become undone. When there are no more battles on the horizon left for him to fight, he'll also turn inward. He'll buckle under the trick that society has played on him. Iago, his standard-bearer, will destroy him. In his hatred of the Moor, he'll convince Othello that Desdemona, his new wife, is deceiving him. Her whiteness, the whiteness of the Venetian aristocracy Othello has married into, will show him up to be the black, barbarous outsider it wants him to be.

This tragedy is hard. I am consumed by it. By the time I place a pillow over the mouth of my sweet, innocent wife and suffocate her before turning a knife on myself, my chest is rising and falling with exhaustion. My knees give way, and I collapse to the ground and lay beside Desdemona's lifeless body. The sweat trickles down my arms.

An anxious pause before the lights illuminate the room. I stand smiling and bow to three hundred faces. Three hundred pairs of hands are clapping. There are whoops and whistles. I feel over-whelmed, and my chest swells with pride. But I know that back-stage, when I sit in front of the mirror and wipe the make-up from my cheeks, I will remind myself that this is not my story. That I will not be applauded for mine. That I died before I ever lived. Still, at my core, I'm rock solid. I am the General that Othello used to be. I am a Soldier.

Chapter 1

Nine Nights

It's June 2000 and I am 29 years old. I'm looking out to a packed hall at Manor Park Crematorium in East London. It is bare but for the noisy, haphazard congregation bursting out from the rows of oak pews stretching up from the small, raised platform where I now stand. The summer sun streams through the stained glass windows—the only real interior decoration signalling that this is a place of devotion. Not that I, or any of my close family, cling to religion. I can relate to Vine Victor Deloria, Jr, the Native American author who said, 'Religion is for those who're afraid to go to hell. Spirituality is for those who've already been there.' Yes, I have been to hell and back.

I take my time, holding the crowd in my gaze. In another England, another person might paper over the cracks. White lies to make the living feel better: the deceased was loved; the deceased was cared for; the family was supported. All the loose ends of their messy lives tied up in a neat bow and delivered to an audience complicit in the deceit. But that is not my England. These are my people, and this is a day for truth—my truth.

This is the day we lay to rest my mother, Joy Rosemary Patricia Brown.[1]

---

1   Both my mother and father had the surname 'Brown'. Although they were never married, throughout the Caribbean the enslaved would be given the surname of their owners. The 'Brown's' owned plantations in Jamaica and Antigua. For years, my biological father believed his surname was Browne with an 'e'. After returning to his birth certificate decades later, he learned this was incorrect. I have inherited my father's ghostly 'e' alongside this history.

People are shifting uncomfortably in their seats now. But I stand firm. I want to look into the eyes of every person before I speak. Some know my story; others have heard paler versions.

Among those who have arrived here on the two coaches are members of my sprawling family, whose tentacles stretch out way beyond my bloodline. On my mother's side, relatives have flown in from New York. My biological father, Anthony, is here too. He also arrived from the States—the first time I have seen him in 12 years. Others have travelled from Birmingham or crossed the river from South London. Then, there are neighbours who, from the windows of their council houses, would have watched my mother for years, striding across the cul-de-sac, pausing on her journey to cuss someone, or something out, returning hours later after she'd walked and walked, often soaked by this country's interminable rain.

One day, she disappeared. I've often wondered whether they noticed straight away, or whether they noticed at all. In the preceding months before Mum's passing, the blisters on her feet, brought on by her diabetes, had gotten so infected she became housebound, like a bird trapped in a cage, at times hardly even bothering to get out of bed.

When news spread that she'd passed they all came, of course. They came out of the woodwork. Over the past two weeks my sisters, Angie and Mini, our younger brother Huggy and I, channelled Mum's once-fearsome spirit. With military precision, and none of the usual bickering, we arranged today's funeral and opened up her home in Hackney for nine consecutive days and nights, as is her Jamaican tradition, a celebration of her life rather than a commiseration of her death. Each day tumbled into the next. The trickle of mourners became a swell, flowing in and out of every room, rising and subsiding from late afternoon into the early hours, the sound of raised animated voices, mingled with the old-school reggae music, bubbling away in the background from Mum's stereo. Any stranger walking past Mum's house would have thought it was more of a party than a funeral.

'Wah-gwan Stan! Long-time, no-see. It's me man, come fi pay mi respects.' They all said this, bumping fists as they ducked under the branches of the big-arse tree that's grown wild and unruly and part-covers Mum's front door. Planted from a single apricot kernel, it was one of Mum's living creations that grew larger than life, taking over the three-foot-square patio, bending the perimeter fence. Now it sits at an angle, twisting like a bonsai tree, precariously supporting heavy new growth.

I know the faces, but I've forgotten many of the names. 'You noh 'member mi but mi know yu from yu ah bwoy. Mi know yu muddah from long, long time,' they said. I hugged them back and gave them my best smile.

My eyes rest on my older sister Angie. Today, she is inconsolable. The tears have made her face puffy and the wetness glistens on her cheeks. She's been like this for days. During Nine Nights, I lost count of the number of times I watched her as she ferried pots of curry goat and rice and peas from the kitchen to the living room, disappeared, and then returned to gather up the empty dishes. She did it with a frown she made no attempt to hide. On the occasions her emotions gave way, she'd collapse into the sofa sobbing while a comforting arm was placed around her. But mainly she kept her grief, and her anger, knotted up inside.

I did the same, but the hollowness of it all had gotten to me, and at times I had to leave. 'I'm gone,' I'd said to Angie in a hushed voice before slipping out, back to the safety of my own flat. Or, taking a breather in the back garden, I'd filled my lungs up with the fresh air to bursting, and slowly exhaled, allowing the tension to soften. I felt suffocated by our sense of duty—by our doing what was expected to be done.

Only a few weeks earlier I was thousands of miles from here, on the first leg of a round-the-world-trip. I had just landed in India and casually checked into an internet cafe in Mumbai filled with backpackers. I clicked on the mouse to fire up the clunky old computer in the booth and waited a lifetime until I could finally open my emails. As the screen flickered, I read and reread Angie's words. Mum had suffered several heart attacks. She'd died on June 11, 2000, at the tender age of 49. 'I'm coming home,' I signed off.

That was weeks ago, but it feels as if it's been years. That day I headed back to my guest house on autopilot, filtering out the sounds of horns and engines from the Mumbai traffic, bumpers nuzzling bumpers and weaving in and out of the long queues of tuk-tuks and chaiwallah stands selling, hot sweet tea. *She's finally gone. She's finally at peace.*

With help from staff, I managed to get myself an emergency ticket home that very same evening. During the night-flight back to London, I'd turned over in my mind the last conversation I had with Mum. I'd felt a compulsion to tell her she'd appeared in our dreams, maybe as a way of protecting her. Fate was circling, ready to swoop down. It was information Mum needed to know and I was confident she'd have no fear. Mum embraced spirituality, and all that it entailed. She would occasionally extradite ghosts—the duppies—from our childhood home in Stoke Newington, telling us they'd got stuck in transition to the other side. 'Please leave now,' she'd say respectfully, as she took a pinch of salt in between her thumb and forefinger and threw it left, then right, across her shoulders.

In my dream, Mum had been suspended above my bed. I laid there mesmerised by her face, not scared, just at ease. 'I'm okay Stan. Don't you worry about me,' she said. Her ghostly presence felt normal, soothing even. When I told my siblings, it turned out they'd all had premonitions, too. Mum had visited them at different times and appeared in different forms, but we all agreed it was a sign. So I took it upon myself to broach the subject of what she might want, should anything happen to her.

'Bon mi, den put mi ashes in di ocean,' she answered matter-of-factly.

'You want to be burned like some witch? Are you sure, Mum?'

'Yes, bon me. I've always wanted to travel but mi never get the chance.'

That thought rested with me. Mum always did have the ability to disarm a person, summing up the complexity of a lifetime with a few choice words. To lighten the mood, I picked her up and swung her around in an embrace which always sent her into a fit of uncontrollable giggles.

'Mum, maybe I shouldn't go backpacking? I can put it off,' I told her.

'Don't be a silly-billy. Make sure that you go. I'll be okay,' she reassured me before grabbing the end of my nose in between her knuckles and giving it a vice-like squeeze that made me feel like a little boy again. That afternoon I sat on the sofa for the longest time, watching her shuffle around the room, turning to smile at me, bringing me cups of tea. For so long Mum's humanity and kindness had been present only in the abstract: qualities that had to be imagined. Not that day, though. I stayed and warmed myself on her rare glow.

That's the Joy they've all come to remember, too. As well as our many cousins, Mum's estranged brothers and sister are here. Mum's long-time friend Auntie Beryl, and our uncle Winston, Mum's first cousin, (but out of respect we call him uncle), now well into his sixties—all have been permanent fixtures on Mum's sofa which is now sitting amongst the ever-increasing bodies all jostling for space in her council house ever since Nine Nights began. The L-shaped living room, where the table and chairs have been positioned at one end, has been commandeered by old men playing dominoes. They sit, slamming down the tiles with cries of 'Take this bwoy!' and 'Gimmie wat mi want!' Others stand around, peering into the hands of each player, chewed up toothpicks protruding from the sides of their mouths. 'Leggo di tile noh man, whappen to yu!'

Many still wear the long trench coats they arrived in, an old-school style of dress, juggling plates of food and, after the clean glasses ran out, teacups of rum balanced awkwardly in their hands. Yes. All the 'long-time, no-sees' have come to resurrect their stories, retelling them, as if for the first time. Beryl's sister, Auntie Pat, was always loud and proud, especially after a few shots of rum: hair pulled back, wide eyes darting around the living room, waiting until she has everyone in the palm of her hand.

'Lawd Jesus! Mi member wen Joy run down di ice-cream van one ah di time because him wouldn't serve her, and she stan-up in front ah di van fi stop im from go anywhere!'

Mum had always stuck two fingers up at the doctors who'd warned her about her diabetes and told her to curb her daily ice-cream fix. There were days when she'd indeed chase down the ice-cream van or push past in front of the waiting kids to guarantee her place at the front of the queue. Sometimes she wouldn't even pay, but the ice-cream man always let her have her way.

'Ahhhhhhh lawd jeeeeezzzus! Mi hear one piece of cussing outside mi house, so mi have to leave to find out whah gwan wid Joy. Mi seh to her, 'Joy, why you not mekking di man do im work and drive di ice-cream van?' She say to me, 'Him need to gimmie mi fucking ice-cream!''

Every story Pat told drew in more listeners. They drifted in from the dominoes end of the room or the kitchen and when there were no more chairs left, they perched on the arms of the sofas, or bunched up like sardines on the coffee table. Every now and then the room would buss-up into laughter. I also found myself squeezed in there, taken in by it all. Seduced.

My dad Anthony had his turn, too. He's always spoken with a fondness for Mum, even though they were never really together.

'Man, I tell you, Joy was something else man. She was soooooo funny.' He has a thick Antiguan accent but he stops himself from speaking patois much of the time as he thinks it's beneath him. He wants to speak the Queen's English, but every now and again patois slips through the net.

'I never met ah woman like Joy ever! Never again, she was ah one-off, and so funny. Dat woman would have you laughing and splitting your sides open in seconds. In seconds, I tell you man! So humorous. So witty, and so smart! Oh my God, Joy was so smart! Her brain was something else, man. You know she used to work in a bank, right? I think she was a bank clerk or sumting like dat...'

He tunes out, tut, tut, tutting and shaking his head from side to side as if he is alone, suspended in his own thoughts.

'Yes... she was a bank clerk. Yes, a bank clerk, dats what I just said, right? Joy was a genius when it came to mats or any kind of equation she could do all dat in her head, meanwhile I'm on mi fingers trying to keep up!'

He's right, Mum is a one-off. *Was* a one-off. He goes on to tell the story of Mum and the lipstick—the lipstick she painted all over her face. It's the first time I've heard it. It acts as evidence that Mum was always different, always precarious, and that what happened wasn't my fault or anybody else's.

'One of di time, we getting ready to go out to dis club, so Joy in the bedroom in front of the mirror, you know, putting on her make-up, so I call out to her to see if she ready yet, as you know woman dem take long. 'I'm ready,' she is shouting.'

His eyes roll, and he waits for the approving grunts from the men in the room before he carries on...

'Anyhow, so I go into di room to see what's keeping her, and Joy is sitting in front of the mirror with the red lipstick in one hand and drawing all over her face with it! I said, 'Joy! What you doing?' She look up at me in the mirror and start laughing her head off. Then she carried on drawing! I shake mi head and say, 'Alright, let me know when yu ready.' What am going to do? I couldn't do notin.'

He makes a sucking sound through his lips and 'kisses his teeth', a well-known gesture by Caribbean people all over the islands. 'But that was Joy. Oh my God, what a woman. What. A. Woman.'

Today, for the formalities at least, he's done away with his usual flowery Hawaiian shirt and cowboy boots and arrived instead in a dark suit and tie. He'll come back to the house after the ceremony, but it's my guess he won't hang around for too long.

Soon after I picked him up from the airport and dropped him off at my flat he opened up his suitcase and held up three of four cheap nylon, brightly coloured dresses—the kind you see hanging from the stalls on Ridley Road Market. I'd clocked on straight away. He'd used Mum's funeral as an excuse to get time off work (he was a security guard at one of the hospitals in Long Island, New York), and have a holiday. 'I have a few old friends to see,' he told me. He meant old flames.

A tranquillity has come over me. It's as if I'm floating. All the feelings that have been waging war inside me these past few days have calmed. I have no formal speech prepared as such, but I haven't left it to chance either. The words have been played with over and over in my mind, shifting tone and sentiment with each passing day. Now I feel liberated by a quiet, powerful rage.

I look around the room one last time. All these people who

have turned up to eat our food and drink our drink; all these people who have brought their stories and played along with the pretence of being part of our lives; all these people who vanished when the going got tough. All these people who claim to be our family.

Now I am ready to say what needs to be said.

'Joy. Rosemary. Patricia. Brown.' I pause, before repeating Mum's name.

'Joy. Rosemary. Patricia. Brown.' It's as if her spirit is inside me now, rising up to engulf me.

'I look around this room,' I say, then scan the faces staring back at me, steady, waiting. 'And I see two coach loads of people, yes?' There are nods and murmurs of agreement.

'Two coach loads…' I repeat. 'Yet where were you?

'Where were you,' I repeat, opening up my chest, 'when she needed you?' People begin looking down now, some shuffling their feet, others rummaging in their pockets for a tissue to wipe their tears.

'Where were you when we were hungry? Where were you when we were taken into the children's homes? Where were you when we needed you?'

'Here, here!' I recognise the voice immediately and glance over at my brother, Huggy. His contorted face is willing me to carry on, and he's nodding his head in approval. Angie and Mini are nodding too. I take my strength from them. I'm speaking for all of us. I point to the three of them. 'Right now, the only family in this room is this family sitting here. Where. Were. You?'

I can feel my jaw quivering now, and the emotion welling up inside of me, but the words are still coming out loud and strong. I tell them about how we'd raised ourselves. About how my sisters and I raised our little brother Huggy, nine years my junior. I describe how they'd all been there for the good times, but how all but a handful had disappeared from our lives. How could they let it happen? How could they let the authorities step in when we had so-called family around us? Where were *my* people? I ask them.

'Yes Stanley! Talk it up!' I hear my Uncle Ashley, who is sat on the wings. He's not blood family, but I acknowledge him as one of the people who tried his best. This slim, wiry Rastaman who used to come to our house to bring us food only to be chased back by Mum again and again.

'Our mummy died a long, long time ago,' I tell them. 'But my heart is full to the brim when I see the legacy in her children and the grandchildren she's left behind. She still lives on in each and every one of us.'

I walk to the back of the platform and stand to the side of Mum, lying in her open casket. She has on a simple blue dress and looks serene, but for the life of me, it seems like the corner of her mouth is turned up ever so slightly into a smile, as if there's a part of her enjoying their discomfort. I bend and give her one final hug. I can almost feel her heartbeat, even though her body is cold.

I'm half-expecting people to stand up, file out in silence, in disgust or denial. Instead, the opposite happens. I hear clapping and turn to see my brother Huggy on his feet clapping wildly by himself. Others follow suit, rising up one by one and joining in the applause. Soon the whole room is on their feet and clapping. I hear, 'Nice one Stan! Nuff respect, Stan,' as I stroll over to my family and put my arms around Huggy and my sisters, squashing my little nephew and niece stuck in the middle. Suddenly, it dawns on me. This is the first time these people have ever heard me. This is the first time they've seen who I truly am. Maybe it's the first time I've really seen myself too.

Chapter 2

Hackney

I was born Stanley James Browne on December 15, 1970, at the Mother's Hospital in Clapton. As with much of London's East End, the building has long since been converted into flats, but it's where I began life—a first son to Joy and a baby brother to my sister Angie, who is one year older. The hospital was built by the Salvation Army more than a hundred years earlier as a maternity home for poor, unmarried mothers. I started out oblivious to those labels. To me, I was one of the lucky ones.

I was three years old when Mum got rehoused. Overnight, we went from a dilapidated council flat several storeys up in the run-down Powell House Estate in Hackney, to a three-bedroomed converted Victorian terrace house at 37B Alkham Road in Stoke Newington: classic London stock brick frontage with a bright green wooden door.

It was only through sheer luck that Mum managed to get it. Auntie Beryl always paced around the front room gazing up at the high ceilings. 'Joy, mi can't believe yu get a big ol 'ouse like this!' she said. As well as being Mum's best friend, Beryl had lived opposite us in Powell House before it got demolished but ended up being relocated to another Hackney council estate. Getting a council house on a residential road was like finding gold dust. People who didn't want to be rehoused in the high-rise blocks of flats often feigned agoraphobia to get a house similar to ours or, worst case scenario, get put on the ground floor of a high rise.

My sister Mini was born one year after me, and she, Angie, and I became a tight-knit trio. Angie was the quieter, moodier sister who joined in but also needed time on her own. Mini was more of a hurricane: quick to lash out and a daredevil, but willing and big-hearted. She took her lead from me: hard-headed, with a swagger mimicked from the men around me, but also caring and eager to please. A therapist would later describe me as 'The Hero Child'—the child who masks a family's dysfunction by showing to the outside world how perfect they are; a child who acts at being brave and strong to save face. There was much truth in that.

We were also different insofar as each of us had different dads—a fact that was never explained to us. It just was. Although they were reunited many years later, Angie's dad, Norman, rarely came to Alkham Road. Like a heavy burden, *my* dad came almost every other Sunday or once per month. He would wait outside in his car with the window rolled down and beep-beep his horn until I bolted down the steps and jumped in. He'd take me back to his place where I'd get plonked on the sofa while he watched the cricket. For me, it was like watching paint dry. He never once did anything with me, fly a kite, kick a ball, nothing, just waited for the time to pass so he could take me back home. Mum called him boring—a regular nine-to-five guy who always worked and never wanted to go out and have fun. They dated briefly before Mum got pregnant with me but by the time I was born, Linton, Mini's dad, was on the scene. My dad hadn't put up a fight. He'd been working an evening job as a club bouncer when an expensive Jaguar pulled up. Linton stepped out—tailored suit, silk shirt and tie and a cashmere coat draped around his shoulders. Mum was on his arm, dolled up to the nines as he bowled into the club, stepping up into my dad's face.

'Ah yu name Anthony? Yu see Joy? Ah my woman now,' Linton announced as they swept past. My dad's response had been a simple shrug. 'What was I gonna do? I'm not gonna fight over a woman with a gangster!' he said retelling me the story.

Alkham Road was a bizarre mix of outsiders shielding themselves from an inhospitable world. Opposite ours there was a three-storey house filled with several generations of one Indian family. Greek Cypriots lived a few doors down to the right. Orthodox Jews with their long beards and tall, black hoiche or squat, fur shtreimel hats passed under our sash windows going to, or returning from, the synagogue up the street. And there were Muslims who wore taqiyah skull caps and long thawb robes that swung freely around their feet when they walked, and there were other Black and mixed-race families. We played and sometimes fought with each other, but mainly we all got on to some degree until the next squabble took place. As young kids, we became walking tea-trays ferrying samosas back to our house gifted by the Indians, or stuffed vine leaves from the Greeks. 'Take this to your mum,' they'd say, and we'd return the favour with fried plantain, or salt fish or banana fritters that were dipped in Mum's special homemade spicy batter and fried until brown and crispy—to take to Mrs So-and-So.

Although it was said that Mum had been a bank clerk, I always picture her at home. Apparently, she had started out working at Lloyds Bank near Liverpool Street, getting her certificate in accountancy, but no one ever mentioned it other than my dad and Aunty Beryl. One of my earliest memories is me being around three years old, of Mum dropping us off at a house and being taken to a basement room where other kids were playing. From the downstairs window I could look up to street level and follow the passing traffic of legs and heels or wide-bottomed trousers. I recognised immediately Mum's slim calves and her boots when she stopped for a moment on her way out before turning and walking away. For the rest of the day, I bawled my eyes out and the child-minder had to keep pulling me away from the glass pane. I have no memory of ever going back after Mum picking us up later that day, noticed we were soiled, and told the woman about herself for not changing our nappies.

Mum walked everywhere and we fell in with her rhythm. We'd accompany her to Stoke Newington High Street—to the butchers with its sawdust floor and pigs' heads hanging on hooks from the ceiling. Or we'd go to Woolworths, or to the Post Office, where Mum would reach into her handbag and draw out her benefit book, which was duly stamped before a bunch of notes slid out from under the glass security screen onto the counter. On the way home, we'd pass the launderettes, the second-hand clothes stores and the cascade of fruits and vegetables stacked up on the pavement outside corner shops. Dirty, derelict buildings with smashed-out windows punctuated the row, but when we turned the corner into the safety of Alkham Road, the huge London plane trees that lined each pavement formed an arch in the middle, as if they were bowing to greet each other. If Mum was feeling naughty, she'd suddenly break free from us, press her forefinger up against her lips, 'Shhhhhhh', and run up and tap a neighbour's letterbox before legging it back down. 'Run!' she'd shout. Whenever she played Knock Down Ginger we knew we had to run for our lives: run and run until that moment when the heavy bolt on our front door banged shut behind us and we could breathe again.

If the street outside had a sameness about it, our house was like stepping inside a kaleidoscope. From our hallway, up the stairs and throughout each room, Mum had decorated with a white and yellowish daisy-flowered wallpaper. The uneven floorboards had been covered with a retro, bright red-and-yellow-flowered lino that you could spill anything on, and with a quick wipe, it would smile right back at you. Yet within the swirl of colour was the uniformity of routine. Mum was up early most mornings to bake bread. By the time we washed, brushed our teeth, combed our hair and had our skins creamed down with Vaseline, the same Vaseline used to moisturise our hair and scalp, which would turn a dull white if my hair was wet and I would have to rub it in for ages to get the shine back, a loaf of bread would be waiting for us and we'd eat it alongside cornmeal porridge stirred in with condensed milk and sprinkled with nutmeg and vanilla essence.

The way she appears to me now, I can see Mum moving effortlessly around that tight galley kitchen. As if she were a goddess. Cornmeal cake would emerge from the oven. Just a simple recipe of cornmeal, sugar, eggs, butter and vanilla, but to us it tasted like heaven. And we'd make each slice last forever, right down to the crumbs. Corned beef from a tin and rice with sweetcorn mixed in, plus fried dumplings on the side dripping in butter—oh man, that was my favourite. And she'd show us simple things: how to soak the red kidney beans for the rice and peas, or how to season the chicken for Sunday dinner. 'Not-ah-lot, but enough.' It was a mantra Mum repeated daily, usually before we were about to eat.

'Not-ah-lot' wasn't measurable to us in any way, but we heard and saw things. Auntie Beryl, for example, came once a week to collect Mum's money for the Pardner—the unofficial bank organised within the Caribbean community. Members would put a tenner or £20 or more in each week depending on which Pardner they were part of, and then take it in turns to draw out a pooled sum. If there were ten members of a £10 Pardner, then each month a member would draw £400 before it moved in rotation to the next person. We always overheard the elders complaining that no bank would ever loan 'people like us' money, but of how they dreamed of putting a deposit on a house or having enough savings to go on holiday.

Whatever Mum could pay for, it was always a struggle to heat the house. Each floor was damp and cold. We only had four heaters, two paraffin and two electric, that we moved from room to room. The electric heaters would only get switched on when our two paraffin heaters ran out of fuel or when guests came. When Mum had parties, known as *blues parties*, one heater would sit downstairs in the hallway, pumping out a steady flow of warm air. Angie and Mini were allowed one in their room too, maybe because there were two of them and only one of me. Or maybe because they were girls and I was expected to tough it out.

On winter nights when I slipped under my damp sheets and my feet hit the cold patch at the bottom of the bed, then snapped into the foetal position, I'd lie there imagining myself tiptoeing up the stairs to my sisters' room, creaking open their heavy asbestos door, wiggling the heater plug from its socket as if it was a loose tooth, and stealing it while they were sleeping. Most of the time this was not merely a fantasy. However, Mum had a habit of checking in on me not long after I'd gone to bed, so I would have to wait for the inspection first before making any moves. The light would flick on and I'd look up at her with squinted eyes, which I'd rub to feign sleep.

'Open yu mouth, liff-up yu arms, good boy.' Mum sniffed me in the same way a lioness does a cub to make sure I'd made good on my promise of washing my body and brushing my teeth. Sometimes she wrapped her lips over her teeth and nuzzled my neck, biting playfully while I shook with laughter.

'Yu-say yu-prayer?' That question always took me by surprise, because if I could get away with not saying them, I would. But Mum made us say *Our Father* every night, plus any other lines she wanted to adlib; it was more out of habit than faith. But she wasn't religious. She told us, this wide and vast universe possessed a power greater than us, and it was busy carrying out humble duties for all of mankind. That's why we had to always give thanks for life.

When we got a little older, she left it up to us to decide whether we went to church. We did go, but it had nothing to do with Jesus. Every Sunday morning without fail, a sky-blue minibus would pull up and collect the Bryce family that lived a few doors down. Identical to us, they were West Indian, but they had four children with the same mum and dad. We were Black, but different. Besides, they had strong boundaries. I never saw the inside of their house. If ever I went to knock for their youngest son Leo, I was made to stand and wait outside the front door. Sometimes, the door wouldn't shut properly and I could sneak a peak of the hallway then pretend I wasn't looking when I heard footsteps coming down the stairs. On Sunday, they would file out in ironed suits and pretty dresses and patent leather shoes. They were perfect and shiny, and we were curious. 'Where do they go dressed up like that?' we asked ourselves. 'What happens at this place called church?'

'We're all part of this universe and don't let anyone tell you any different,' Mum repeated to us after we pleaded to join them. She must have known that this place we wanted to see wasn't going to welcome us in with open arms, even though it was full of people who sang and prayed to the Lord Jesus and pretended that their shit didn't stink. She was right. It didn't take us long to see, but more than that, *feel*, that this was not our tribe. We didn't have shiny suits and dresses, though Mum would have made sure we dressed up smart.

Worse than that, the musky smell of pews and the high arches seemed so alien; everything was grey and dim, as if watching TV in black and white, compared to the warmth and colour of our house, with its array of friends and family members who came and went. And the gospel according to Mum. Thou shalt not lie, cheat, cuss each other out and definitely not cuss elders or call them by their first names. Manners and politeness mattered. Everyone who came to visit, blood related or not, was to be called Auntie or Uncle, otherwise we'd get a box across the head. For the neighbours, Mr or Mrs would suffice. Children should be seen and not heard; this was sacrosanct.

On my first day at church, I got told off by a fat woman for swinging my legs. Mum never had a rule for that. And after a second visit to Sunday school, I refused to go back. Mum's school was disciplined but it was never boring. Quite the opposite, it was stimulating and I loved it.

The first word of more than a syllable that I ever learned to spell was 'electricity'. It's hard to imagine how I'd remembered it, but I suspect it was because it always tripped me up and Mum made me repeat it when we had to do spelling competitions between us. Before we started school, we could read, spell and write. She would line us up against the flowered wallpaper in the living room and, at breakneck speed, move from me to Angie to Mini asking us to spell 'school' or 'banana' or 'electricity'. At the slightest hesitation, one child would be immediately dismissed and she'd move on to the next to pick up where the other had faltered. Mum, trying to keep a straight face, impersonated a sergeant major, saluting and marching up and down the line while we poked each other behind our backs to stop ourselves from sniggering.

Mum also introduced me to my first superhero, Brah Anansi the Spider ('Brah'—short for Brother), the character from old West African folklore, brought to Jamaica by my enslaved ancestors, the Trickster with eight legs and a human face, who outsmarted everyone with his cunning and creativity. Angie and Mini got their bedtime story first, and I waited patiently for mine. I hung on Mum's every line, engrossed in Anansi's next adventure. I thought it was great that he never went to school. Instead, he made up his own rules and used his knowledge to outsmart those more power-ful than him by 'playing fool fi catch wise', a Jamaican idiom. His wisdom sounded the same as Mum's—not the stories we heard at Sunday school. Anansi was otherworldly and fun and had the wherewithal to work the system. We'd have to be like Anansi, too, Mum said. Nothing was ever going to be handed to us on a plate. I made a mental note to be just like Brah Anansi.

Chapter 3

Blues

A blanket of smoke fills our front room, coming from the long, cone-shaped spliffs, dancing, curling, and twisting in slow motion, almost in time with the deep, hypnotic reggae beat. It floats up towards the dim ray of light from a bulb dangling from the ceiling, which glows lantern-like and has a brown paper bag covering it. Moving shadows loom large against the walls. The bulb is supposed to be blue. Blue bulbs for blues parties. But blue-coloured bulbs are hard to come by, Mum says. So, she improvises.

Earlier, I helped her fetch the cotton bedsheets that she hung across the bay windows, 'To keep the nosy neighbours out', but it's also to contain the sweet, deep smell of the weed and dull the pulsing reggae bass reverberating through the walls. The Hawthorns, the white elderly couple who live in the basement flat, are always banging a broom handle on their ceiling if voices get too rowdy or if the music is too loud, screaming for Mum to turn the music down or, if we're running on the stairs, for us to stop that bloody noise. On occasion, they've even called the police, which Mum hates. We're not at war with them, though. There are days we lend each other teabags, or a cup of sugar, or Mum gets us to knock on their door to see if they need anything from the corner shop. This always confuses me, how they can be so cold on one hand, and so neighbourly on the other, yet Mum still talks to them as if nothing's happened.

Pushed back into the sides of the room are the sofa, the mahogany dining table, and the TV, housed in a mahogany box on wheels. Along one wall, the record player sits on top of square pieces of thick foam placed on a stool. Just for extra measure, Mum's Sellotaped a two-pence piece onto the arm of the record player to weigh it down, to stop it from jumping and scratching the vinyl, once the revellers start rocking and whining their waists to the heavy baseline. Oh bwoy, if anyone ever gets even the tiniest scratch on Mum's record, they will feel her wrath. For us, it's an instant arse-whooping. The minute she hears it jump, she's in to check, holding the vinyl up to the light, inspecting every inch and dusting it off with her special yellow microfibre cleaning cloth that's like a magnet to any specks.

'Which one of unno scratch mi record? Ehhh? What mi tell unno? Don't play wid mi records, dem is not play toys, yu ear mi?'

She's taught me how to slip the vinyl out from its sleeve, not to touch any part of the black bit with the lines, but cup it between each palm and place it gently onto the turntable. I do this ever so slowly, and carefully, so as not to upset her, and always under supervision. When it's time to change the song, my fingers slightly tremble while lifting the needle from the record. I immediately break out into a sweat, hoping I don't drop the arm back down onto the spinning vinyl.

Mum loves her music. We go with her to the record shop on Church Street in Stoke Newington and have to pass by Fitzroy's barber shop where Mum takes me for my haircuts and sometimes leaves me by myself while she goes to pick up a few bits, making me feel like a grown up. I love being in there with its old, beaten up, deep-red leather chairs that spin around and the white roll of paper the barber puts around my neck that looks like Christmas decorations and the smell of it all mixed in with hair oil and after-shave, and the music of laughter and the running commentary about anything and everything. I am kept entertained and observe keenly, the soft piles of black hair on the floor being swept into a corner, the small brush used to lather up a man's face, then the cut-throat razor blade being drawn across the pulled, stretched skin, scraping the snow-like stuff away. The way a leather strap is used to sharpen the razor, then left dangling on the side of the barber chair, and Fitzroy swiftly passes a small mirror around the back of the clients' head, not stopping long enough to show them the finished haircut.

I stare at Fitzroy's goofy teeth protruding from his top lip, like white pillows peaking from under the quilt covers, his thin pencil moustache, and slanted eyes on a narrow face, his silver hair, and his tall, slim frame. He *can* talk, and when he does, it's nonstop chat no matter what the subject is. And always smartly dressed, with shirt and tie, wearing black leather sandals that pass as shoes. He carries them off well, and they look cool with the hem of his pinstriped bell-bottoms hovering over them.

The small glass-fronted shop has four barber chairs, and mirrors that run the length of the wall on both sides, making it look bigger than it is. Pictures of boxers: Muhammad Ali, Sony Liston, and Marvellous Marvin Hagler are displayed on one side and a map of Jamaica on another. A kettle with teacups stands neatly cleaned in a corner on a tray, with a bag of white sugar, a teaspoon, and a box of Tetley tea bags. In the drawer next to the kettle, Fitzroy kept a bottle of white rum to add a splash to his tea. A poster of Black men with all types of haircuts and fades sticks to the wall in front of the chairs.

I like going to Fitzroy's and wish Mum could stop there on the way instead. When we arrive at the record shop, Mum spends ages thumbing through the LPs lined up in milk crates on makeshift tables. The shop is so tiny that there's no room for us so we hang by the door while Mum jostles past customers in the narrow aisles. A very male-centric place, they are silent and focussed, lost in a library of sound, yet nothing intimidates Mum. She commands the space, chatting to the man behind the counter, or singing along when he plays her a B-side on the countertop turntable. The same happens when we go see Uncle Winston's mum, Auntie Hattie, in Brixton and Mum stops at the market stalls. At home, she plays Elvis Presley and Frank Sinatra. Sometimes she even blasts out big classical orchestras, but most of the time she plays reggae and dub and lovers rock. I know all the artists: Gregory Isaacs; Rupie Edwards; Dennis Brown; and of course, Bob Marley, who we call Uncle Bob Marley, as if he's one of Mum's elders we have to show respect to.

I am five years old.

Tonight, the first guests are arriving. I look up to the bodies brushing past each other in the hallway as tall as pillars. I move among them as if I'm lost in a forest of people. Angie and Mini are sometimes lost in them, too, but I choose not to seek them out. Among the men in particular, I'm special. I'm their protégé, being schooled in our secret language. Gold krugerrands dangle loosely around necks, fingers weighed down by signet rings and sovereigns set in gold, pat my afro hair as I move through them, squeezing past cashmere coats balancing on shoulders, or the silver, silk suits that shimmer in the charcoal shade. Gold teeth of every type sparkle in sunshine smiles or opened-mouthed laughter. Beaver hats are perched ever so slightly to one side of the head, giving off a cool and deadly, bad man look.

Uncle Winston is here too—crocodile shoes are polished to a mirror shine. I love him and I fear him. He's Mum's first cousin, and she always recalls that when she first came from Jamaica, Uncle Winston looked out for her, like a brother. He has three scars: two etched down the left side of his face and one on the right, all going from his temple to his jawline, and I always manoeuvre round the back of him to see the wheel of his ratchet knife peeking out of the corner of his rear pocket, next to his silk hankie. I know about ratchet knives. Fishermen in Jamaica use them to scale fish, but I also overhear Mum and Auntie Beryl talking about Winston. He's an old-school gangster—a man who wouldn't flinch to bruck you up or whet you up with a knife, meaning to draw blood. He moves with a couple of Yardies, a nickname for rude bwoy Jamaicans, who have arrived fresh from back home 'back ah yard', sticking up the underground dance halls and shebeens, robbing the night-time revellers of gold chains, watches, rings and anything else of value, men who would travel the length and breadth of the UK, raiding, wearing NFL football caps with the Raiders logo on it, showing a guy with a patch over one eye and two cutlass swords crossing behind him, looking like a modern-day pirate.

In the kitchen, the air is soaked with ganja mist. It, and bottles of white rum, have been smuggled in from Jamaica courtesy of a British Airways flight, and are lined up on the side next to a row of mixers. Brandy, whisky, vodka and Guinness also litter the worktop and, in the ashtrays, spliffs burn like incense sticks. They are passed through hands and fingers or dangle from lips. The smell feels welcoming. I'm used to it, and it strokes the back of my throat as I breathe it in. I wanted to try and smoke one, but Mum would give me a good licking if I got caught, no questions asked.

Mum and Auntie Beryl are always talking about how the blues parties give us that little bit extra in life, and as Mum has one of the largest front rooms, she is usually the one to hold them. To supplement any money coming in, she uses these parties to sell weed. She calls it 'juggling' as it's like a part-time job. It can be considered rude for guests to bring their own ganja, instead they buy it from the host as a sign of respect for opening their house.

Sometimes, I see Mum in her bedroom preparing it: unwrapping the layers of newspaper and brown paper, as if she's playing pass the parcel. It takes her a while to get down to the block sealed in cling film. To me, the block looks dark and matted like a lady's wig, and it's Mum's job to detangle the mess and make sense of it all. There are often lots of small seeds which she has to pick out before she can cut it up. She doesn't mind me watching so long as I keep quiet, and occasionally, if a block arrives that's too matted I'm allowed to help her by boiling the kettle. Then I wait with her as she pours the scalding water into a large saucepan, pulls a tea cloth over the top and sits the weed in the middle, steaming it until it's soft and spongy and easier to pull apart. If she's in a good mood, she lets me cut strips of magazine paper, usually from the *TV Times*, into which she places a pinch of weed before she folds each parcel tightly into a small rectangle, ready to be sold.

The music is pulling me towards the front room now, and I weave my way further in. On the makeshift dance floor, Rasta locks swing out from under wide-brimmed hats with small peacock feathers on the side. Afro wigs bob up and down and high-heeled boots beat out a rhythm on the floor. Mixed in with the smell of weed is the smell of sweat and excitement, and I take my place, right in centre of the action. The tune stretches and pulls back like elastic, while it's slow, sweet groove echoes out. I'm skanking now. My hips are twisting down and I close my eyes, trying to feel the pulse of the beat vibrate through me. My movements are deliberate, exaggerated. I'm on one foot now, arms outstretched on either side. I look up. A crowd has gathered around me, smiling down and floating their arms up, mirroring my moves. My body rises and drops as I move from foot to foot. Then I hear the cries. 'Skank! Skank!' They flick their wrists, which makes a snapping sound in their fingers, to show their delight in the Jamaican way. It feels like slow motion. It feels like flying.

Just as Mum juggles her weed, I juggle entertainment. Attention is my drug of choice and it earns me good money. Fifty pence pieces and £1 notes land at my feet as the crowd bounces with me. 'Goh-deah! Goh-deah!' The men and women are shouting, and I play to them. I become their reflection and they go wild. I pinch my right thumb and my forefinger together, raise them up to my mouth and mimic taking a long, cool draw on a pretend spliff before dropping my head back, closing my eyes and exhaling.

This routine has been practised over and over.

I often put on shows for Mum and my sisters. I mimic Uncle Ashley, Mum's friend who she rents a room to, and treats him more like a brother, even though he secretly fancies Mum, she's not interested. He's a Rastaman, who is always smoking spliffs and complaining about Babylon and the system. 'Babylon ah go bon down. Jah is watching every-ting them ah do, mi ah tell yu. Yu noh see it?' He's easy to imitate. I pull a black T-shirt over my head to fake his long locks and place one of his crochet hats on top that I've sneaked out of his bedroom. I stand proud and pretend to smoke and cuss and complain as he does. Or I slip into Mum's wardrobe and pull out her wigs and high-heeled boots, stick my bum out and catwalk down an imaginary street pretending to be Auntie Beryl. Mum and Angie and Mini roll around on Mum's bed, pissing themselves.

The women are edging their way closer to me on the dance floor now. Their breasts sit directly above my eye-line and their long legs rise up. I've seen how they dance 'nasty' with the men, and again, I mimic it, sending my audience into hysterics. I press up against them, wind my tiny hips around their thighs, and bump and grind, moving in a slow, circular motion. I can't be more than waist height, but I keep going, burrowing my face into their short dresses, looking round now and again to check that the crowd is still with me.

I'm just getting warmed up, when suddenly I feel a firm hand clasped under my armpit, prising me off. It's Mum. She's heard the shouting from the kitchen and she's come to see what's happening. 'Joy! Joy! Leave de-bwoy!' I hear some of the men plead with her, but at the same time they agree that it's way past my bedtime. Reluctantly, I know my time is up. I bend and collect tonight's earnings, the money thrown at my feet for my performance; I feel like I've won gold in a competition. I'm patted and cheered. Kisses are placed on my cheek from the women, wet with rum and brandy that leave a lipstick trace, as I'm led out by my collar.

'Mek sure yu brush yur teet and wash yur arm-pits before you go to bed!' Mum says as she sends me up the stairs with a guiding slap to my bum. I'm still sweating as I stand in the bathroom with the cool flannel gliding over my skin and feeling like Stanley, the champion of the world!

Chapter 4

Back Ah Yard

We knew we weren't English. Everyone in Mum's circle was Jamaican other than Angie's dad who was Grenadian and my dad who was from Antigua. That's why we three siblings are all different skin tones and the different island names meant nothing to us; as far as we were concerned, we were Jamaican. Through Mum, and by extension, we had been sent from paradise—paradise, Jam-down, Back ah Yard, Home, Jamaica, Mum was magical in that way. I never thought of her as vulnerable.

Mum didn't look the same as the others. She wasn't dark-skinned. Instead, she was caramel with wide almond-shaped eyes, and she dressed in the most beautiful clothes. Her best dresses had fireflies embroidered into them, or patterns with delicate flowers that looked like hibiscus. Then, there were her short miniskirts and plunging necklines which she saved for the blues parties or for the dance halls or if she was in the mood, to wear up the high street. To us, she was a mystery that needed to be solved, a person we had to piece together, bit by bit.

Every month, a parcel turned up from paradise, from our Great- Great-Grandma Harriet, who we only knew from a photo that sat on top of the mahogany gas fire mantelpiece in the living room. This old, mulatto-looking woman with long, spindly fingers placed neatly in her lap, wearing a white cloth pinafore and a white head wrap, sat on a rocking chair, almost as if she was hovering, eyes penetrating, looking very much like a ghost from the past. With every parcel we were able to add another piece to the puzzle. As Mum untied the string we pressed our noses against it and guessed at all the different smells. We also knew receiving it put Mum in a good mood. The second she saw the stamps and the postmark, it was as if someone was handing her a lost fragment of her heart, a fragment that made her more complete. She softened, opened up a little, moving in and out of patois and the Queen's English. Angie, Mini and I would sit with her round the kitchen table and she'd teach us.

'Ummmm, smell this kids.'

'Ummmm.'

'What's that called? Can you remember?'

'Mint?'

'Yes, that's right, it's fresh mint to make tea. When I was living in Jamaica I'd drink this before I went to school in the morning. Sometimes this is all we had for breakfast if there was no flour in the house. We would drink it with lots of condensed milk, bwoy it sweet!'

'Is it the same as what we have?'

'Yes, just like I give to you guys. Aright, who can tell me what this is?'

'Is that ginger?'

'Yes, son... and we have nutmeg, and, ahh... Who can tell me what this is?'

'Is it a branch from a tree?'

'It's not a tree, Mini!'

'What is it, Mum?'

'This is chocolate!'

'Chocolate!?'

'Yes, but you can't eat it like that. You have to grate it into boiling hot milk to turn it into chocolate. Then add vanilla, nutmeg, cinnamon and a likkle honey.'

'Can we taste it?'

'If you want, but it's bitter...'

'Yuk!' I said, being the guinea pig.

'Let me taste! Urrrrrr...' said Mini. 'Try it Ang.'

'Urrrrrrr, yucky. Puhh. It's bitter!'

'I told you, you can't eat it like that. You have to boil it up. When I was in Jamaica we used to have this in the evening before we went to bed. This is the real natural chocolate, not that stuff they sell in the supermarket.'

'What's this bushy thing, Mum?'

'That's called cerasee bush. It's what I give to you to clean you out, remember how bitter it is? But it's good for yu blood system!'

'That's what makes us poo in the morning!?'

'Yes, and that's good for your body! Nana Harriet use to give this to me at night before bed, just as I do with you. She mix it with other bitter bush teas that was so bitter, you had to wait until it cool down and pinch your nose so you could swallow it down in one go. We use to shiver when we saw it boiling on the pot! But it's to make you strong, especially living here when you're not getting enough sunshine. In Jamaica we had sunshine every day. I never knew snow until I came to this country. Man, what a shock! How could something look that innocent, so fluffy, but be so cold? Not for me bwoy!'

'What was the sunshine like in Jamaica?'

'Oh bwoy, I miss that sunshine, because it is a different kind of sunshine to the one here in England. There is a natural breeze that makes it feel warm on your body and skin, mek yu feel nice! We could play until late and mi and mi friends would go pick fruit and climb the orange trees. Where I grew up is in the west of Jamaica, in the Parish of Manchester, a place called Devons. They call it 'orange country', because of all the orange trees, and it's cooler because the breeze from the mountains, just cool yu down, bwoy. And we used to wake up early in the morning around 5 AM to feed the goats and the pigs before going to school because those were our chores, and you had to do your chores.'

'Wow! Goats *and* pigs?'

'We had goats and pigs and cockerels, and when we need milk we would milk the goat, and use it to make tea and chocolate. Sometimes we drank it straight from the pail, while it's still warm from the goat's body. It's the best milk to drink. You would love it too if you tried it. When we need meat, they slaughter the pig to fry up bacon and they eat the pig foot. Me!? I never liked pig foot but Harriet, she force me to eat it. Oh bwoy, that pig foot sticking out of the pot would frighten me and put me off. My favourite was always her cornmeal porridge...'

'Yeah, we love that too.'

'I'll make it for you tomorrow... but, you know, I never want to come to England, but Greta, she sent for me.'

'Wasn't Harriet... sad?'

'She was, but Harriet was not my mum. I never knew that in Jamaica, she raised me as her daughter. It was only when I come here that I get to find out Greta was my real mum. Man, she work mi! She was wicked, man. She's one tough woman. She hated me being her daughter. I couldn't do anything right. Nothing. Nothing I did was right, bwoy, dat woman wicked you see!'

'So, Harriet's not your mum?'

'No son, I thought Harriet was mi mum all my life, so I was sad when I find out she was mi great grandmother. What a shock to the system, man! She told me when I was sent for by Greta. I'll never forget it. She say, "Yu mum in-ah Hngland send ah ticket for yu." That was it. She told mi she was mi great grandmother, and mi real mum was called Greta an living in England. Oh man, I cry! I leggo one piece of bawling, I bawl, I bawl, I bawl. I never want to go. But everyone was saying, 'You should go Joy, you should go.' Everyone wanted to come to England for the opportunity, so I came. I wish I never did now. For me, Harriet, was mi real mum and she raise mi from a baby. I never know Greta. I only met her when I came off the plane. An I never been on a plane until I took that ride with the British Overseas Airways Corporation. All I could see below was water for miles. Just water and clouds, it was scary, I can't swim to save mi life! But man it was tough, really tough. I missed home right from the time I look back and the island disappeared from sight.'

'Where's Greta, Mum?'

'She's here, son. She here in London, but I don't see her. I don't know if I ever will see Greta again… she's not mi mudder.'

Chapter 5

The Globe

The auditorium is deserted. Only the steady drone of aeroplanes high above, following the path of the Thames in the midday sun, breaks the stillness. Under my weight, the wooden boards creak as I hop up onto the stage and explore every inch of this hallowed platform. I run my fingers across the Pillars of Hercules, carved out from a single oak and rendered as marble. Above me, the painted heavens of the canopy are clear and brilliant in the light.

There's an old Jamaican saying: 'Everything happens for a reason and nothing happens before the time.' And this is my time, serendipity. The actor who is to play the part of Friar Laurence in *Romeo and Juliet* at London's Globe Theatre has been called away and may have to cancel his run. The cast has been rehearsing for six weeks, but I have been brought in as the understudy with only two weeks' notice. I am offered by the company to go on stage with book in hand and read the lines, but I politely decline. I put my head down and get off book. I've learned my lines and the jig they do at the end—no script needed.

It's as if the part chose me. Friar Laurence: the fixer, the caretaker, the man who gives wise counsel to Romeo and assists the marriage of the forbidden lovers in his desire for peace, to settle the feud between the Montagues and the Capulets. A man who understands how easily virtue, when abused, can become vice. On the stage I practise, and project my voice out into the open space, imagining hundreds of faces staring back at me in the cool evening light.

> *For naught so vile that on the Earth doth live*
> *But to the Earth some special good doth give;*
> *Nor aught so good but, strained from that fair use,*
> *Revolts from true birth, stumbling on abuse.*
> *Virtue itself turns vice, being misapplied,*
> *And vice sometime by action dignified.*

As a kid, I never knew how the caretaker could become the destroyer: a risk taker who can gamble everything, a person who has the power to heal and to hurt. Friar Laurence will hand Juliet the poison herbs to feign her death rather than marry Paris, her suitor. He will set the scene for her eventual suicide alongside Romeo's. Through unintended consequences, his actions will lead them to their ultimate fate.

My fellow actors in the green room are still having lunch. I use this time to imagine the performance from the audience's perspective. I jump down and stand in the yard, where ordinary people watch. Then, I move up the tiers, hopping from seat to seat, weighing up the stage from every angle, from left to right, from the lowest to the highest vantage point.

It is 2019 and I am 48 years old. I am the understudy, but in this moment, I have no intention of waiting in the wings. As the cast trickles back from their break to take their positions, I prepare to deliver my lines for a special dress rehearsal organised by the director with the cast just for me. The cast are anxious because of the short notice, they are unsure of what my performance will be, or if I will remember all those lines and entrances and exits for the entire show. I know this character inside and out: the caretaker; the fixer; the hero child. But instead of him crippling me, I own this experience. He is mine. I won over the cast who are elated at what I produce and celebrate in a group hug, the relief pouring from their shoulders, knowing they can finally relax and let go. I feel accepted and a part of this tribe.

In the end, the actor is called away, and I play the part of Friar Laurence for four nights with one matinee. At the end of each performance, the cast members pull me towards the front of the stage to take my own bow. I welled up and fought back the tears when the applause from both the cast and the audience hit me. They tell me they have seen no one step in and learn a part so quickly and perform it with such passion. And that they could never have done that themselves in such a short time frame. Only I know how long I have prepared myself for this moment and how hard my journey has been to get here. Mum's words echo in my mind: everything happens for a reason and nothing happens before the time.

Chapter 6

Sesame Street

In my mind, there was a before and there was an after: life before the day that Mum got sick and every day since. It wasn't exactly like that, though. Mum wasn't just okay one minute and not the next, but that's never how I choose to remember it. Even now, when Angie and Mini and I comb through the past, 'before' takes on the form of a super-saturated film—linear, a storyline we can follow, exaggerated in glorious technicolour, as if we're on the set of the Spike Lee movie *Do the Right Thing*. It was London 1976, but it could easily have been Brooklyn 1986.

That summer was the hottest on record for more than three centuries. From mid-June to August, temperatures soared to above 36 degrees Celsius. On our road, all the neighbours were out from afternoon until late evening to escape the stickiness of indoors. Men sat lazily on the porches in their shorts and vests on upturned crates, playing dominoes, wiping the beads of sweat from their brows with a flannel that hung over their shoulders. They talked about the blistering heat or discussed politics while women in summer dresses and saris fanned themselves and swapped stories and recipes. Plates of mangoes and pineapples, peeled and chopped, got brought from our house, while the Greeks sliced up juicy watermelons and the Indians shared savoury snacks. In the background there was the constant squeal of kids chasing each other on the hot paving. Water fights were plenty and we armed ourselves with balloons to use as water bombs or ambushed the enemy by squirting water from reused Robinsons squash bottles and cheap water pistols from Woolworths. Occasionally there was a sudden cry if a kid leapt from wall to wall, misjudging the gaps where gates once hung and falling to graze a knee or shinbone. In the sunshine, we were all equal. I felt like I was living on Sesame Street. A multicultural, melting pot of ethnicities living in our own concrete jungle of pavements, roads, and bricks.

Before then, we never strayed past the boundaries of Cazenove Road which intersected Alkham Road at the north end and Northwold Road to the south. If we did go past the imaginary demarcation line, it was always with Mum or Auntie Beryl. Although our street safely contained us, Mum, or another parent, would always keep a watchful eye over us. Everyone looked out for each other's children. There wasn't the 'stranger danger' kids are fed today. At the same time, Mum never told us who we could, or could not, play with. She let us decide. Most of the time that included all the children who lived near us, but I guess some families, like the Bryces, had their own unspoken rules.

As for racism, the word became a part of our everyday language, even though we didn't fully understand what it meant. Hell yes, it existed. The elders described it as 'wickedness'. We overheard them talking about 'Dem wicked people.' Or, they called them 'Dem wicked white people' who just don't like Black people or anyone from a different culture. We listened intently to their stories, and sometimes they wouldn't even notice that we'd stopped playing. Then, out of the blue, we got chaperoned away with a firm hand. 'Go remove yourselves and play. This is big people talk!'

Wickedness only ever happened outside the front door, but I never heard it on Alkham Road. There were wicked people on the high street, I was certain about that. Auntie Beryl told me that while she was out shopping one time a white man strolled right up to her and spat in her face. 'You Nigg-nog!' he hissed, before calmly walking off. What stuck in my mind more was that Auntie Beryl said she just froze. She thought the man was going to ask her for directions or the time. And then she managed to respond with some verbal abuse after wiping the phlegm from her face, but it was too late, he was halfway up the street. She said the rage she felt afterwards, she could have murdered someone. When we lived on the Powell House Estate, Beryl's upstairs neighbour, an African woman, once left her bath running and it seeped into Beryl's ceiling. Her eldest daughter was home and knocked to ask the woman to turn her bath off, but the door was slammed in her face telling her to mind her own business. When Beryl eventually caught up with the woman in the central courtyard, everyone watched as Beryl, judge, jury and executioner, battered the woman's head with her shoe-heel until she drew blood. But freeze? That wasn't Auntie Beryl's style, she was renowned for fighting anyone including men, and the police.

Angie, Mini and I were best friends with three kids from a family who lived a few doors down called the Thompsons. Forget the Famous Five. Angie, Mini and I, alongside Wayne, Paul and Emma called ourselves the Famous Six. We played tin can alley, tag or kiss chase, and because no one in London's newly built high-rise flats had been allowed to keep their pets, our road was littered with stray mongrels searching for a home. We always had a few dogs in tow. One was vicious with a red coat. We named him Rex. We had our own dog too, with a coat like a golden retriever. He reminded me of the dogs on the Andrex toilet paper advert. We christened him Samson. Years later, we got a black shabby mongrel and called her Sammy in memory of Samson.

Wayne, Paul, and Emma were mixed-race kids and we took it

for granted that their white mum Deborah was their real mother. No one told us any differently. Later on it turned out that not only was she their step-mother but she was also an alcoholic, too. So was their dad, Solomon. Behind the scenes, the Thompsons were as messy a family as we were. We heard about their drunken arguments from Wayne, Paul and Emma and occasionally the police got called to their house, but kids don't place labels on people the way adults do. To me, she was just Mrs Thompson, and the Thompsons weren't mixed-race either—if anything, they were 'Black' like us. Solomon dressed as a cowboy, with proper cowboy boots, and wore the shirts with the bolo tie leather string that dangles at the front. He had a lap steel guitar which he played horizontally on a bench with a metal slide on his index finger. In summer, he would throw open his front room windows and let the melodic blue grass music drift down the road.

We hung around together at every opportunity, and soon the Famous Six started pushing the boundaries of the demarcation line. We went off picking wild blackberries on the railway sidings, one street away. Or we climbed the apple trees overhanging the synagogue walls or picked the pears also growing there. We stuffed as many as we could in our pockets before we got chased away. And we loved bringing them back to our mums for them to make fruit pie.

At home, I became more important: the man of the house. Even though Uncle Winston occasionally stayed with us after Uncle Ashley moved out, there was never any doubt that I had responsibilities. One of my chores was to go to the paraffin man and fill up our plastic containers with fuel for the heaters. They were gigantic and came up to my waist. Normally, he delivered, but Mum had fallen out with him—we never knew why—and so she sent me instead. Worst of all was visiting him in the winter. I had no gloves, and so I'd wrap the cuff of my jumper around my fist and then thread the jumper through the plastic handles, and lug the bottles home, stopping every two minutes to catch my breath but determined not to let Mum down. One time it was snowing and I lugged the bottles all the way home, up the icy steps, and got to the front door when I realised the change that was wrapped up in Mum's note to the paraffin man had vanished. My heart jumped into my mouth and I could hear it pounding in my ears. I knew what was waiting for me if I went into the house without Mum's change, and I couldn't leave the paraffin on the doorsteps otherwise someone might steal it. So I lugged the bottles down the icy steps, and retraced my footprints in the snow all the way back near the garage. Thankfully, the white paper note lay camouflaged on the side of the pavement half covered in snow, as if it was waiting for me to come and collect it.

How I felt about being 'the man of the house' depended on what day it was. Part of me hated it. Mum always had a list for me as long as her arm, but I also wore the title with pride. Like it or not, I took on every job with a perfectionism that I've never been able to break free of, and back then it gave me a satisfied feeling: the caretaker, the fixer. Because I was helping Mum, I kept in her good books, but I was also taking care of my sisters. Angie was one year older, but I still felt protective towards her and Mini.

My jobs also included emptying the bins and sweeping down the three flights of stairs. Easy-peasy when the stairs had been bare wood, but not such a breeze when, as soon as she could afford to, Mum had a burgundy, swirly-patterned carpet fitted. Suddenly, the dustpan and brush with its worn out bristles got heavier and didn't do the job so well; dust would be flying everywhere and it seemed to take double the time. I would cough my lungs out from the particles that also made me wheeze, finding it difficult to breathe at times, and am sure this was the reason for my asthma to this day.

The man of the house also had to make sure the lights were

turned off, especially before bed. This was by far the toughest job. Downstairs, the light switch sat by the main door. Getting there was no problem, but when it came to finding my way back, the stairway now pitch black, I near enough shit myself. My head was filled with images of King Kong rampaging through New York City having broken free of his chains. And Godzilla, the king of the monsters, woken from sleep and emerging from the sea, ready to wreak havoc on everything in his path. Mum fed us on a diet of scary black-and-white movies. She'd bring blankets from upstairs and we'd watch them huddled on the floor, rigid with fear. Halfway through the films, when nature called, we'd insist on going to the toilet in pairs.

Now though, I was alone in the dark with only the faintest light from the upstairs landing as my guide. Sometimes I panicked so much I lost my footing in the scramble and slipped back on the steps, grabbing the carpet with my fingernails, all the time imagining a monster's claws sinking into me and dragging me down. Just to be extra mean, Mum and Angie and Mini would switch the landing light off and jump out on me at the top of the stairs and I would react with such fright, a deathly roar would escape from the pit of my stomach.

When things got tough, Mum would shout, 'Go fetch the hammer!'

By far my favourite job was finding the hammer and passing it to Mum while she climbed up a wooden ladder and kept smashing the padlock off the side of the electric meter until it broke. The meter sat high up near the front door and got filled with 50p pieces. She did the same with the gas meter in the kitchen cupboard, and the TV, which she hired from Radio Rentals. It had a slot at the back that got emptied once a month. Fifty pence bought us four precious hours of TV, but with the back smashed off, we could watch it forever. She'd always leave one 50p coin hidden on top of the kitchen unit so we wouldn't spend it by accident; this we fed through each slot, catching it as it fell from the meters when we needed to top up on anything. When the gas or electricity man turned up, or the TV hire guy, our script was well-rehearsed. There'd been another break in. We were the unluckiest family on the street—so many burglaries at our house! The box would get replaced and filled up again until Mum shouted out of frustration, 'Go fetch the hammer!'

This was a sign that money was tight. Once we got the money out, we hit the high street to go shopping or we got sent to the local shops to buy the essentials—bread, condensed milk, butter, eggs and self-raising flour. Not that this was the beginning of the end of Mum as we knew her. Although, strange things had started happening. We often sat upstairs whispering about them, but we were too young to understand what they meant, or even if they meant anything at all. They were just more pieces of Mum that we couldn't fit neatly together. For example, Mum had always hand-washed our clothes in the bath, but from time-to-time they'd sit in the half-filled tub for days: dye running, mildew growing with a fusty smell that seeped into our noses. The sink got piled high with dishes, stinking out the kitchen and hallway. Sometimes dirty dishes sat in the bath among the clothes when the kitchen sink got too full.

These things all seemed to coincide with a letter Mum received from Jamaica to say that Great-Great-Grandma Harriet had passed. We wouldn't be receiving Harriet's parcels anymore. Mum said she was really sad, but her sadness seemed deeper, more profound. There were days when she didn't get out of bed, and we'd have to bring her Sugar Puffs, her favourite cereal that she would eat straight from the box while we waited anxiously for her to take us to school, which often didn't happen until we figured out we would have to take ourselves, if we wanted to go.

From the stairs, we also watched Mum talking to herself. 'Who is Mum talking to? There's no one there! Mum's gone crazy, man,' we whispered. To be clear, we didn't fully understand what *crazy* really meant. Growing up in Hackney, we had seen lots of crazy people on the streets and would point at them. Auntie Beryl did, though. Like a sister, Beryl was staunchly loyal to Mum and she started to appear at our house more often. She quietly let the plug out of the bath, and washed the dishes while Mum stayed in her room. We noticed that the floor in the kitchen had been mopped, or the laundry had been done. Beryl tried to sweep Mum's decline under the carpet, until the day when there was no place left to sweep it. Years later Beryl told me how she'd wrestled with her decision to stage an intervention. But stage an intervention she did, albeit a misjudged one.

One afternoon Beryl took the bold move of turning up at the house with Mum's doctor, a blunt man with a large moon face called Dr Egbonwon, who was African and couldn't hide his disdain for us West Indians. We weren't at school: another day when Mum hadn't got up and walked us to the gates or when we woke too late to take ourselves. 'Yu eaten? Who put on yu clothes? Where's yu mudder?' Auntie Beryl fired off a dozen questions as I let her in. *Had I done something wrong?* I wondered. Like her sister Pat, Beryl had eyes that could trespass on your soul.

Mum was in bed. 'Who is it?' we heard her call as Beryl and the doctor stood outside her room knocking on the door.

'Mi bring the doctor fi see you,' Beryl replied. No response.

Mum took ages and kept them waiting, but when she finally did appear, her hair was perfectly scraped back into a bun. She had a dress on, nylon stockings, heels and make-up. 'Hey Beryl, everything alright?' she asked in the Queen's English, precise and punctuated as if her words were gliding on air. She and Beryl always spoke thick patois together, each sentence moulded to the next with no full stops.

45

While Dr Egbonwon and Mum disappeared into the living room, Beryl, Angie, Mini and I hovered around outside the door to listen in. Part of me was hoping that Beryl would just take us home with her. We were like family and called each other cousins. Her son Nicky was around my age and we was thick as thieves when we were in each other's company. Beryl's place was our home from home already. We even bathed together with her younger kids when we visited. She had five. Maybe we could stay there for a while, until Mum became *our* Mum again? Auntie Beryl tried to take us *once*, but Mum wasn't having it. And in future whenever Beryl recounted the story she said she still couldn't believe what happened—how smart and devious Mum could be, and how she had begged Mum to let her have us kids until she got back on her feet.

Just as Dr Egbonwon was about to leave, a debate sparked up in the hallway.

'I can't see much wrong here. If a woman wants to stop doing her washing up now and again, she is entitled to!' Dr Egbonwon told Beryl, as if she'd just wasted his time. 'How have *you* been keeping?' he went on to Beryl.

'What yu asking mi dis question for! I'm fine,' Beryl insisted, looking confused.

'Miss Brown tells me you have some anger problems,' the doctor continued, which enraged Beryl to the point where she lost control and started cussing the doctor out. It seemed to prove Mum right.

'Told you so,' she nodded knowingly to the doctor. Then, Mum went straight for Beryl's jugular.

'Look at me. Do I look ill? No, Beryl. It's you who is not well. It's you who is imagining things. You need help, Beryl. Please Beryl, let the doctor help you.'

Elizabeth Taylor had nothing on my Mum. She played the

part, alright, skilfully gaslighting everyone around her. Maybe that's what made what eventually happened all the more confusing. Maybe that's why I always see a clear before and after and never a fraying around the edges of Mum's mental health.

Chapter 7

Cowboys and Indians

We are under siege. On the frontier. We've seen them from the window in their cars looking up, clicking the ends of their ballpoint pens. Inside, Mum is pacing like a lion. She moves in circles around the kitchen, then back to the window again, marking out her territory, protecting her pride.

They've knocked once already, but Mum wouldn't answer. She won't open the door to anyone. One of them called up through the letterbox. 'Miss Brown? Miss Brown? We're here from social services. We're here to help you.' Angie, Mini and I have no idea who social services are. All we can see from the top kitchen window is a huddle of white people talking below. They look official: suited and determined. Mum keeps repeating that we're not going anywhere. We're sticking to our guns. I believe her, but secretly I want to disobey her and hand myself in. I know that white people aren't to be trusted, but I have a feeling in my belly that I should run downstairs, let them in, and tell them that Mum is not acting like our mum anymore and needs fixing. Who is going to fix my mum?

The standoff becomes a stare out: them looking up, Mum staring down from the sash window which is wide open. Angie is crying. Mini is standing near the kitchen door, silent. I am frozen, but I'm also cowed by shame. Mum is calling the white people every name under the sun out the window and her cussing is bringing the neighbours onto their front steps. I can see people talking and pointing, some are our own friends looking sorry for us. In between, she ducks back in and continues to circle. 'I'm not letting them.' She's talking to herself again.

We didn't know it then, but this would become a cycle that would repeat itself throughout our young lives. These strangers with their clipboards would become regular visitors. We'd get to know them by name. But now, we don't know how they got here. How do they know where Mum lives? Why are they here? What have we done? What have I done? I'm scrolling through the past few days in my mind. Beryl came with the doctor, but she hasn't come back since. I've not been bad at school. We've hardly been to school. Angie is a goodie-two-shoes most of the time. Mini is Mini, but Mum always gives us a good licking if any of us step out of line.

I make my way towards the window and peer down as if I'm on a canyon ledge, uncertain of the drop. Now, they're backing off into their cars. Beating a retreat. They won't come again, Mum says. She's made sure of it, but I want to check that they've driven off, just for Mum. At the same time, I'm unsure I want to see the cars go. Most of all, I want to protect my sisters. I'm the man of the house and protecting them is one of my duties. 'Move from the bloodclart window!' Mum screams out of the blue. I jump out of my skin and leap back. Nothing I'm doing seems to be helping. I'm not protecting anyone.

Minutes have gone past now, but the cars remain parked outside with them in it. The white people haven't left. They're waiting. I step out onto the landing but just as I do the letter box bangs again, sending a shudder through the house. 'Miss Brown? Please open the door. We're here to help you. If you don't we'll be forced to break it down,' one of them shouts. I put one foot forward, uncertain of which direction to go in. Should I do as they say, or do as Mum says? Who's the baddie here? Are both the law? In the kitchen, Mum is back on lookout. A torrent of abuse rains down on them. 'Go fuck yourselves, and fuck your mothers, bumbaclart, rassclart, pussyclart.'

The white people have been joined by men in uniform. The Babylon. The pigs, as we have come to know them. I can see the tops of their round police helmets but not their faces. I know their MO. Uncle Ashley calls them 'Dutty Babylon' and Uncle Winston always talks about how they keep stopping him in the street. They beat brothers up. Brothers even die on the road or in their custody. 'Dem are the wickedest of people,' they say. 'Come here kids. They're not taking you away,' Mum repeats. There's a fierceness in her eyes that we've not seen before, but that we would also come to know.

Mum is on the landing now. She's holding the piss basin that she's slid out from under her bed. It's a plastic washing-up bowl she pisses into at night because it's too cold to go downstairs to the bathroom toilet. We all have a piss basin under our beds, but sometimes I don't use mine. I have a small back window in my room that I wedge open before stretching myself up and aiming outside into the bushy unkempt garden below, whilst still wrapped in my bed clothes to keep the warmth in.

'Mi seh move from mi fucking bloodclart door!' Mum yells and hurls the stinking contents of the bowl out onto the authorities. We hear shouts and squeals from below as it lands with a splatter. This is followed moments later by cries of disgust—the realisation that this is not water. It's urine.

Boom! All at once the front door caves in and footsteps pound up each step. I'm not torn by indecision anymore. I know whose side I'm on. I'm a cowboy. These are *my* sisters and *my* mum, and if the sheriff and all his deputies come anywhere near them, they'll have to get past me first. The footsteps are getting closer now and bodies swarm onto the upstairs landing. Angie's cries have morphed into shrieks. Inside, I am paddling furiously, but I know not to flinch in the face of danger. My face is emotionless, chest pushed out with a hint of contempt. If I had a thin, black cigar, I'd spark up a match on the kitchen worktop, light it up and take a long, slow drag. I'd tip the brim of my Stetson. If they shoot to kill, they'd better aim at the heart.

'Miss Brown! We have to do this. We're here to help you,' they say. But the white people don't storm the kitchen. Instead, they talk softly, cautiously, edging their way forward on the stairs. My eyes are fixed on them. Then, without warning, I'm uprooted from my vantage point in the doorway. Mum is dragging all three of us towards her and she clasps us tightly under her forearm.

'Move back, yu hear me. I say move yuself back!'

She's pulled out a kitchen knife, which she holds in one hand while she slowly manoeuvres us behind her body with the other. Dressed in a long kaftan that reaches below her knees, her hair tied up in a head scarf, she's turned herself into a human shield. She's not scared. She's having fun with them, disarming them.

'Look pon yu? Yu tink yu smarter than mi? Eh? How can you be smart wid ears like dat? How dem let yu in the police force looking like dat!?'

She keeps the knife held up and taunts the officers, picking out their every physical defect, making fun of them. They stare back, bemused.

'I don't know wat yu laughing at, look pon yu nose hole! How come yu ave a nose hole so big?'

'Yes, that's right I have a big nose. Very mature this conversation, isn't it?' one officer replies, which only makes Mum worse.

'What yu know bout mature? Eh? Yu tink yu ah big man? Yu

51

not a big man. Yu ah bwoy to mi. Yu is a likkle bwoy! Are yu di one in charge? Are you a sergeant wid yu stripes pon yu arm? Yeah, yu tink yu bad? Eh? Yu tink yu badder than mi? Come try take mi pikney if yu tink yu bad. Mi will cut out yu troat. Yeah come noh!' She tells them this, almost in a whisper, while squinting her eyes and biting her lower lip for good measure.

'Madam, you need to calm down,' the officer replies. The problem is, Mum is calm. We've never seen her this serene. Her voice has a deathly undertone that signals she means business.

Of the white people the doctor steps forward. 'Miss Brown, please listen to the officers. Think of your children.' His words silently wound me and I feel hot with shame that this is our Mum and I'm not a cowboy.

'Don't call mi no Miss Brown!'

'Joy, let us help you. That's why we are here. We want to help you.'

'Yu know mi?! Ey?! Don't call mi by mi fucking name, okay? I'm not your fucking friend! Nuthing wrong with me. Just come out of my house so I can feed mi kids alright, all of unno come out of mi yard! Leave before one of unno get hurt!'

A woman steps forward introducing herself as a nurse. Again, she tries to get Mum to see sense, while the officers back off and linger in the hallway, radios crackling, instructions flying back and forth. Time is dragging on and everyone is getting tired of this Mexican standoff. We've been here for a lifetime now, maybe two. There's stretches of silence, conversations in hushed tones, attempts to talk Mum down.

Something is now happening in the hallway. The officers are shifting from the stairs, stepping up the tempo. Mum senses it too and she starts shouting, grasping the knife tighter. Before she can move, three officers rush in. One circles her on one side and pulls back her empty hand while the other wrestles the blade from her.

They yank her forward onto the floor while we are herded out from behind in single file. I don't want to go. I want to stay and fight for Mum but no one is listening. As I turn, Mum is pinned to the floor and her twisted body is writhing among boots and uniforms as they hold her face down.

Seeing Mum like this is too much for me to take. I hear her scream, 'You're hurting me!' And something in me snaps. A primal rage overtakes my rational. And in the spur of the moment, I break free from the stranger's arm and run back towards my mummy.

'Leave my fucking mum alone, leave her alone, fucking leave my mum alone!' I am bawling and fighting, kicking and punching with my arms flailing, but I don't get far. I am yanked back and restrained, held on the landing with my sisters before we are marched downstairs and led towards a waiting car. No one has told us where we are going. All we know is that we're leaving Mum, and the eyes of the street are fixed on us. Angie, Mini and I sit in the backseat, heads bowed, tears pouring down our cheeks. The authorities don't look tough. They look as shaken as we are. In this standoff there's no clear victor. Maybe they're going to try and fix my mum?

Chapter 8

The World Turns Upside Down

At seven years old I was angry with the whole, wide world which began and ended in Stoke Newington, N16. What was happening to us at home began spilling over into school. The beatings became more severe when we were there. It was as if mum didn't recognise us as her children at times, and treated us like complete strangers. I couldn't contain it. Yet if you'd asked me how I felt, I wouldn't have known. Don't-give-a-fuck numb is how I'd describe it now. Not that anyone did ask. Ever. We were only told things. *Mum's not well. We're looking after you. Tomorrow you're being sent home.*

Thirty-three Forest Road in Dalston was the first children's home that we got taken to: a building that, from the outside, looked like an old people's home—a yellowish brick modern-build with a sloping roof set behind imposing walls. Its outer glass door was reinforced with wire square meshing. Inside, it had an equally sterile interior: monotonous magnolia washed through the corridor walls, the reception area, TV room, and the dining hall which was set out with fake wood grain Formica tables covered in plastic cloth. Upstairs, the dormitories were split into boys and girls. No pictures or posters were allowed, so the walls lay bare, and you could feel the metal springs of the beds poking through the thin mattresses as we shuffled uncomfortably at night. At first, we stayed there for around two months. 'Mum can't look after you,' became a familiar message, but why remained unclear. Mum loved us, so that was bewildering. But most confusing was that we'd been plucked from Alkham Road with no compass with which to find our way back, no reference points to map a return to our lives. Through Mum, we'd lived and breathed Jamaica. Our house was a mini-Jamaica. Patois ricocheted around every room. The elders' stories were etched in our memories, alongside Mum's blues parties, the baked bread and the parcels from Harriet. Instead, on one of our first evenings in Forest Road, we sat in front of *Top of the Pops* watching Status Quo sing 'Rockin' All Over the World', while the staff hummed and sang along. Reggae and dancehall didn't have a home here, and aside from Uncle Bob Marley, they weren't visible on mainstream TV. Here, 1977 was the year of the Sex Pistols and the Queen's Silver Jubilee. Culturally, we'd fallen into an abyss.

Every morning, at around 7 AM, we were woken with a knock at our dormitory door. We then filed to the bathroom, and then to the dining hall. Everything, even the staff, smelled of frowsy milk—the same distinctive smell that always hits my nostrils whenever I went to a white friend's house. Other than for porridge and tea, Mum rarely used fresh milk. She used the sweet, condensed milk from the tin that she watered down. Or we Browns drank sugared water or homemade lemonade. And yoghurt was something we only had at school. Salad and spaghetti bolognese were enigmas on a plate. It felt like we were being fed school dinners as the set up was the same, with the same tasteless, simple ingredients. No seasoning. That said, Betty, the cook, had a special place in her heart for me and my siblings, especially Huggy after he was born. A strong, heavy set, dark-skinned, Jamaican woman, she swung between being soft as pie and hard as a rock when she needed to be. Occasionally we would sneak in the back door and raid food from the cupboards if she wasn't around, but Betty always gave us second helpings reminding us that 'food should not be wasted'. She became one constant in an ever-changing world.

While we made friends with other kids, nothing lasted. The children's home was like a revolving door. Sheryl, Charmaine, Aisha, Turik, Steven, Sean and the two Sues, along with ourselves, became regulars. One Sue was deaf and we learned basic sign language to talk to her. I made sure I learnt how to sign 'cake', so I could get her pudding. Brah Anansi taught me well. Even the Thompson kids, Wayne, Paul and Emma, turned up one time for a short spell; it was the best time of our lives! All together again, the Famous Six reunited. Kids got shipped in and out. We got shipped in and out: adapting, fitting in, adjusting to a new set of rules wherever we went.

The only positive was that we'd been assigned a West Indian social worker called Andrea. She had a warm face, and she wore long skirts with boots that made her look more like a headmistress than a social worker. In this disorientating newness, Andrea became a connection to our tribe, even though she was a stranger. Over those years she was attached to our case, she had a sixth sense— an understanding that it was our circumstance that resigned us to where we were, rather than it being *who* we were. During the periods when we were allowed home, she seemed to turn a blind eye to some of Mum's behaviour to prevent us from being separated for good. I sensed that as a Black woman in that job, she knew and understood how harshly Mum would be treated in the system and was attempting to soften the reality.

After a couple of weeks at Forest Road we were allowed to see Mum. She'd been sectioned in the psychiatric ward at Homerton Hospital in Hackney and she'd be there for a while. Being led through the eerie ward, past the beds and vacant stares, and finally seeing Mum, barely recognisable, it crippled us. Runny noses and silent tears trickled down from our tiny faces in our attempt to act brave and grown up. Mum's features had completely changed. Gaunt and hollow, with nobody home. What's more, her eyelids would repeatedly blink as if they had a life of their own, something we had never seen Mum do before. Her hospital robe sat askew on her shoulder, and the exposed skin had become dry and flaky. I couldn't take my eyes off her long unkempt nails and the dark, browny-yellow of her nicotine-stained fingers that had burn marks on the tips, when the cigarettes singed her skin before she had a chance to extinguish them in the ashtray.

This was our introduction to Mum on medication. We were innocents in a hardcore world of the unwell. Even the air of that ward felt sedated. When she attempted to lean over and hug me, I felt sorry for Mum but I felt guilt, too. I hid it, but every sinew wanted to recoil from her. She appeared an empty shell, moving in cinematic slo-mo, arms heavy and lumbering, with a voice that sounded like an underwater echo: distant, monotone, drowning.

'Staaaaan. Miiiiin. Annnnnge. You okaaaaay? You all okaaaaay? It's okaaaaay. Come. Come. It's okaaaaay.'

The hardest part was reconciling our heavily medicated mother with the animated woman we knew: the mum that played Knock-Down Ginger and lined us up against the living room wall, ready for our spelling tests. Naturally, I assumed that version of Mum would be back soon, but that's what a seven-year-old would think.

At first, my dad, Anthony, came to see me once or twice at the children's home on Forest Road. He brought a brown paper bag filled with sweets, with extras for Angie and Mini, and we'd sit in the TV room in staggered silences. 'Oh bwoy. Oh man. What we gonna do with your mother like this?' he'd tut and suck his teeth. According to him, he had a plan. He and his girlfriend Olivia, whom he now lived with in Edmonton, were going to bring me back to their house, maybe even have me live there permanently.

Up for debate was whether Angie and Mini would join me, but I didn't want to push my luck, nor would I leave without them. At first, I believed him—or I wanted to believe him—but as the weeks wore on, he didn't come back. I doubt now whether there ever was any serious attempt. Sometimes I want to imagine that my dad was unrelenting in his pursuit to rescue me, that his failure was down to a cruel system, or 'dem wicked people' who stopped it, but that wouldn't be the whole truth.

In the course of time, the hospital let Mum out to visit us at the home too, but she had to return at the end of the day. She'd sit in the small TV room from morning to evening barely moving a muscle, just smoking. The staff would let her join us for food, and then she would slowly shuffle back to her spot in the TV room, lighting up cigarette after cigarette, her fingers trembling and so numbed out on medication, that she wouldn't notice when they kept burning down, scorching her skin. I would have to tap her on the arm for her to put the cigarette out. Once Mum wet herself, so I covered up the patch on her dress so no one could see, by tying her jumper around her waist when it was time for her to leave. Whenever she was well enough and got sent home from hospital, we were fetched by the social worker from Forest Road and taken back to Alkham Road. No one came. No one offered to scoop us up and take us in, even though we hoped that they would.

While we lived at the children's home, we didn't attend our regular primary school. Instead, we got temporarily enrolled in the school opposite, called Holy Trinity. When it came to telling the other kids where I was from I buried that we lived in care. On one parents' evening, when the care-home manager Felicity stood in as my substitute mother, the charade became too painful for me. I hung back, slumped against the corridor wall outside the classroom, refusing to stand beside her while she thumbed through my work, set out for inspection by my teacher.

I didn't warm to Felicity or trust her. She was built like the Michelin Man with rolls of fat for legs and her arms bloated, looking like pillows, with a small head too that seemed out of place on such a large body. She resembled a female version of the wrestler Giant Haystacks. She wore round, black-rimmed glasses and had a tiny terrier dog, Dennis, always running behind her that stank to high heaven! Her word was the final word. 'It's up to you' was her catchphrase, always delivered with nasty sarcasm.

'Here you are again in front of me for yet another problem, Stanley. I can sit here all day. It's up to you.' Cue an awkward silence while I nonchalantly kicked around my options.

'I can see with that attitude, you don't want supper tonight, Stanley. It's up to you.' That one was easy, supper was a yogurt, tangerine and a pack of crisps.

On one occasion she got wind that I'd spat at another kid, but instead of summoning me to her office, she hunted me down in the smoking room, hanging out with the older kids, listening to music. I was sprawled out on a single armchair enjoying the jokes and feeling like I was a teenager. Slowly, she lowered herself to my level and leaned closer into my face.

'Don't... You... Ever...', she spoke menacingly, before I felt a large, wet glob of phlegm spatter my face, 'Do... That... Again,' she concluded, before levering herself up and swinging her lumpish frame out of the room. The violation left me feeling utterly powerless in front of my peers. A massive argument ensued when the teenagers kicked off and were up in arms, challenging her for what she did to me. But she simply folded her arms and stood her ground without a care in the world, exerting her authority, and reminding them who was in charge.

Felicity said everything was up to us, except it wasn't. For starters, being there was not a choice at all, precisely nothing was up to us. It didn't take me long to cotton on that I was at the whim of people who pushed me, pulled me, ferried me around, got me settled in and then upturned my world. In spite of that, I was expected to carry on as normal: be a good, balanced child who could make choices that would serve me well. Sure, our caregivers were well-meaning, but they didn't understand us. Behind their backs I called them the 'goodie-goodie white people'. All our talk of home and our so-called family and of cornmeal porridge and Uncle Bob Marley was met with the polite veneer of incomprehension. Yet all we were doing was comforting ourselves, clinging on to Mum's ties and the scraps of everything we knew.

When 33 Forest Road was full we got sent to a holding pen, a temporary children's home at Mathias Road, also in Stoke Newington. It had yellow walls for the girls' dorm and blue for the boys' with a middle section of old Victorian baths. Procedure was procedure. We were registered, questions asked, boxes ticked, forms signed and afterwards we got taken to be bathed. We always had a bath upon arrival and the soap felt luxurious. Whenever Mum ran out of soap at home she used washing-up liquid on our skin and hair.

As we always arrived with no possessions other than the clothes we had on, we had to dress up in other people's hand-me-downs. At the top of the stairs, in a big cupboard, there was a lost property box of mismatched children's clothes, full of pyjama tops and bottoms, skirts, trousers, and T-shirts. We even wore other people's knickers and underpants. I felt like the scarecrow character Worzel Gummidge, trying on different personalities for size, rifling through, holding up outfits, throwing them on just to come to life again.

The words, 'You're going home today, Mum can look after you now,' should have been a relief, and at first they were. That was until we fully understood what going home meant. Any routine was short-lived. Our lives stopped, started, sped up, slowed down, careered around corners, crashed and burned. Going back to our family home in Alkham Road became a literal Joy ride.

* * *

Angie is screaming at the top of her lungs. She is naked and desperately trying to break free. She has been caught by Mum at the bottom of the stairs and she is crouching, curled tight in a hedgehog ball, to shield herself from the blows. A thick, black leather trouser belt that Mum has cut in half, splices the air and makes a whistling sound before it slowly thwacks against my sister's skin. Mum has named the belt Roots after a TV programme about an African man called Kunta Kinte who has been sold into slavery and is whipped for refusing to say his slave name, Toby. Roots hangs on a long nail above the light switch next to the kitchen and has five eyes and a V-shaped tongue. Even while sleeping, he looks menacing.

I've heard Angie's frantic cries from my bedroom and I am trembling by the time I reach the landing. I know these beatings well. I can almost taste the blood in my mouth. Sometimes, if I know I'm in line for one, I race into my room and throw on layer upon layer of jumpers to pad myself out, and stuff a towel into the back of my trousers to protect my arse.

Angie is nine years old, so skinny that her spine forms a perfect arch when she hugs her knees. You could walk up it vertebra by vertebra. She's seen me from the corner of her eye. 'Help me, Stanley!' she screams as she turns her head. I see a trickle of blood coming from her nose. Once again, I feel that primal rage coming to the surface from inside of me, and I feel powerless to stop myself. I edge my way down not sure of what I will do, but I'm stopped by Mum, who looks dead into my eyes. Keeping one hand clasped on Angie's neck, she points to me with the other, and squints as if she's sizing me up.

'So, you tink you are a man?' Her voice is low and deliberate. Her eyes are full of this sickness: fierce, yet vacant, and they have made me wet myself in the past. I decide to front it out and move down one step further. At this, Mum's mood changes. She releases her grip on Angie before stretching out a hand to help her up. 'I'm not going to hurt you, silly. Come on. Get up and go upstairs to your room.' Mum's voice is gentle, almost childlike and the same Queen's English she put on when the doctor came. My sister is cautious. She flinches at Mum's every move and doesn't get up. Instead, she stays crouched, fixated on Mum's eyes.

Without warning, Mum loses patience. Her hand slaps the side of Angie's face. She didn't see it coming. Neither did I. Angie breaks free and bolts up the stairs as if Mum is pursuing her, but she doesn't follow. Her attention turns to me. She softens, stretches out her hand to touch me, which I instantly back away from.

'It's okay, relax yourself. Relax man. Relax,' she says. It's as if she's a snake charmer. Before I can move, her hands are on my shoulders massaging them, working on my body until I allow myself to uncoil a fraction. She repeats the same words, hypnotising me, before she guides me so I'm flush against the landing wall. 'Straighten yourself. Relax,' she says, but I can't help myself. I let out a stifled laugh. I'm scared, but I'm also embarrassed. I feel I am about to wet myself, so I concentrate when she asks me to look into her eyes, trying hard not to giggle. There is something about looking into someone's eyes, especially your own mother's that makes me want to laugh. I'm searching hard, but I can't see Mum. Instead I see the illness that has inhabited her being and left her an empty shell, void of compassion and love. Where is my mummy?

Booof! The blow to my stomach. I was so busy looking for Mum that it takes the breath right out of me. A dull ache spreads through my body. I try to breathe. Nothing. I try again. Nothing. My body slowly melts to the floor and lying on my back, I look up at my two sisters who are looking down between the banisters on the stairs. They look cloudy, and are upside down.

It's okay Mummy. It's okay. I love you Mummy. It's not your fault. It's not your fault. I repeat this in my head before silently saying goodbye to Angie and Mini, telepathically, staring into their upside-down eyes. I start to blackout.

'Breathe! Breathe!' The words come in short, sharp bursts. Mum is shaking me, eyes locked onto me. Now I can see concern, fear, and the love. 'Breathe, son, breathe!' she is whispering. Did she *really* just call me son?

It didn't take long for me to work out that school wasn't a place to learn anything. It was a means to an end. I got fed, I could escape from home, but most of all, I could take out my frustrations on whoever crossed me. At Fountayne Road primary, Mrs Hassocks was my head teacher. On top she had brunette mopped hair, and she wore horn-rimmed spectacles, trousers and a suit jacket which she constantly adjusted and picked at fluff that wasn't there. She had a special place for me in her life: a desk directly outside her office, a permanent fixture, where I was sent when the teachers had enough of me. There, I started to push down every emotion. I became a walking reaction to whatever presented itself at home, or at school, where I attracted a different kind of attention.

In the playground, I collected a new family. These friends were the school cast-offs—the weaker kids of all colours and shapes and sizes that I called my cousins, and woe betide anyone who messed with any of them. Being the caretaker that I was, I would defend and protect. Because I was taller and looked much older than my years, gazing in the mirror at myself, I saw the frown of degradation etched on my face, the void in my eyes, my nappy black hair, and the light patches scattered around my skin. I had nothing to lose and thought nothing of picking a fight. I had punch-ups lined up almost every day of the week. I would fight kids on my lunch breaks, milk breaks, another after school when the bell rang at 3:30 PM. If anyone thought about cussing me or my family out, they would be punished before the insult even landed. If a kid was being bullied, I was the go-to. Even though I was feared by some kids and seen as a bully myself, I would beat up the bullies, which made me a bit of a hypocrite, but I didn't see it that way at the time. I was being bullied at home which was nothing compared to what I was doing at school. I forced kids to give me their puddings and made their lives hell if I was having a bad day. Teachers didn't want me in their classes, and I was constantly being suspended. I felt the power over others when I was powerless over my own destiny and whether or not I would sleep in my own bed. I arrived at a place where I no longer cared if I lived or died.

Even my best friend at school, Grant Davis, wasn't immune. He was a gangly kid who lived around the corner on Osbaldeston Road and walked as if he was made of plasticine. We bonded because we were both fast runners, but Grant was the angel to my devil: high spirited, always laughing at things that weren't even funny, and making me laugh too, but ultimately a kid who toed the line. When trouble landed, usually because of me, he was out of there. I admired him for that, but he also took seriously the job of keeping me on the straight and narrow and talking to me as if he was my dad, giving me unsolicited advice.

One time when Mum went through a phase of making clothes for us from any material she could find, she sent me to school with trousers made from curtains: thick gabardine with a flowery pattern. Covering up his open mouth with both hands, trying his best to stifle a grin, Grant's jaw dropped with disbelief. But he also wanted to protect me. He knew I'd be embarrassed. 'Stanley man, they look like... Cur...?' Yes, they were curtains, but I couldn't bear to hear him say it out loud, nor did I want him to make me say it. My defences were up and before I knew it, I punched him straight in the face. I immediately saw the shock in his eyes and felt the hurt from his tears. He had seen me attack other kids, but he didn't expect me to ever turn on him.

Even though Mum brought us up with a clear sense of right and wrong, I began to 'borrow' items from the classroom. At first I started borrowing plastic toy cars to take home. Then, it progressed to dinner money. As a way of cajoling me into the system, and to make me feel included because I was otherwise always in trouble, my teacher gave me the 'very important job' of transporting the class dinner money to the secretary's office each morning. The money was kept in brown envelopes placed inside a wall-papered tin. Unbeknownst to her, this was setting me up to fail. These slim, brown envelopes were bursting with the £1 notes and 50p pieces that made our TV or gas or electricity switch on at home. So, I stopped off at the boys' toilets, gently unpeeled the seal, and shoved a few coins into my pockets making sure I pressed the open envelopes back together, smoothing them with my fingers, before handing the tin to the secretary. Later, I banked them under the lino in my bedroom. When nothing happened, I graduated to the £1 notes. The day Angie discovered me counting my loot and told Mum was the day I thought I would die from the beating. Yet, on this occasion, Mum didn't bring out Roots or the curtain rod, another weapon that made a whipping noise as it licked against your skin. 'Get your coats kids, we're going out,' she shouted from the living room. 'Stanley, bring everything you have.' I thought great, Mum was going to spend the money on food. She marched us up to Stoke Newington High Street, but marched right past all the shops and into a large, grey building. P-O-L-I-C-E. It took me a moment to read then register the sign. Holy shit!

'My son has something to tell you,' she announced to the desk sergeant. I looked at him blankly as if Mum was delusional and looked back up at Mum with the same look. 'WACK!' She slapped me so hard across the face that my legs buckled. I started talking in tongues and confessing to all that I had done.

Once Mum made me recite my crime and empty out my pockets, the sergeant walked me to one of the cells as a scare tactic. Instead of feeling scared, I celebrated. As soon as the cell door banged shut, I stretched myself out on the concrete slab. Thank God I hadn't got a beating. It was peaceful in there, and as I read the graffiti covering the walls—So-and-So woz here, 1964—so I too etched my name with my belt buckle. I felt I'd just been inducted into a hall of fame. I was special.

I am standing with Mum at the Post Office in Stoke Newington. It's a busy lunchtime and it's filled with people. The Asian man behind the counter is telling Mum she can't claim her benefit today, that her DHSS book has expired and she needs to go to the benefits office and wait in the queue to get a new one. But Mum wasn't having it. I'm not concentrating on the detail, instead I'm waiting and watching her mood. I know the signs; I know the moment when Mum is about to rage. My heart begins to race and I see the scene unfold before me, the switch having been flicked. Mum is shouting at the man behind the protective glass. *Rassclart, bumbleclart, motherfucker.* The room is silent and everyone is staring. Once again the shame is burning a hole in me. I want the ground to swallow me up. The man behind the counter is sitting still trying to calm Mum but he's only making the situation worse. He's going to regret he ever refused her the money. Mum is bending down. She's taking off her shoe. She's hammering the heel against the glass pane. Hammering. Hammering. When is this going to end. People are calling out from the queue now. It's an incident and someone needs to call the police. The glass is shattering into pieces. The police have been called and we can hear the sirens outside. Now we're in the back of a police van. Mum is handcuffed to the seat. The officer is making polite conversation but Mum is cussing her out. *Yu stinking pussyclart. Don't fucking smile at my kids, yu fucking stinking pussyclart.* The WPC officer is looking at me and she looks sorry, she looks sorry that this is my mother. I'm sorry too. I'm sorry about the officer and I'm sorry about Mum. But I have no feeling left to be sorry about *me*. I feel like the protective glass, shattered.

Maybe if someone had spoken to me about how I felt, I might have told them how I lay awake longing for life to go back to the way it was; how I was terrified of Mum; how I worried about her, too, and my sisters; how I had a constant grinding in my belly; how I didn't understand that Mum couldn't simply be fixed. Mum's illness didn't even have a name. A broken arm, you can mend. A broken mind can't be glued back together. Why can't they just fix my Mum?

Chapter 9

Elvis

We are home and Mum is well enough to look after us again. She is cooking, but these days it's hardly ever for us. Our kitchen is no longer filled with the smell of baking bread and mint tea from Harriet. Tonight, Elvis Presley is Mum's only dinner guest. She loses herself in him, and hums along to his songs spilling from the record player while chicken is marinating, rice and peas boil on the stove and dumplings are lowered into sizzling oil.

From the landing stairs Angie, Mini and I can see Mum's large shadow twisting to the rhythm. Mum isn't the woman with the slim calves and high-heeled boots anymore. Her eyes are puffy and red and she's stopped taking the medication. Her clothes have gotten ragged, as if she's washed up on a desert island.

Our kitchen has no door. Mum ripped it from its hinges ages ago and hung bamboo beads in its place which, at the slightest touch, rattle loudly like a maracas shaker. The stairs have become our permanent safe harbour from which where we rarely venture when Mum is raging. At times, we huddle together on the top step with the free Kays Catalogue on our knees, thumbing to the back where the food hampers ooze promise: tinned hams, exotic fruits, continental cakes, Terry's chocolate. We take it in turns and pretend to scoop up each item and cram it into our mouths: 'Oooh yummy'.

We play with our imaginary food, chew on it, smack our lips until we are full. It's remarkable that this play-acting actually makes us feel full, but the feeling doesn't last. When the acid fire in our bellies reminds us we haven't eaten all day and missed school, we tiptoe to the bathroom, crane our necks over the basin and slurp cold water from the running tap. Water acts as a poor substitute for the satisfaction of sinking our teeth into a warm fried dumpling or any of the delicious food we remember emanating from Mum's kitchen, but it brings a temporary comfort and helps soothe the burn.

We sing, too. Sing for our supper. Our heads sway in unison, right then left and back. We repeat the chorus of Uncle Bob Marley's 'Three Little Birds' over and over. Then, we take it in turns to sing a verse, or harmonise to pass the time until we grow weary of singing, and of hunger. It's now 9 PM, and there is no sign that Elvis is leaving anytime soon.

Eventually, on nights like these, asking Mum for food is our next move. We also take this in turns, but as I am the man of the house, mostly I assume the responsibility of walking the line between expectation and rejection—the hero child, restoring order and dignity to our fractured lives. But this decision always comes after some bickering.

'You ask!'

'No, I did it last time...'

'No you didn't. I asked Mum. It's your turn...'

It's usually me and with the decision made, I creep downstairs, approaching the beaded curtain side on. Pausing briefly, I weigh up the right moment to make my entrance so as not to disturb Mum's reverie. The last thing I want to do is surprise Mum or appear a threat. I breathe deeply, puff out my chest but keep my head bowed. I've figured out a way to announce I'm there before I step into the half-light. One glance towards the stairs where Angie and Mini are egging me on seals my mission. Their eyebrows, raised with urgency, insist, 'Go on.' I can do this. I am ready. Gently, I clear my throat, but as I turn, I am paralysed. Mum has already clocked me, and from behind the beads her deathly stare is bearing down into my gaze. I know that if I stare back too long she'll lash out. She has a rule that none of us are allowed to look into her eyes anymore. Every part of my body twists. My thoughts are scrambled. I've been caught off guard, and I can't get the lines I've rehearsed out of my mouth. She holds my gaze until I remember the rule and my eyes frantically dart around the floor trying to avoid any eye contact. I can sense her still staring until she breaks off, starts to hum again, and floats back inside the kitchen as if I wasn't there. The smell of potential violence lingers in the doorway.

The line has been crossed, though, and I now stay rooted to the spot in no man's land. I've come too far to re-join Angie and Mini but I can't move forward to ask Mum for food, either. Not in the way I'd imagined. I am diminished. A poor Oliver Twist, rags hanging, palms cupped to the heavens.

'Kids. Go to bed. School in the morning!' Mum calls breezily. We know this voice well now, but we still attach hope to it. The tone of her words suggests affection and it still triggers a self-deception that I play out in my head—the deception that proves Mum still loves us. *That's it! Mum has forgotten to feed us, and now the ghost of Elvis has turned up with his lonesome lullabies and his 'Love Me Tender'. If I remind her nicely...*

I clear my throat again, hoping the words might tumble out, but instead my voice fades to a whisper. 'Muuuuummmm, can we have some foooooood pleeeeeeese?' This, too, is ignored. I hate Elvis. He always has Mum's attention when we are hungry. Tonight I grow impatient, vexed at his presence. Unscripted, I lose my inhibitions for one careless moment and a defiant Oliver erupts—not begging, but making a stand against this clear injustice. '*Mum!* Can we have some food pl...'

Mum spins around, crackling and spitting. 'I said go to your fucking bed! School tomorrow. Don't ask me anything more. Hurry up! Bloodclart, rassclart, come disturb mi spirit.'

Elvis doesn't only visit Mum in the kitchen. He's creeps into other rooms, too. He steals other needs. Most of all, he steals love. It took me many years to understand complicity, but we weren't complicit—we were an audience to Mum's fantasies, participants, tangled up in them. Not that I blame us for that. We were kids. It wasn't so long ago that Mum talking to herself was funny, before it got underpinned by a mute horror.

As far as food is concerned, Mum's wedding day—her most elaborate fantasy—has been the only time we've got to share anything with Elvis: dumplings, plantains, fried chicken, all laid out for us in a never-ending spread. We had a feast!

As for the ceremony, the only inkling we had that something was afoot was the sound of Mum's sewing machine, fired hour after hour like an M16 automatic rifle, punctuated by the silence of it being reloaded. Then one Sunday, we were woken early, made to take a bath, washed, dried and creamed with Vaseline. Our hair was combed and plaited and we were each handed homemade outfits: dresses for the girls and a suit for me, all made from sheeny curtain material—the product of Mum's night shifts.

She made a dress for herself, too: its bodice and train fashioned from net curtains that had hung from the large sash windows around the house. They screened us from the outside world, but without them, the windows looked naked. The summer sunshine streams through, exposing a truth and making the living room stagnant and oppressive, and the faux leather sofa sticky.

Just before Mum made her grand entrance, we're made to stand to attention, our mouths dropping as she turned the corner. Little by little, she made her way across the room in pigeon steps, the whiteness of the net brilliant against the retro red linoleum, mopped clean especially for the occasion. Never mind that the veil trailed metres outside the door and onto the landing. Mum didn't care about that. It was all about the wedding.

Her vows were timed to coincide with the Elvis double bill that happened every week on the BBC. But Mum was so early that we were made to rehearse over and over while she hummed 'Here Comes the Bride' and staged her entrance. All the while, the sunlight streamed in, torturing us with the knowledge that our friends were out playing. Why were we indoors, bored and frustrated? Why were we trapped in a carnival of the grotesque, a scene more outlandish than our imaginations could stretch?

Moments before the matinee started, Mum instructed us to wait outside the living room door and clutch her train. The 20th Century Fox fanfare sounded and the famous searchlight swept across the screen as Mum stepped her perfect steps, reaching the TV set as a young Elvis, dressed as a GI in uniform with a peaked cap, launched into song. Standing side on, as if he were facing her, she spoke solemnly, 'For better, for worse, for richer, for poorer, in sickness and in health, to love and to cherish, till death us do part,' she said, concluding with 'I do'.

Our uncontrollable giggles stopped long ago and now we glanced at each other with disgust. Was this actually happening? Was Mum married to Elvis now? In her mind, yes, but it didn't last. Not long afterwards, Mum kicked him out. We found her one afternoon yelling that he'd kissed one too many white actresses. All his vinyl records got smashed to smithereens with the hammer and thrown away. That was it. Elvis had left the building.

Tonight, though, it is all about survival. With no food to bring Angie and Mini, I watch as they trudge up the next flight of stairs which leads to their room. Mum went on a painting escapade recently, and painted over our bright wallpaper with a dark, mauve, purple and the skirting a fluorescent-looking lime green.

She dismantled her double-sided wardrobe into bits and used some of the bigger pieces to paint pictures on. Mum's a good artist, to this day we have kept her work. The house is dark and eerie, it feels colder, damper, more uninhabitable. When it rains outside, it rains inside. In winter, we can see our breath as we lie in our dew-soaked sheets waiting for first light.

'Night night' I mouth to them, but I see tears in Angie's eyes. Inside, I'm squirming. I've let them down. The man of the house can't even bring his sisters food. But there's one last weapon left in my armoury: the food will have to be stolen.

I've become good at stealing. I've been practising for a while now, sharpening my skills on the streets on the days when Elvis visits or there is no food in the fridge. Out there, I'm the concrete jungle 'Invisible Man', from one of my favourite TV shows. Some mornings, I wake instinctively and lie in bed waiting until the tinkling of milk bottles is almost detectable. There it is, 'chink chink', followed by the faint whirr of the electric float making its way up our street. 'Chink chink'. There it is again. I spring into action, pull my clothes on over my pyjamas and creep out of my room onto the landing and down the stairs. I know all the musical notes of these stairs off by heart—the creaks and groans that if landed on could wake my beloved sick mother who would certainly give me a beating.

Often, it's still black outside when I force my feet into my Woolworths' plimsolls that have cardboard stopping up the holes and follow the fog of my breath into the open air. I glide along the pavement keeping as close to any bushes so as not to be seen. Ahead, in the middle of the road, I can make out the glow leaking from the float's headlights. I sink into the foliage and watch as my prey is methodically carried up each set of stairs and placed outside the doors.

On occasions, panic lurches through me. Did I remember

to take the latch off our front door and wedge it shut with the folded-up cardboard? Will the wind blow it open and wake my mother? Or, worse, the Hawthorns downstairs? Worse still, alert the milkman? I stamp down these doubts immediately. My sisters are counting on me. I cross Alkham Road and jump the wall to reach Kyverdale Road where that morning's deliveries have already been made. There they are, all lined up, illuminated by the streetlight. There's not only bottles of milk, but there's eggs, bread, orange juice and butter, but I don't have the heart to take everything from one house, which would be easier. Instead, I hunt the hard way. Bread from one step, milk from another, continuing along until my arms can't carry anymore.

As soon as I've gathered enough, I head back. There's eggs to boil and bread to eat, which we wash down with the milk and orange juice before school. I always want to tell my sisters the story of how I criss-crossed from house to house, invisible, evading capture, but there's never any time. We have to eat before Mum stirs. Often, there's enough bread left over, so I store it under my bed for the rest of the week wrapped in my clothes, hoping the rats don't get to it first. I'm the breadwinner and I love the feeling whenever I reveal this stash to my sisters, applying a finger to my lips. 'Shshhhhhhhhh'. It's a feeling that I always want to feel, and this evening is no different. Like a caveman discovering fire. Me. Man. Feed family!

It's late now, well after 10 PM, and I lay on my bed and wait for Mum to leave the kitchen. I strain to hear, but I can make out a final rattle of the beads and the ker-clunk of the bathroom light switching off.

I leap into action. Now, I am the domestic commando, the home-front hero. The beads fall a foot from the ground leaving a gap wide enough to low-crawl underneath. I spotted this opportunity soon after Mum ripped the door off, and I've become an expert at levering my body under with my elbows and dragging myself across the floor careful not to hit a single bead, as if I'm playing buzz-wire.

Yet for all that, I need an accomplice for this job. It will have to be Mini. She is braver, and she now has a nickname: Robin. I am Batman, she is Robin. Angie also has a nickname, Bob, after Uncle Bob Marley, on account of her long plaits that resemble dreadlocks when they are pulled out.

I enter their room. 'I need someone to help me get food from the kitchen?' I whisper. I flick on the light momentarily but Angie cusses me out to turn it off. She's tired and resigned to hunger. Besides, she plays by the rules, except 'the rules' have become arbitrary since Mum's illness. 'We're not allowed without asking Mummy,' she tells me, but I know better the necessity of this noble cause corruption. So does Robin, who, led by her instincts and her hunger, responds by climbing from her bed and following me move for move as we zig-zag *en pointe* down the stairs.

She waits barefoot in her nighty at the top of the landing, so that when it's time to pass the plates out she can tiptoe down and collect them. Also, there's more chance she can escape undetected if Mum makes an appearance. Meanwhile, I continue down the next flight of steps. With Mum's bedroom to the side of the kitchen, I see there is light peeking from under her door that illuminates in the hallway for me. It's safe. Pausing first to tuck my trousers into my socks and my T-shirt into my trousers so there's no risk of snagging, I lower myself onto my front and ease and slide my way under the beads: head; shoulders; elbows; waist; hips; back of knees and finally, ankles and socked feet.

All of a sudden I hear Mum shuffling in her room. Prickles of sweat needle my skin. Shit! Is she getting up to use the toilet? Thinking fast, I push myself up to the other side of the beads and slide under the kitchen table, reaching a safe spot as her bedroom door flies open. *Boom*! Mum is in the kitchen. I dare not look up. The beads are singing loudly now, swaying from side to side, and Mum is still humming. Her feet make their way to the kitchen sink and the faucet opens to fill a glass with water. She strides back. The beads are just coming to a standstill when *Boom*! she sends them bouncing again, the sound reverberating as adrenaline rips through me. The dim light in the passage which guided me down has now gone pitch black after Mum turns her light off, and I am left there, curled under the table unable to see anything in front of me.

With Mum settled back in her room, my eyes adjust to the darkness and I start to see shadowy outlines with the help of the faint streetlight glowing through the window. The cupboards, cooker, sink, all become vaguely visible, and the purr of the fridge soothes me sounding much louder than usual. I just need to get the food from the pots and onto a plate. If I fail, the food will stay there all night before it is decanted into the fridge and eaten only by her. Sometimes, it will stay there for days, congealing and growing mould until Mum throws it out.

Slowly, I prise a plate from the top of the stack by the sink before I make my way to the stove. I edge one lid up. Maybe I'll need a spoon for this, but I decide against it on account of the noise and settle on using my fingers as a scoop. Rice and peas land on the plate. I eat some as I go along, making sure that I pat the rice down when I am done so as to make it look untouched. Next, I move to the chicken, which is sealed in a cast iron Dutch pot used in Caribbean households to cook meat in. Mum says the food tastes better than using the English pots. The Dutch pot is heavy and trickier to manoeuvre without the metal clattering, and it takes me twice as long to replace the lid.

I go to slide the mountain of food under the beads but now I hesitate over the fried dumplings, which lay on the table in a bowl covered by a tea towel. Would Mum have counted them? I decide she hasn't and take one from the bottom of the pile, careful to rearrange them afterwards.

Back on the landing, I am now willing my mother to move around so I can sense which part of her room she is in. When her light is on, I can tell from the shapes cast under the doorway. Tonight, there is no beam guiding me on my first step to freedom. With a full plate in hand, I have to feel my way in the dark back up the stairs. Robin's tiny figure startles me. She has been waiting patiently all this time. 'Come,' I whisper and we sit in the girls' room and quietly share the food using only our fingers. There are no words, only slurping and swallowing as we sit over the plate, taking it in turns to scoop up each mouthful.

Once it's licked clean, my sisters climb back into bed and I head down to my room with the plate wedged under my armpit. I slide into my damp tomb for the night and hide the plate under my bed. I am glowing with success. Just as I am sinking into sleep, my body tenses and my eyes fly open. My heart is beating fast as another shot of adrenaline passes through me. Did I remember to cover over the dumplings with the tea towel?

Chapter 10

Jah! Rastafari!

Nineteen seventy-eight was the winter of our discontent. Rubbish piled up outside Victorian terraces waiting for striking bin men to return to work. Stoke Newington Common, at the bottom of Alkham Road, was a mountain of cardboard and bin bags and car tyres, all teeming with rats. On the high street, the derelict shops with their smashed-out windows were now corrugated iron fortresses. Our decay was part of something bigger, more powerful.

Time dragged by and at nine-and-a-half-years old, I was trying to find my way back home. As Mum had introduced us to the TV series based on the Alex Haley novel *Roots*, I imagined myself to be the slave Kunta Kinte: sold in Africa and shipped to a Virginia plantation to be worked and whipped and beaten, in the end relinquishing all hope of ever returning. I was in awe of the leading actor, LeVar Burton: bare-chested, chained by a yoke to a new way of life, alien to anything he'd known, searching for belonging in a cruel world.

Mum's illness now had a name—the doctors called it schizophrenia, which wasn't a word we understood. And no one ever said it. Whenever Mum's illness got discussed, there were pauses and ambiguity. People spoke under their breath. 'Some-ting do

Joy, man. She noh right.' She was supposed to have drug injections. She kept it up at first, but we always knew when Mum stopped going for them. That was when our home descended into chaos. Mum would be hospitalised again, and we would be shuttled between Forest Road and Mathias Road Children's Homes.

As for visitors, Mum expelled most people from her life. Auntie Beryl came occasionally, but Mum hardly ever answered the door. Uncle Ashley persisted, but Mum threw her basins of piss on him too. Anyone else got chased back with a broom handle. We existed inside our own fortress, and that winter the cold bit hard.

By then, I was turning up to school just enough to escape serious trouble, but not enough to be present. I decided I had a more important mission. Stealing food only went so far, and without regular heating it was time to find work. On the corner, there was a shop run by a Greek lady called Minerva. She shared the same name as my sister, and she always mentioned it when we went there, so I figured I had an 'in' already.

'What age are you son?' She laughed when I lied about being 12 and announced that I was looking for a job.

'If you're looking for work, you have to say: 'Do you have any vacancies please?'' she smiled, as if I were playing a game.

'Vay-can-kie please,' I repeated back to her.

'Try again, son. It's Vac an-cie.'

My newfound word took me in and out of shops up one side of Stoke Newington High Street and back down the other, until I reached the health food shop. Outside, there was a Rastaman leaned up against the doorway who had an air of ownership about him. I'd never seen a Black shop owner before, only ever workers, and it drew me in. Besides, I loved the Rasta men in their red, gold and green hats. There was one who often greeted me on my way to school: 'Irie, yut man. Jah guide and protect, sceen.' He looked so calm, bouncing, leaning back on his Clarkes shoes, as if buoyed by invisible springs, while his bright Rasta belt loosely swayed from his hip. Everything about him was so cool and relaxed, even the way he walked and talked. I loved the way the Rasta colours weaved in and out of each other against the backdrop of London grey. And I thought he might make a good boyfriend for Mum, and a good dad for us. Maybe I can introduce him to Mum somehow?

Although we never thought of him as Mum's boyfriend, the main man who came to our house was Mini's dad, Linton. Before Mum's illness, he'd arrive ad hoc with gifts for us and a large wad of cash for Mum, which he'd slapped down on the table. Mostly, he was drunk. Sometimes I found him funny, but in a pathetic way. His appearances mostly coincided with him wanting to be fed but seared into my memory was one occasion when he lurched through our front door drunk as a skunk, after banging on it for ages, and shouting through our letterbox, loud enough to disturb the neighbours. There he sat at Mum's table, demanding food.

'Joy, where mi dinner deh? Why yu tek long fi open di door?' he slurred.

'It's in the pot. If you want it, go help yourself!' Mum replied. Angie, Mini and I laughed our heads off at Mum's response. He saw the funny side, too, bit his bottom lip, and began to chuckle with us, then we all sat there laughing in stitches. Even Mum joined in.

'Mi mus help myself? Yu tink that's funny?' he repeated, slouching back on his chair, looking at each of us and rubbing his crutch, which made us giggle even more, and the way he kept saying it.

At that, he slowly leaned over, still chuckling, picked up the now empty Ribena bottle from the table, and smashed it across Mum's forehead, splitting it open. There was blood everywhere. We kids froze. Like rabbits caught in the headlights, petrified. 'Go clean yuself up and go get mi dinner,' he said in a matter-of-fact way. In the silence of her moans, Mum raised herself up from the table, walked to the sink, bandaged her head with a tea towel, reached for a plate and then dished up Linton's dinner before sitting back down as if nothing had happened, her blood dripping down the side of her face. After that, when Linton was being funny or pathetic, I never forgot that he had a brutal edge to him and I secretly vowed to make him pay for what he did to Mum that day.

Uncle Ashley, the Rastaman, was probably our most stable influence. Although he was never Mum's boyfriend, it wasn't for the lack of him trying. Animated with a slim frame and skin that glowed a smooth dark velvet, he was the epitome of health. Just like the Rastas who came in and out of the health food shop, he ate only Ital food, deriving from the English word 'vital': vegan, before veganism ever became fashionable. When he said, 'Jah guide and protect,' he meant the universe would guide and protect us. A painter and decorator by trade, he'd often teach me skills. And, despite his conspiracy theories about Babylon and di system, he never forgot that we were children who needed looking after.

When I eventually reached the health food shop to ask if they had any vacancies, the Rastaman leaning outside reminded me of Uncle Ashley.

'How old are you?' he looked down. The 'I'm 12' trick didn't wash and after bartering me down to the truth, he asked, 'Why you not in school bwoy?' I told him about Mum and that she was ill and that I needed money. And he listened. But he didn't own the shop, he explained. Instead, he worked for a white owner, but if I started sweeping the floor, he would pay me out of his own wages. 'Yes Uncle,' I replied, but he didn't want me to call him that. His name was Rasta Mark, and when I told him about Uncle Ashley, he knew who he was. 'Yeah mon, mi know brodder Ashley!' Finally, I had an 'in' to an even better family.

For months, there wasn't a day when I didn't turn up at the

health food shop, either after school or when I was supposed to be in class. Rasta Mark fascinated me. I often watched him sitting, smoking his spliff and stroking his thin beard, lost in his thoughts. He came from Ghana. A real live Kunta Kinte, full of wise words gleaned from experience that only elders knew. He said words like, 'Don't watch me. Watch yuself, Stanley. Dis country man. I tell yu. It's dread. Dreader than dred, bwoy. Yu have to be mindful how you trad inah Babylon! Serious tings!'

Rasta Mark lived above the shop and after I finished my work, he invited me to eat with him. He served food in a Calabash bowl, made from the husk of a fruit called a long melon. He taught me how to hold a guitar and pluck the strings to Uncle Bob Marley's 'Redemption Song'. He showed me the Old Testament, the part of the Bible Rastafarians adhere to. Chiefly, he taught me about the book of Revelations and about the prediction that a Black Messiah would come to Earth, and how this Messiah had arrived in the form of Haile Selassie, the Ethiopian emperor. He was our link back to Africa: the Black redeemer, our Jesus, who would spirit the descendants of slaves, like Mum's family, out of the shit and back to their spiritual homeland.

'Don't mek anyone tell you is only the white man dat is wicked. Black man is also wicked,' he cautioned, teaching me that our own people sold us into slavery, too.

After a few weeks, I'd progressed from sweeping the floor to packing shelves and before long I was working behind the till. I was polite and helpful and customers came into the shop to be served by me. I stopped combing my hair and let it grow into short dreadlocks and I became a part of the Rastafarian Tribe. I felt alive and respected. Not only was I earning money for Mum, but these men gave me attention. They schooled me, not in maths and English and the lessons I hated, but in who I was. In the care system, nothing was my own. My heritage was quietly snatched away from me. At home, my dignity got trashed. To survive, I had to be so many different people. But these quiet, humble, warriors became the architects of an identity that felt steadfast to me—an identity that was real.

Most of all, I could fail in front of them, free from judgement.

One time, I sat with the tribe of elders, listening to them discuss life and Jah and the Babylonian ways. The chalice, the Rastafarian equivalent of the shisha pipe, was homemade. It was tall and had a long wooden stem sticking out from the side with a base made from the husk of a coconut decorated with carvings. There was a cone shaped funnel that sat on top at one end where they put in the herbs. In the belly of the empty coconut they added water so the smoke could fill up quickly as they drew in a lungful of Ganja. It always made a gurgling sound whenever they inhaled. This was passed around and I watched as the herbs got loaded and lit. As the smoke billowed out of each man's nostrils and mouth, it gave me goosebumps. And as it made its way around to me, I couldn't believe that I was part of their inner circle, about to experience a ritual reserved only for men.

'Hold on dere! Yu can't give di yut man di chalice fi smoke!' Just as I was about to take my turn, a debate sparked up about whether I was old enough to smoke this contraption that was almost as tall as me. After a long reasoning amongst themselves, someone had the good mind to ask me what I wanted to do.

'Are you ready to smoke di chalice. Are you ready to become man?'

Naturally, I said yes. I composed myself cross-legged, exactly the same as the elders, and drew on the pipe until it hissed and bubbled. At first, the smoke brushed my throat, but suddenly, my chest and lungs were on fire. I tried so hard to hold the smoke in, and stifled a cough, but the minute I exhaled, I started spluttering and couldn't catch my breath. 'He a man now!' They roared with laughter as Rasta Mark led me onto the balcony to gulp in the fresh air. Yet, I wasn't embarrassed or ashamed. I was with my tribe who were supporting me through my transition to manhood.

Another of the Rastas who also took me under his wing was called Simeon. Whereas Rasta Mark was a short, stocky, outspoken man, Simeon was an almost biblical vision: a Black Moses, a Bobo Shanti, one of the most orthodox Rastafarians. Of all of the brothers, Simeon appeared as a father figure. He dressed in a cloak robe and even walked with a staff, his locks wrapped up in a red cloth balanced like a cone on his head. He smelled of coconut oil, earthy and inviting. And his wisdom went back even further than the Old Testament, to the Books of the Maccabees and the 12 Tribes of Israel.

'Waht di I name?' he tested me.

'Stanley.'

'Waht month yu barn?'

'December.'

'Ahh sceen, so di I is Asher tribe. Yeah man. December is Asher. From now on me will call di I Asher. Trow away dat slave name 'Stanley!' You ah Asher, now sceen?'

Asher meant 'happy' and although I didn't think the name Asher was particularly cool, and would much rather have one of the other tribe names, I didn't care. What mattered more was that I was being taken into the bosom of Rastafari.

'Do you overstand?' Simeon asked me after every lesson, meaning did I understand? And he always put the question 'sceen' at the end of his sentences, as if my eyes should always be open: 'Rastaman don't deal with under. We go over. Sceen? We don't understand, we overstand, bwoy!'

Best of all, he hollered out 'Jah Rastafari' in the middle of the street while he was walking. I loved that so much and I often did the same on my way home. The words made me feel invincible and I didn't care that people looked at me as if I was crazy. 'Jah! Rastafari!' I shouted louder.

Riding on the front of Simeon's bicycle was like being transported to new worlds. He'd painted it Rasta colours: red for the blood of our ancestors, gold for the wealth of Ethiopia, and green for the vegetation of Jamaica and the end of Black suppression. 'Come yut-man, climb up on di chariot!' he said, as he lifted me onto its bars and showed me how to sit with my legs dangling to one side while I held onto the middle of the handlebars. As we rode he bellowed out 'Rastaman Chant', a song about the angel with the seven seals in the Bible.

When I was with him I was greeted as a prince. He cycled me to where the sound systems were set up on Hackney Downs park, with the towering speaker boxes pumping out Rastaman roots dub music. Jah Shaka is one of the biggest sound systems there. Whenever he met his Rastafarian bredren's, Simeon bowed slightly from the waist and touched his heart with a clenched fist. I copied him and did the same. Simeon didn't have only one girlfriend, he had many, who he called his queens, most of whom had children by him. 'Inna Africa, we are kings and queens. We don't deal wid Babylon system and Babylon ways,' he said. 'As kings we have many queens and live according to our African roots and heritage.' At first, I was in awe of this. My new family wasn't only a family of brothers who had taken me under their wing. This was a sprawling family, the same as my own, but living in beautiful harmony.

Sister Isacher, Simeon's main queen, was short with black freckles on a pretty, round face. She was always smiling, and I was drawn to her. She could easily have been Mum. She had four children, three of them by Simeon and she entrusted me to babysit the kids, all as pretty as her, with glowing skin and beautiful locks that had a sheen from the coconut oil she applied. They looked up to me as a big brother and sometimes, Sister Isacher would let me stay over at her house on Mildmay Grove, overlooking the railway track near Dalston. She let me in on a secret. Not everything was as harmonious as it seemed, and Sister Isacher complained that she was left to look after the children while Simeon came and went.

'Asher. Yu find yourself a good woman and stick to one. Yu don't need more than one queen, trust me my brudder, it cause too much heart ache and too much problem!'

Only Simeon knew my home situation. And when Sister Isacher became concerned that my mum must be wondering where I was, Simeon revealed it, without my permission. 'Him mudder sick, she mind not there!' I felt exposed, as the nine-and-a-half-year-old I actually was. A little big man, pricked by tears. Sister Isacher wrapped her arms around me and said I was welcome to stay at her house whenever I wanted, but that if she were my mother, she would be worried sick.

That night, she suggested Simeon take me back home to Alkham Road and I didn't have the guts to say it was the last thing I wanted. I didn't want anyone to step inside our front door and see the purple hallway and the rubbish piled up, or for them to feel the bitter chill. As I ate with the family, I told them about Angie and Mini and how I tried to look after them, and about the children's homes and school. Simeon said I had a deep purpose in life, and that he respected me for working at the health food shop to help Mum out.

When it came time to leave, Sister Isacher packed up fruits and nuts and berries in a calabash bowl wrapped in foil for me to take home. Outside, the rain was hammering down and I hoped the whole journey would be called off because of it, but Simeon said, 'Don't be afraid of Jah rain. Only the wicked run from the rain. It's Jah blessing.' He then gestured for me to climb on board his chariot. It felt like the longest ride of my life. As we zigzagged through the streets of Hackney, up Kingsland High Road and right onto Northwold Road, I imagined I was on a ship sailing across an endless sea, embracing the world with open arms as the rain belted across our faces and we sang at the top of our voices, drenched. I felt a sense of freedom I had never experienced before.

Immediately, my belly tensed as we turned the corner into my street. I knew the ride was over. How would Mum react to a stranger bringing her son home this late at night? Would she chase him from the door? What would Simeon think when he saw her? Or saw how we lived? I hoped that Angie or Mini would answer the door and I could slip in quietly without Mum ever knowing.

'Evening sister,' Simeon introduced himself as Mum opened the door ajar and peered into the night. My heart sank. Mum appeared calm. She listened intently as Simeon made a speech about how I was a special young man, about how we'd met and how he'd invited me to stay, but that it was time to bring me home. I hadn't been back for two days.

All the time I watched Mum's eyes. 'Come out of the rain,' she said, welcoming him in, prolonging my ordeal. Instantly I saw that he noticed the water dripping down the banister from the leaky roof at the top of the landing. Simeon's voice softened as if he now understood. 'Nice place yu ave sister. Big 'ouse,' he said before asking Mum if it was alright for me to show him my room, which I had told him about. When he peeked around the door I showed off my single bed and my small drawer unit, and he introduced himself to Angie and Mini who had come out onto the landing to see who was there. By this time they had grown accustomed to see me coming and going and had heard my stories about Simeon and my Rasta family. They knew I would be coming home with goodies and waved at him excitedly and went back in their bedroom.

When he left, his cloak flapped against his ankles as he bounced down the steps. 'Okay yut-man, mi have to trad back to di queen and kids dem, come check mi tomorrow at deh house, sceen?' he said aloud. Suddenly, I didn't want him to leave. And he sensed it, because when I followed him to the front door, head bowed, to say goodbye, he said, 'Hold yu head up yut-man. Never look down. Always look up to the heavens and receive the blessings, sceen?' As he lifted up his chariot to carry it down the front steps, he whispered, 'Mi see wha yu ah deal wid here. Yu come to di house any time. Jah guide and protect.' I didn't know it then, but I would be 15 years old before I ever saw Simeon or the family again.

I loved working in the health food shop, but my time there came to an abrupt end. I was so eager to please, to be a responsible part of my newfound family, that I messed up big time. After weeks of the rubbish mounting up, the bin men eventually came. There must have been around 20 black bags stacked high in the alleyway by the shop's side entrance. Rasta Mark had stepped out momentarily and, as I was left there alone, I gave them permission to take the lot, thinking I was doing the right thing, clueless to the trouble I would be in.

'What happened to the black bags?' the white shop owner quizzed me when he passed by minutes later. I was so proud of the decision I'd made that I announced it with fanfare, expecting him to praise me for being a mature young man. Instead, he erupted, turning red with rage. 'You stupid, stupid, stupid, little boy!' I froze, looking up at this tall, frizzled haired, angry white man that wore a long coat down to his shoes with the longest scarf hanging around his neck, like Dr Who. I felt I was in school being told off by the headmaster. Then, I felt my eyes watering and tried to be brave and not let them fall. I was wounded by his reaction. Apparently, the bags had been filled with white cabbages, imported from West Africa. I'd cost him valuable stock.

When Rasta Mark reappeared he defended me, telling the owner never to talk to me that way and that I was only a boy who'd been trying his best. Rasta Mark told him to go fuck himself. The owner could stick his job where the sun didn't shine. That made me feel even worse. My job was done, but I'd lost an elder a job. But Rasta Mark didn't seem that bothered and he said he despised working for the man anyway, that he was mean and stingy with money. Then he gave me one last life lesson: 'Mek mi tell yu what is more important, is dat yu always stand up strong and keep yu integrity. Don't mek anybody talk to yu like that again, yu hear mi?' And then he explained what integrity meant.

Chapter 11

The Town Hall

Alan Mackie stinks of goodie white people: early 30s, double corduroy—jacket *and* trousers—and sandy suede desert boots. He has ginger hair and a ginger beard and drives a VW Beetle. He might as well have 'save a Black family' stamped on his forehead. I don't know why he's been assigned to our case, or when, but he's become another fixture, a second social worker alongside Andrea. I'm wary of Alan. I'm wary of any white authority. There is always a part of me ready to fight.

Even the staff in the children's homes who have gotten to know me understand how I can flip. Josie and Dean, who work under Felicity at Forest Road, are a double act of good cop, bad cop. If boundaries are crossed, Dean comes down hard while Josie is a softy—the kind you can wrap around your little finger. Mostly, Josie likes me but if I kick off I'm as fierce as a bulldog, snarling and squaring up to anyone, until she calls the cavalry to pin me down. Not long ago, when she was wearing flip-flops in summer, I bit down hard on her big toe as I lay prostrate, wrestled to the dormitory floor, a pile of staff bodies on top of me, knees in my back and hands pressing down on my legs. 'Get out of my room!' I barked from the side of my mouth, still clenching Josie's toe in my teeth. I refused to let it go until my demands were met, all the while she screamed.

90

Just like them, Alan drops in and out of our lives. At heart, I know he wanted to understand me, but he can't. He isn't one of us and I feel reluctant to let him in. Although I believe he does root for me. Maybe everyone who comes to our home does.

There have been other social workers, but they've never lasted the distance—not like Andrea and Alan. The basin of piss, the cussing, the broom handle, these send them all packing. Still, it amazes me how well-mannered they are. They never give Mum what for. They can never bring themselves to sever the invisible umbilical cord between her and us, the cord that her illness cannot reach or control. Even when Mum is spread-eagled on the floor, writhing among the blur of boots, her wrists bent back by police, they speak politely, apologetically. I think secretly, they are terrified of her.

I've learned from Mum, though. She goes for anything in sight when fighting for her life: a foot, an ear, a nose. Since the first time we got taken, the social services always arrive with the police and a doctor in tow. Sometimes they have to inject her with a sedative to take her back to the psychiatric ward. Every standoff takes hours. It feels freakish, yet at the same time, routine. We've come to expect it. Sometimes we hope for it. But when it comes, Mum flexes every muscle to stop us from being taken away from her.

Wherever we go, Angie, Mini and I always remain together: we come as a package. The only time we are separated is at night, when they leave to sleep in the girls' dormitory and I head for the boys'. Mostly, they are in my sightline. Like a hunter, neck craned, eyes darting, I check for them at breakfast, in the playground at school, and at dinner. The second my eyes lock on to them, I can relax. I do it because we don't have anyone else looking out for us, so I make sure I look out for them. We have telepathy between us.

Tonight, Mum had another psychotic episode and the neighbours have called the authorities. It's after hours, so Alan hasn't come. Instead, Josie is here, direct from the children's home to collect us in the bright blue minibus. It's not a chariot. It never feels free. We hate being driven anywhere in it, especially to school. It looks so uncool, like an advert for our dysfunction and we bow our heads so none of our friends will recognise us. It is well after midnight when we arrive and Josie is overrun with apologies after speaking with another member of staff. Apparently, I have to go to Mathias Road while the girls stay at Forest Road, which is too full to accommodate us all.

I feel sorry for Josie, so I don't kick up a fuss. Neither does Angie or Mini. Instead, we sit in the van in silence soaking up the news. When my sisters finally file out, feet shuffling, we stare at each other through the back window where I've been left. 'Please don't go,' I mutely tell them, but a moment later they have disappeared. I've never felt this feeling before. This is a new emotional desert. There's a hurt inside me that comes in waves. I'm alone. The only two people in the whole wide world who I allow myself to love have vanished. Years later, when I broke up from my first long-term relationship, I recognised that feeling again and realised I was heartbroken.

The door slides shut and the minibus roars to life. It's raining. Streetlights, parked cars, buildings, shops, neon signs, zebra crossings with yellow beacons flashing. I know the way to Mathias Road off by heart now, but tonight the journey feels unreal. As we approach the front entrance, the driver winds down his window. One of the night-staff is already on the pavement waiting. While they talk, I'm gazing at my reflection in the window.

'Nahhhhh, you're kidding me, right?' I can hear the driver discussing me as if I'm not there.

'Bloody 'ell. Where is he to go, then. Eh...? To what...? The town 'all? At this time? 'Av you been in touch? Are they expecting us?'

Who or what is at the town hall is not explained, but the driver is now giving the staff a proper tongue-lashing. He says I'm only a kid and that it's not fair for me to be shipped around in this way, what with it being the early hours of the morning. When he turns the key in the ignition he reassures me that one day all of this will blow over, although I have no idea what that means.

We've been one other place than the children's homes before, and nothing blew over. Nothing at all. Not long ago, when Mum was sent to Homerton for a prolonged spell, we got temporarily fostered out with a fireman and his wife. All three of us. Alan said if we fitted in, and the couple liked us, then we might stay longer. But it didn't last. We got taken to Brentwood to a cul-de-sac of new-builds, not a Black face in sight. The kids from the school we were sent to followed us around as if we were royalty, after we got a name for ourselves being the fastest runners, beating anyone in a race, girls or boys. Strangely, they seemed in awe of our colour and appeared to really like us. The headteacher called me into his office one afternoon and sat me down. I hadn't been in any trouble so I was confused with why he wanted to see me. He said, 'The children here look up to you, Stanley, be careful not to abuse your power.' I didn't understand what he meant, and just nodded my head in agreement.

On the weekends we played with the kids from the close and made small fires in the woods nearby, but one afternoon a gang of white boys circled us on their bikes, shouting out names and laughing at us, while riding round and round. 'Nigger!' 'Sambo!' 'Get back on the jam jar, you fucking Golliwogs.' Wickedness is alive and kicking in suburbia. My urge to protect Angie and Mini overwhelmed me, and I felt the primal fight or flight rage rear up inside. Before they could attack, I grabbed a thin branch we had put in the fire and waited for one of them to come closer, before lashing out and poking it in one boy's face, burning him under his eye. Next thing we knew, we were leaving.

We're nearing our final destination now, and as the minibus pulls up there's a couple stood on the pavement in their dressing gowns. They look dishevelled, as if they've escaped from a haunted house and they're flagging down any vehicle in sight. Looming in the background behind them is Stoke Newington Town Hall, with its oblong concrete frontage, rising up from the bottom of Albion Road. I know this place, but under the sodium glow it looks different, like the TV house where the Addam's Family lived.

This is Molly and Bill. They're going to fix me up a nice bowl of cereal when we get inside, but I'm panicking already. I don't know Molly and Bill. Besides, they are old enough to be someone's grandparents. The gulf between us is too wide and there's no bridge for me to reach them. I don't want to be left here with these strangers. Mostly, I can't get Angie and Mini out of my head, and the worry in their eyes as they looked back at me.

'When am I going to see my sisters? When am I going to be with my sisters?' I plead.

As the driver fills Molly and Bill in on what's happened, I hear them soften, spreading on an extra thick layer of kindness, as smooth as butter.

''Ello Staaaanley. Watcha want to be called? Is it Staaaanley? Or Staaaan?'

'Poor soul, eh? Watcha want for breakfast? What's your favourite food?'

'Beeeeens on toast,' I mumble.

'That's our favourite, too.'

We enter into the marble hallway with pillars and a large mahogany countertop desk. I think they must be well rich to live in a place like this. Even the lift is carpeted and fitted with wooden panels and mirrors that gleam.

'Go on! Press the top button. We're going right to the top. All the way to the penthouse. We call it that, don't we Molly?'

'That's right, Bill. It's our little penthouse.'

The lift doors gently slide open and the couple lead me into a small flat, plush and perfect, with a mantelpiece lined with ornaments. Off the living room is a kitchen and an even smaller bedroom. I can't seem to eat anything they offer, so they put me straight to bed, but the covers feel stiff and cold and the noise of the traffic outside on the main road is unfamiliar. I can hear Molly and Bill talking as I lie awake, afraid to shut my eyes and surrender to sleep.

In the morning, my body feels heavy and I still don't have an appetite. I can hardly step a foot out of bed. This is also a new feeling. When Molly and Bill eventually lead me into the living room, I'm bawling my eyes out nonstop, but can't understand why.

'Don't you cry, son. We've made your favourite. Beans on toast,' says Bill, but it only makes me cry even more. He is short and dapper with his hair combed over and dressed in smart trousers with a black top hat and a red tailcoat jacket. Soon he'll have to go to work which is downstairs at the town hall. He's the doorman who welcomes visitors through its revolving door.

'What's your favourite TV show?' Molly follows on in quick step. Both have thick cockney accents. I tell her it's *Starsky and Hutch*. It's on too late to watch in the children's homes but Mum lets us stay up. After every episode, I dream of being a detective. I imagine I've been handed a case and spend ages working out how to go about solving it. I like Starsky best. He is way cooler than Hutch: impulsive, quick-tempered and funny, and he always gets the girls. Mum bought me a toy Ford Gran Torino with a white stripe on both sides for my birthday when I was around six.

Later, Molly and Bill let me watch it. I sit quietly and it distracts me for a while, but it's not the same. The whole flat feels empty. More than that, I feel empty. Angie and Mini aren't beside me tugging at the blanket that's keeping us warm. There's no shouts of 'Whhhooooaaaaaa!' as cars being chased screech round corners, or 'Uhhh-ohhh' the minute we know Starsky and Hutch are in trouble. When I look to Molly and Bill, perched neatly on the sofa, there's no laughter breaking on their faces when Huggy Bear appears—the character we all love because he looks like us—and leaves us in stitches because he's so funny and cool at the same time. Best of all, he's a jive-talking hustler, the same as Linton and Uncle Winston.

I stay with Molly and Bill for three days. Every morning, Bill takes me downstairs and lets me spin around the revolving doors while he doffs his top hat to everyone who steps in and out. I know Molly and Bill are trying their best. In a way, that makes it worse. I feel awkward and self-conscious, as if I'm not worthy of their kindness. They cook for me, but I can't touch my food. I break down constantly. It's as if I'm having an out-of-body experience, going through the motions. I want my sisters back. I would do anything to be with them again. They are only a ten-minute drive from me, but it feels as though we're separated by continents. When we are finally reunited, I don't tell them about my ordeal. It feels too surreal, and I'm embarrassed that I've cried the whole time. I don't tell anyone. I hug them tight, then I put my armour back on.

Chapter 12

Belly Bump

Just as spring broke the following year, Mum announced that she was pregnant. In the autumn we would have a new baby brother or sister, she smiled, patting her belly. We struggled to take in the news.

However distant I felt to Mum when she wasn't well, I comforted myself with the knowledge that she tried her best. Other people said it too: Mum wasn't in control and she didn't mean the things she said or did. Part of me believed it because when she hurt us, she became like a creature driven by a raging spirit—an Incredible Hulk caught up in a strange scientific experiment: half human, half beast, subdued only by drugs and injections. On one of these occasions, I was playing on the stairs when Mum approached. I was more or less standing at the same height as her because I was on a step. Her eyes were wide and vicious, so I averted my gaze for fear of putting more wood on the fire. Before I knew it, Mum had grabbed the back of my trousers with one hand, giving me a wedgy, and bunched up my jumper on my chest with the other, and then hurled me through the air. I was airborne. I could see the corner of the door frame to the front room approaching me, and remember being unable to stop, or stop it from coming towards me. Then blackout. Mum had rendered me unconscious. I came around on the sofa looking up at Mum standing over me with a tub of butter, and Angie and Mini staring at me wide-eyed, as if I'd just come back from the dead. I had a massive bump the size of my fist in the middle of my forehead, and she was rubbing the butter on it to bring the swelling down.

But this pregnancy felt different. This felt deliberate. This felt as if she'd made a choice. At first Angie, Mini and I were baffled. How could she even have a baby when she was this sick? Then the realisation kicked in. Mum could barely look after us, or herself. As her belly grew, we understood that it would fall to us to shoulder the responsibility. Being the most sensible, Angie was first to grasp this. During our conferences on the landing she concluded, 'You know what it means, innit? We'll have to look after it.' Also up for debate: who was the daddy? That was something else in Mum's life we had to piece together. A few names got bandied around, but we were convinced it was a guy called Lenny. Mum had known him from back in the day, and he'd been hanging around the house— the only constant visitor Mum had had in a long time.

My feelings of anger towards mum only surfaced years later. At the time, this all felt more like weary defeat. We were not even teenagers, trying to feed and clothe ourselves and help Mum with her heating and electricity. We kept running but the goal- posts kept shifting. We could never keep up. The last thing we needed was another mouth to feed, another life to be saved. But my anger towards Lenny was crystal clear then. I despised him. How could he do this? Couldn't he see that Mum wasn't well? Wasn't it obvious that our family needed help? Couldn't he smell the dereliction of Alkham Road every time he stepped inside our hallway? What kind of man lays with a sick woman?

In truth, Lenny was a difficult man to figure out. An oddball. He kept himself to himself—never part of the street scene but hovered around the edges. There was nothing gangster about him, even though he had drifted in and out of Mum's blues parties years before. He was tall and slim with inky black skin and small oval glasses that he kept pushing up onto his face whenever he spoke. According to Auntie Beryl, he fancied himself as a bit of an intellectual, always doing courses at the Open University. Like Mum, he could effortlessly move between patois and the Queen's English. His manner was thoughtful and beguiling. Maybe it wasn't a surprise that women fell for him, including Auntie Beryl, who's flat he used to visit on a regular basis while he sneaked around at Mum's. But no one actually trusted him.

'Dat man is a fox. He so sly and slippery,' Beryl would say. Apparently, she'd bumped into Mum on Stoke Newington High Street when her belly was so big it looked like a balloon about to be popped. 'She tell mi seh she was pregnant for Lenny, but I never believe her, true seh she sick.' Auntie Beryl confessed. She even confronted Lenny. 'Mi ask him if he sleep wid Joy, him look mi dead in nah mi eye and tell mi straight, 'Don't be silly Beryl, how you going to listen to a mad woman!?'' It wasn't until our little brother was born and Beryl saw him in his pram for the first time, that it was obvious he and Lenny had the same angular face and nose. Mum hadn't been making it up after all and was telling the truth all along.

Lenny hardly said anything to me or my sisters when he visited before Mum got pregnant. I doubt that he had much interest in kids, period. Even Mini's dad, Linton, would playfully sidle up next to me, press his face up close to mine, and ask me what I'd learned at school. No sooner had Lenny come through our front door, then he quickly slipped into Mum's room to avoid us. At times I could hear her giggling, and I stood outside, anger surging through me. When it got too much to bear, I flung open the door to see him grinding on top of her, sheets all messed up.

'Joy, man. Tell him to come out of di room. Jesus!' he

complained. Mum laughed her head off, so I went with it. 'Mum, can we go to Woolies for sweets tomorrow?' Or, 'Mum can we watch films on TV?' Never-ending questions, but I didn't care. I was the man of the house, stood bold as brass at the foot of Mum's bed while a naked Lenny clung to the sheets. The moment Mum agreed to my demands I slowly strolled out, purposely leaving the bedroom door wide open. 'Tell 'im to shut di door, noh Joy?!' I heard Lenny plead as I climbed the stairs to my room. Even when I got called back to close it, I wasn't going to let him get the better of me. I let the latch rest against the lock, knowing full well that its weight would cause it to swing back open of its own accord. I did it to put him off and let him know that he wasn't welcome on my territory.

As the months wore on, I caught glimpses of Mum's growing bump and was puzzled by the dark line that ran down the middle of her belly. She let us touch her sometimes and put our ears against it so we could listen to the baby move. The bump felt hard and unalterable. Sometimes we would hear her in her bedroom telling the baby off for kicking her, and she said it was definitely a boy because he never stayed still.

On the day our brother arrived, we got taken to the same Mother's Hospital that we'd been born in to see Mum. We'd only ever visited her on the psychiatric ward before, so this felt different, maybe more hopeful, but none of us were sure. Corridor after corridor. Through double doors with big panes of glass in them so you could see into the wards, and when we found her, she was sitting up in a small bed in this vast space with its shiny, mopped floors. It struck me how high the beds were off the floor, so high you could see the length of the ward stretching out beyond it. Beside her in a cot was the baby, fast asleep.

No sooner had we arrived, Mum became desperate that the nurse leave, asking for some privacy so we could all be together.

We hovered awkwardly around the cot, but Mum didn't introduce us. Nor did she pick the baby up and hold him or place him in our arms. Instead, as soon as the nurse disappeared from view Mum whipped back her bed sheet, swung her legs around and hopped down, touching her bare feet on the cold floor. In the rush, her hospital gown dropped down from her shoulders to reveal her nakedness, but she didn't pull it back. Instead, she reached for her clothes from the side cabinet and began pulling on her knickers and bra, then her dress. Mum was on a mission.

'I'm calling him Hogarth Neville Brown,' she announced as she grabbed her jacket and slipped her feet into shoes. Just as the nurse padded back, Mum swooped down into the cot and scooped up the baby.

'Miss Brown, where are you going?' the nurse said anxiously.

'I'm going home. Now move out mi fucking way woman.'

'Please Miss Brown, let me call the sister so you can speak with her first. Please Miss Brown, you've just had a baby!'

Mum acted as if the nurse was invisible, pushed past her and marched us down the corridor and out into the evening dark. And by the time the nurse had caught up and was shouting for her to come back, Mum had already flagged down a black taxi. '37B Alkham Road, Stoke Newington, please,' she said to the cabbie as we all piled in.

All that night we heard our newborn brother, who we nick-named Huggy, cry and stir. At first he slept with Mum in her bed. She breastfed him and taught us how to wind him, by propping him up on our knees and patting his back until he burped. Then, we got sent to the kitchen to fetch a glass. Any excess milk would be expressed into it before she passed it along the line of Angie, Mini and me while we all took a sip. 'It's good for your bones and your health,' Mum said, but it tasted warm and sour and we held our noses while we drank it down.

Huggy stayed in Mum's room, but as we feared, we were called on more and more to help out. Mum showed us how to change him—a white terry towelling cloth that first got folded into a neat upside-down triangle and then positioned under his bottom to fold the flaps like an envelope. The last flap between his legs got folded up on to his tummy, then we pinned all three flaps together, while trying to hold down his tiny legs to stop him from wriggling. It was hard work, man. Dirty nappies got soaked and washed in a white, tin bucket in the bathroom, which mum called 'The Pail' before it was put to boil on the cooker to sterilise them. One time when I accidentally pricked Huggy with the large nappy pin, I quickly placed my hand over his mouth to stifle his shrieks, terrified that I'd be in serious trouble for hurting him and get some 'righteous licks', as Mum likes to call it.

I gently rubbed Bonjela onto his gums when he was teething. I tried it out myself, it tasted disgusting, but it stopped Huggy from crying.

I measured out milk powder to mix in his bottle when Mum was too tired to breast feed. When there was no food for us, I nibbled on his Farley's Rusks before crushing them into warm milk to make his porridge cereal. We took it in turns to feed him, burp him and play with him, while Mum withdrew, leaving us to Huggy's survival.

Unsurprisingly, Lenny did a disappearing act. I only ever recall him coming to see Mum once after my brother was born, and we listened in while he and Mum argued about whether he was Huggy's dad.

After around half an hour, he slipped out of the house and out of our lives.

Having Huggy in my life was an emotional tug of war. I loved him. It was impossible not to. He looked at me with expectant eyes, innocent, wanting to be loved and nurtured like me. One of his favourite pastimes was throwing his bottle from his cot whenever I turned my back on him. I couldn't ignore him, as the minute he got picked up and cuddled his tantrums stopped. But I resented him, too. If I was feeling vexed, I teased him with his bottle, letting him suckle on it before pulling it out from his mouth, then feeling sorry and letting him have the milk. There were times I felt so frustrated with the whole mess that I smashed up my toys in my room or buried my face deep in my pillow and screamed into it so that Mum couldn't hear.

We also argued between ourselves, about who would stay home from school to look after him. Or, we'd debate on the stairs until Mum randomly yelled out a name from her bedroom.

'Stop di bloodclart noise! Stanley, you stay home. The rest of unno go to school. Hurry up and don't disturb mi spirit!'

The unfairness of that stung. Any one of us could be called back to care for Huggy even when it wasn't our turn. Whenever Mum did this, my first impulse was to tell her where to stick it, but the fear of her was too real for such words to ever tumble from my mouth. Instead, I kicked my PE bag against the wall or stood behind her bedroom door silently giving her the finger and pulling faces, cussing her in mime.

Missing school because I bunked off was one thing but missing it because I had a baby to look after was taking the piss. Being under the watch of social services, my teachers must have known, but I don't remember anyone ever talking to me about it. All I saw were the pained expressions, the looks of pity if a teacher ever had to deal with me.

I didn't tell any friends at school; only the kids I hung out with on our street knew. I didn't even tell my friend Grant Davies. The shame of us all having different dads was already a weight to bear; to then have a mentally ill mum was bad enough, but a mentally ill mum with a baby by a fourth man was off the Richter scale. Other kids looked like each other and had a proper home with the same mums and same dads who picked them up from school.

My own dad had never even been to my school, and I fantasised about walking out of the gates to see his purple Volvo estate parked and idling, waiting to pick me up. Before Mum's illness, she had dropped us off and collected us, but I felt embarrassed when she wore miniskirts with afro wigs and men wolf-whistled at her.

I felt more isolated than ever. Because of the new responsibility, I started missing sports days and school trips. One outing was to the Natural History Museum, before we broke up for the summer holidays. The stuffed animals and the solar system and who did what on the way there all got relayed to me secondhand. In the playground, I still managed to maintain order: defend myself, defend my patchwork family of cousins and my sisters and preserve my don't-give-a-fuck reputation. But now a new threat was biting. Before this, I'd experienced racism as something random, words spouted out by kids on bikes or people on the high street. Now it moved in packs with boots and braces.

I understood who was in the National Front way before I understood fully its reason for being: to drive blacks and Asians out of Britain. All along Stoke Newington High Street the letters NF were sprayed in red and black graffiti across shop shutters and walls. I'd heard about the fights and the stabbings and the men having to retaliate if 'dem wicked white ball-heads' ever attacked, but I never felt hunted down as prey by English dogs, yet.

At school, I knew of one kid from an NF family: a guy called Brett who had four older brothers. Their racist shorthand was a shaved head, a bomber jacket, red braces and a pair of Dr Martens boots with red shoelaces: red being code for bloodshed. When another kid, Bobby Wilson, started hanging out with Brett I suddenly understood that the target of attack was me.

Bobby and I were friends at first, and we had had our run-ins and he was scared of me, but now he taunted me. He boasted that he was getting his head shaved too, and openly asked why was I even in this country when my parents arrived on a banana boat? Uncle Ashley had warned me that wicked people rarely attacked one-on-one. I had to be prepared. They were cowards who needed to be in gangs and I guess Bobby found his gang.

One lunchtime he and I got into an argument.

'You fucking coon!' he yelled at me.

'Yeah—come and say that to my face you fucking pig.'

'Golliwog, Sambo, Nigg-nog. Uhh, uhh, uhhh…' Bobby stood at a safe distance and made the sound of a gorilla, pretending to knuckle-walk and scratch under his arms.

'Come fight me like a man if you think you're so hard! Meet me at the gate after school, you fucking white honky!' I shot back.

I knew Bobby wouldn't be alone after school, so I had to make an example of him. After that, no skinhead would want to mess with me or any Black person again. During the lunch break I jogged home, snuck in the house and opened the kitchen drawer to pull out Mum's sharpest knife—the one with the black handle she used for cutting up meat. I jogged back, scaling the school walls to avoid being caught by the playground helpers, and wrapped the knife in the swimming towel in my bag. Nobody knew other than Grant Davis. But that afternoon, I heard whispers circulating that I had a knife. Fucking Grant with his big mouth, I should have known better than to have shown him the knife. When it came to a fight, he always got scared. Sooner or later news of the knife was bound to reach a teacher, so I lodged it up the sleeve of my jumper and buried it under a tree in the playground—after I'd pretended I wanted to go to the toilets. Kids never imagine they are going to get found out. I thought I was as safe as houses. But it wasn't long before I got summoned to Mrs Hassocks's office, the slow, silent wagging of her finger acting as the universal sign for 'in serious shit'. The whisper had come to her ears, she explained, leaning across her desk, arms outstretched with fingers interlaced. I feigned surprise and fronted it out.

'What? *A knife?*' My eyes popped out of my head.

'Yes, Stanley. A knife with a black handle.'

'Nah miss. That was liquorice. I got it from the shop on the way to school.' Who was I kidding?

'Stanley. I want you to listen very carefully. If you have brought a knife to school, I must know.' Mrs Hassocks removed her glasses and rubbed her eyes. She continued with the Spanish inquisition, before pulling out her ace card. 'Do you want one of the littler kids to find it and hurt themselves?'

For all my tough-street exterior, Mrs Hassocks had located my soft spot. Right there. The idea that my actions could hurt the little kids pricked me. She knew it would. No one would be allowed home until the knife was found. That was another good manipulation: the guilt I would have felt if I made everyone stay behind. Nice one.

'Will I be expelled, Miss?' I asked.

'No, but I need to know where the knife is.'

'Behind the tree in the playground,' I eventually admitted.

'Stanley, I need you to go and get it and bring it to my office please. Can you do that?' This she said in a very slow manner as if the words were a lit bomb.

Mrs Hassocks changed her mind and accompanied me to the spot, and when we returned I sat at the desk outside her office that was reserved for me. The bell rang, classroom doors flew open, kids ran down corridors, engines roared. Then the void, as everyone scattered back to their nuclear families, and then the cleaners moved in, sweeping up around me.

This was the first time I'd been held back for so long. By now

Bobby Wilson and Brett and their crew with their angry, shaven heads would be wondering where I was. I'd be a laughingstock. There was one thing worse than being a kid: it was being a chicken-shit kid. When Mrs Hassocks finally emerged from her office, she was running her fingers across a long white sealed envelope.

'Stanley. This letter must be given to your mother immediately. Do not come to school tomorrow without your mother. Understand?'

I was too late. No one was waiting to fight me at the school gates. And whatever fight I was due to have with the NF, I still had Mum to deal with. 'That Jewish bitch,' Mum snarled as she read the letter. 'Who she think she is to expel you from school like that? You watch when we go up there tomorrow. I'm going to tell her about her bumbleclart self.'

Chapter 13

Therapy

It is 1994 and I am 24 years old. Marion, my first counsellor, is teaching me about co-dependency. She wants me to recognise that from a young age, I've taken care of others despite this being harmful to myself. She says I'm stuck in a cycle of seeking out people to care for even if they abuse me. She introduces me to little Stanley, the hero child, the people pleaser, and asks me to write a letter to Mum as if I wasn't going to send it. Because the letter won't be sent, I can write what I want. A catharsis. But I end up sending mine. One day, I leave it on Mum's bedside table, even though I don't expect her to read it. She is in the full throng of her illness so it was as good as not sending it at all.

This isn't the exact letter. It's what I can piece together from my memories. It's what happens when you get moved around from place to place, especially those early years in the care system. Yet they are all I have to understand who I am. Not long after I left the letter at Mum's, I bumped into her in the local park at London Fields. At first, she walked right past me after I greeted her, as she usually did. But then she stopped and turned around, and in a rare moment of clarity, she acknowledged that she'd read my letter. 'It's okay, son, you did your best for the family,' she said, and then gently held me while I sobbed my eyes out before walking off again as if nothing had happened, leaving me sitting dumbfounded on the park bench.

Dear Mum,

Why did you get sick? Why did you have a breakdown? Why did this happen to you and to our family? I love you Mummy and it breaks my heart. We loved you and we still love you. As I write this now I am crying because of the pain I still feel from the trauma I have suffered.

I was scared of you Mummy. At times I was petrified because you were so ruthless. I didn't know who you were or what you were going to do to me or my sisters when you had an episode. You inflicted so much torture on us, and then switched back to the mummy we loved and missed. I hate your illness, and I blame your illness for all the suffering I went through. Do you have any idea what it was like to be put in children's homes? To sleep in strange beds with strange smells? To eat different foods and be tucked into bed by strangers? Or to move from home to home when none of these were our home?

Why did you have four kids with four different men? What were you thinking? Do you have any idea of the shame I felt when school friends asked me and my sisters why we didn't look like each other? I would fight anyone. In the end I hated school and I hated being in class-rooms. I couldn't concentrate. Teachers always said I had the potential to do better, but I couldn't focus.

I wanted to be normal. I wanted to be a kid who played like other kids, who didn't have to worry whether there was food in the cupboard or anything in the fridge. Why did we even have a fridge when it had no food in it? I wanted to be free, Mummy. I didn't want to stay home to look after my younger brother after you got pregnant. Why did you get pregnant knowing that you were not well and needed help?

Angie, Mini and I knew that the burden of raising Huggy would fall on our shoulders, and it did. We had to stay home from school because you would not leave your bed. You demanded it. I missed out on school trips, swimming, fun things. I know it's not your fault and I am sorry for writing you this letter, but you need to know how it was for me. And I need to let you know so I can move on with my life and put the past to rest.

Mummy, I have such a mountain to climb that some days I don't think I can make it. I am scared of ever being diagnosed as a schizophrenic: of inheriting your illness. I'm scared of ever being a husband or being a father. I am scared to pass on my dysfunctional behaviour. I am a caretaker and I've been taking care of our family from such a young age, but I never took care of myself.

I can't turn back time. What's done is done. I know you are still unwell but I need to say this to you for myself. I need to untangle the spaghetti of feelings that overwhelm me every day. I am lucky. I have found people who I can share with. My counsellor is helping me face my demons, which is why I have written this letter to you. I love you Mummy and I always will, and I miss you so much. I know who you really are, and I will never forget.

I don't know what the future holds, Mummy, but I am trying my best to live one day at a time without harming myself or others. I am sorry if this letter upsets you, but I need you to understand that I must recover. I need to heal.

Love from your son,

Stanley

Chapter 14

Chaos Rains!

I am trying to stay as still as a statue. I can't move a muscle in case a twig snaps or a leaf rustles. Deborah Thompson is crouched beside me, shielded from the pavement on Alkham Road by a neighbour's hedge. Her hand is covering my mouth. 'Don't make a sound,' she is whispering to me.

She was out chatting late in the evening sun, when I nose-dived like a goalie down our porch steps, the front door pulled wide open. *Whoooooosh*, the breeze of Mum's rolling pin brushing past my ear as I leapt.

It's July 1980, and the summer is hot and muggy. Home has become hell. This is not because I've been expelled, but because it's the holidays and there's no school to go to. Mum tried to fight my expulsion by saying that I was only a boy and so what if I'd hidden a knife. She cussed out Mrs Hassocks so badly it brought teachers out from their classrooms. 'You white people are always looking to find fault,' she said, then called her 'an uptight bitch' right to her face.

'There's nothing more I can do. Please, Miss Brown. I have tried to help Stanley on many occasions by allowing him to continue to stay at the school but, a knife is a knife,' Mrs Hassocks replied calmly, before giving me the pitying look, adjusting her jacket, and picking at fluff that wasn't there.

Mum's funny like that. She can beat the living crap out of us on a whim, but if an outsider so much as tries to bad-mouth us or lay a finger on us, she will defend us to the hilt. I didn't even get a beating.

I don't know which school I will go to come September but, for now, I don't care. On summer nights like this I am out with the other kids in the street playing football or cricket against the back wall of the train tracks, not getting home until around 8 PM. Usually, if it's later, I can make it to my room without Mum noticing. Tonight, though, I stayed out way past curfew. As I climb the stairs to the second-floor landing, I can see Mum's shadow, she's standing outside the kitchen waiting for me. Instinctively, I scan her armoury. One glance at the wall: Roots is still asleep on his nail. Yet Mum stood awkwardly to block my way, one hand behind her back.

'What time you call this? Eh? Where you been?'

'I... I...' *Having fun*, I wanted to say, but I didn't because it would be pointless. Before I could answer she revealed the thick wooden rolling pin, as big as a baseball bat. She then lunged at me. These days my reflexes are honed, the same as a boxer's. I can bob and weave, flinch and duck when the beatings rain down on me. Tonight, I blocked the blow: I raised my arm in front of my face and let the rolling pin ricochet off my elbow. My life flashed before me and the pain opened my bladder. I wet myself. This is not the first time Mum has made me pee my pants, or that I've felt the warm liquid oozing out of me, trickling down my legs, powerless to stop it. Powerless to control myself. I could see in Mum's eyes that she doesn't understand that this weapon is another level of punishment and the force of its blow could kill me.

I can't explain it, but something changed inside of me. Right now, a switch has been flicked. There's nothing tethering me, no connection. Normally, I'd stay rooted to the spot and take the beating, but for the first time, I felt an urgency to run. But it was more than running. Like ammo from a slingshot, I launched myself so fast down the stairs that my body somersaulted over my legs and I roly-polied down the last few steps to freedom. By the time I flew out of the house Mum was almost on top of me, slashing the rolling pin in the air. But I kept running.

Everyone outside on their porches saw what was happening and shouted for me to run. Some are sympathetic, and protect us when they can: tonight, Deborah is my getaway driver. As I raced past her, her impulse was to run with me, grabbing me by my hand and pulling me further down the street before leading me behind a hedge. Mum saw us run. Now, she's hunting us down.

'Stan... Stan... your dinner's on the table. Come on, Son.' Mum's voice is melodic and we can sense she's moving closer as we finally see her dressing gown through the hedges. I know I can't stay here forever. I debate whether I should surrender, walk out, hands in the air, white flag flying. But Deborah gestures for me to stay put, as Mum's tone changes and we spy the wooden pin in her hand, dangling by her side.

'Deborah. Give me back my son. Don't fuck with me,' she growls. I'm anticipating Mum peering over the hedge any second, but she doesn't. Instead, her footsteps retreat towards the pockets of onlookers gathered on their doorsteps, some shouting for her to leave me alone, and Mum responding, but I can't make out the conversations in the distance. The tension softens in my body, enough for me to feel the throbbing in my elbow from the impact of the rolling pin. Now it is limp and hurts when I move it.

Suddenly, Mum shouts out. 'Deborah. Mi have yu daughter. When yu ready to give mi back mi son, yu can have her back!' Silence descends over the street like a storm cloud. Deborah's eyes dart around as the words sink in, and her face contorts with horror. Mum's got Emma. Has she kidnapped her?! Deborah can't hide any longer. She's let go of me and she's sprinting towards our house. I'm behind her, but Mum's bolted the door shut. The neighbours are shouting. Apparently, Mum went straight up to Emma who was sitting on our neighbour's porch and asked if she wanted to have dinner at our house. Blindly, Emma said yes, because she'd eaten with us many a time before Mum got this sick. Mum held her hand and walked back home with her.

Within minutes sirens are wailing. And Deborah's husband Solomon has been called. He's drunk and wild with rage and he's sent Wayne, their eldest son, to fetch the axe he keeps indoors so he can break down Mum's door. The neighbours watch as Solomon swings the axe into the wooden panels over and over, while Deborah cries out for Mum to give Emma back. The scene unfolding is so surreal I feel like I'm in a movie or stuck in a bad TV series. Maybe I should have just taken the licks? Maybe, by now, I'd be in the safety of my room nursing my wounds? Maybe if I had, all these people wouldn't be out on the street? Maybe I should have kept running?

Police. Ambulance. Fire Brigade. The holy trinity of emergency services have all been called in quick succession. Solomon is being restrained by the police and firemen are ramming down our door. I am pointed out by one of the neighbours and led into the back of the ambulance to be checked over. The paramedic speaks to me in a babyish voice and I respond by laying it on extra thick, wincing and yelping as he touches my elbow, which has swollen up and is painful when I try to move it.

In that moment, all I want is sympathy. I want to feel that someone is taking care of me. I want to be loved. What I don't realise is that this stunt, compared to all the other stunts in the world that I've ever performed, will change the course of my whole life forever. It will take me away from my sisters and baby brother and everything I know.

'Okay, son. We're taking you to the hospital for an X-ray. Let's get this checked out, eh?' the paramedic says, shaking his head pityingly. The ambulance doors close. It's the last time I set foot in Alkham Road for the next six years. No one accompanies me.

Chapter 15

Nottingham

I ended up staying on Connaught Ward at the Queen Elizabeth Hospital for Children in Bethnal Green for around two weeks, even though there was little wrong with me. Mum was sectioned again, and Angie, Mini and Huggy were temporarily sent to a nunnery before being sent off to Forest Road. I was to learn this information decades later, that history had repeated itself. I remember Alan Mackie turning up, looking concerned and reeking of coffee, asking if Mum had any relatives who could take me in for a while as the children's homes were full. No one had stepped forward so far. I shrugged. I badly wanted to go home and be with my sisters and play outside with the kids on the street. I was missing the summer holidays stuck in here and missed my family, including Mum. I couldn't accept what I was being told. My mind started conjuring up different ideas for Alan so he'd send me back. My dad had a sister Martha who I stayed with once in Nottingham, so I told Alan her name. I never thought he would actually go and find her. It was meant as a decoy because she lived so far away.

A few days before I got discharged, a heavy-set woman emerged through the double doors and shuffled her way along the ward with Alan in hot pursuit. Holy shit! It was my Auntie Martha. Alan

116

explained that she and her husband Ray had agreed to take me until the authorities could find something more permanent. And on the day I left Connaught Ward, Alan drove me to Nottingham in his VW Beetle.

'Why do I have to go? It's so far from London,' I complained. I knew I couldn't go back to Alkham Road but I'd actually gotten used to being in the hospital. I was on a small ward with around 20 beds. The nurses fussed over me. My bed had crisp white sheets and a soft baby-blue blanket, and the central heating was turned up so high that I had the luxury of kicking the sheets off at night. Plus, I got fed three meals every day with pudding.

Alan kept saying that it's kind of Auntie Martha and Uncle Ray to take me, and that I'd be reunited with my sisters and brother soon.

'It's the best we can do for now, but if you hate it we can try to move you somewhere else,' Alan reassured me.

'Promise?'

'Promise.'

Auntie Martha and Uncle Ray were in their late 50s and lived on a row of terraces north of the city centre: redbrick and uniform with cobbled stone alleyways running down the side. Alongside the Roads and Streets, there were Avenues, Drives, Groves and Crescents, the sort of lower middle-class suburb where a trumpet plays a sullen melody as a camera pans across wet rooftops, like the beginning of *Coronation Street*. Most striking was their house: three bedrooms, two living rooms, sanitised, and blessed by Jesus. Piercing blue eyes followed you from every angle: Jesus on the cross; Jesus at the Last Supper. And quotes: Jesus loves you; He died for you so you may live.

Just after we arrived, Alan and I got ushered into living room number one and Alan sipped coffee from a china cup. When he left, that room became off bounds, reserved only for special guests or church folk. I'd never seen a floral sofa covered in thick, protective plastic before, or hard crochet mats—miniature mats for sitting plants and ornaments on, and an identical mat on the floor, only bigger. Crochet dolls, too. Everywhere. Once a week, Martha dusted them but mostly the room stayed locked, as if she was hiding the Queen's jewels.

On my first night, I got shown upstairs to the spare room. Rule number two: no shoes on the upstairs carpets. I liked the feel of the carpet—it was spongy when you sank your feet into it—but like most young boys I was in a rush and I would zip up and down the stairs, constantly being told off for forgetting rule number two. My room had a wardrobe, a chest of drawers and a double bed, also something I'd never had before. The only time I'd ever slept in a bed that big was Mum's bed in Alkham Road, which we'd all pile into when the nights got really cold. At first, all this space felt wasted. I missed Angie and Mini beside me, and even the screams of baby Huggy. To fill the nothingness, I curled my legs around my pillow, tucking it in close to my chest for comfort and put another one close to my back as if it were them.

Although Martha was inviting, I had bad feelings about her from the get-go. Not long after I arrived, Uncle Ray cut off my little dreadlocks, apparently under her orders. He was apologetic about it. 'You can't go around with your hair like that,' he said, explaining that dreads might be okay in the big city but here, it was frowned upon as dirty and unwashed. Martha said she couldn't fathom how Mum had let my hair grow that way. She served West Indian food but processed food, too. From tins. And bacon. All the warning signs were there, and I recalled everything Rasta Mark and Simeon had taught me about eating pure, home-cooked food and no meat. 'Dem people. Di Babylon system corrupt der mind. Dey lost their way,' they had warned.

Every Sunday Martha took me to the Methodist Church

around the corner and afterwards to Sunday school. She loved to show me off. A self-approving glow spread over her face when church folk commented on what a good, Christian woman she was by taking me in. Then one evening, Martha brought me to a friend's house. She must have told the elders beforehand that I was her son because I heard them questioning her. 'Martha ! You too untrue! Who is di bwoy? This is not your son. Talk di truth!' But Martha insisted. 'Her son?' I thought angrily, as I sat on the living room floor, listening to them talk as if I wasn't there. I was secretly pleased when one of them had the sense to ask me. 'No. She's my Auntie,' I replied, moodily. On the way home, she grabbed my ear and twisted it round between her fat fingers.

'You don't tell people my business,' she cautioned me.

'Fuck off! I know who my mum is,' I shouted, running into the road, threatening to tell my social worker. Martha never called me her son again.

As a couple, Martha and Ray were the exact opposites. Martha was short and barrel-round with a moustache shadow on her upper lip and chin stubble. She was also a woman who couldn't let things lie. Maybe it was because she complained so much that she and Ray slept in separate bedrooms. At the time I didn't think much of it. Uncle Ray, on the other hand, was tall and slim with a gentle Jamaican accent and an even gentler nature. Immediately, I latched on to him as a father figure, and I became the son he never had

Rule number three concerned the TV, which sat in the back living room beside the kitchen. 'Shhhhhhhh, *the news* is on,' Martha always said. There was absolutely no talking allowed while the news was on. Martha and Ray didn't power their TV with 50p pieces. They could watch all the films and detective programmes they wanted, yet mostly they watched *the news*, which I found really boring. To rub salt into the wound, Uncle Ray would then explain the news, to educate me. I knew that Margaret Thatcher was prime minister; unemployment was at a record high; a serial killer was on the loose in Yorkshire and a guy from The Beetles band called John Lennon got shot in New York just before my tenth birthday. And that summer, Uncle Ray also sat glued to the cricket, rejoicing. The West Indies toured its dream team all over the country and mainly whooped England's arse.

Days became weeks at Ray and Martha's and there was no mention of me going back to London. Then weeks became months. Alan drove up occasionally and sat in the forbidden living room and said that since Martha and Ray were happy to take me then I should stay there. Apparently, Martha couldn't have children and Ray felt a duty to help because of Mum. All I could say was that I missed my siblings. There was no one to share anything with, not even my thoughts. And, what really vexed me was that I'd miss Uncle Bob Marley play at the Crystal Palace Bowl. All the Rastafarian elders had been talking about his Uprising tour when I was amongst them. I couldn't believe he was actually going to be in London. I hadn't figured out how, but I was making plans to cross the river south with my tribe to see my hero in the flesh, no matter what.

It was May 11, 1981. We were watching the news when they announced that Uncle Bob had died. I was devastated. Heartbroken. Another loss, another blow. I ran upstairs to my room. I was inconsolable, knowing now I would never have that chance to see him live. He became my guardian angel, and wherever I went he kept me company, and I would hear his songs being played on the radio in different places at the oddest times. That was my sign that he was still here, watching over me.

I got enrolled in the local school, Douglas primary. Another school to add to my list. And I made a new friend, Carlton, who lived across the road. At first, friendships were hard. In Stoke

Newington, everyone knew me at school. Here, I had no imme-
diate place in the pecking order. Worse still, I stuck out like a
sore thumb. I was among a handful of Black kids and no one
spoke the same as me at all. In Nottingham, they had a strong
East Midlands accent, people called each other 'Duckie', and when
they greeted each other they said, 'Ayup Midduck.' They used the
word 'summat' for 'something' and had strange phrases like 'you
mucky bugger'.

Carlton played cricket in the cobble alleyways between two
houses with the other kids, which was wide enough to pitch and
bat a ball. Soon after we started hanging out, I realised that me
being from London made me cool. Instead of ignoring me, kids
gravitated towards me. My difference made me a hit, so I played
to it. I held onto my accent and I even beefed it up a bit whenever
the need arose. And because I was a fast runner I also used that as
a way of fitting in. At cross-country I broke free ahead of the pack:
no social workers, no dramas, just the wind and the forest, the flex
of my muscles and the rhythm of my breath. I ran to forget where
I was and to forget what I'd left behind. Once I started I felt I
could keep going forever, not wanting to stop for *no one*.

Quickly, I sniffed out my tribe. Carlton, who was two years
older, played the role Grant Davis had had in my life: the kid who
I liked and respected but who tried to keep me on the straight and
narrow. The kid who, when it came to mischief, would bow out
gratefully, saying, 'My dad will kill me.' *Why would you listen to
your parents?* I remember thinking.

Another boy was called Brian. He lived a couple of roads down
from me. I captured him, in the same way I'd captured my band of
cousins at Fountayne Road primary. He represented a version of
me on the mornings Mum had stayed in bed and I'd had to dress
myself: shirt hanging out of his trousers, collar pointing upwards,
odd socks. He was as light-headed as helium, always laughing until

he almost pissed himself. I could smell his vulnerability. Later, I found out that he lived with his grandmother, and the woman who he called Auntie was actually his mum who'd given birth to him as a teenager. He got added to my list of protected species, and if anyone picked on him, they had me to deal with first.

One time, on our way home from school, I was behind when I saw Brian get jumped by one of the older neighbourhood kids. Brian was caught in a headlock, struggling to wriggle free, his hopelessness on display to the whole street. Instinctively, I charged from behind, smashed my fist into the kid's face before legging it down the street. Instead of thanking me, Brian shouted out, 'What did you do that for?!' I was confused, then, before I knew it, the bully was chasing after me. As I glanced over my shoulder to see how far away he was, I felt the blow to my face. My nose was busted. I kept on running with blood spattered over my hands and my white school shirt, and when I got home, I locked the bathroom door, filled the sink up with water and tried to scrub it out with soap. But my nose wouldn't stop bleeding. When Martha and Ray asked me about it later I lied and said that I'd fallen. My lesson for that day? Maybe I wasn't as hard as I thought. I made a mental note to take more care about who I lashed out at. Nottingham was a hard-faced brawler town. In many ways, kids were way tougher than in Stoke Newington. I was in unfamiliar territory.

While I was marking out an identity for myself on the street, Ray was quietly shaping one for me at home. Martha worked as a nurse at Nottingham General Hospital and he worked at the Raleigh bike factory, around the corner. They managed their shifts around me, so in the evenings we'd drive Martha to the hospital at around 9 PM. The next morning, she'd arrive home as Uncle Ray was putting on his jacket and heading out to work. It was a constantly revolving door. Also on repeat, was Martha's list of make-sures which she rattled off on the 20-minute journey to the hospital.

'Ray, make sure you put the bins out tonight... Ray, make sure there's enough cereal for Stanley's breakfast... Ray, make sure there's enough in the account to pay the mortgage this month...'

Mostly, Uncle Ray let Martha fill up the air while I sat silent on the backseat, but I loved it when he occasionally put his foot down.

'Christ woman! How many times mi have to tell yu! Don't talk to me as if mi ah some likkle pikney.'

They were always arguing about something or the other, and often about the mortgage for the house, or about me. Ray wasn't allowed to smoke in his own car, or play his music loud. But the minute Martha disappeared, he wound down the windows, lit up a Rothmans cigarette, cranked up the volume, and gestured for me to climb over into the front seat. Sometimes no words were exchanged. We sat there, the breeze on our faces, heads lolling to the lilt of country and western blues. Later, he would boil up milk to make Ovaltine on the stove until it frothed on top and we enjoyed it with a late-night toastie before bed.

Similar to Mum, Ray had stories about Jamaica. How he'd grown up there poor, but carefree, and the shock of arriving in England on a boat in the 1950s with the other West Indians to share a room with eight men.

'When that ship dock in London, everyting was grey, the sky grey, the people dem grey, the houses grey, no fanfare waiting to greet us. It was every man for dem selves, son, until we realise it would be better if we all stick together.'

He recalled the signs in the windows. *No Irish. No Dogs. No Blacks*. 'Even the dogs came before us,' he laughed. He swore that one day, he'd go home to die. 'Mi have to rest me bones back home in the sunshine!' he dreamed. And, in the end, he did.

As far as racist comments were concerned, he said if anyone said anything, I wasn't to pay them any mind. It was people trying to get a reaction. They did it because they feared us and they didn't understand us. 'People are people wherever you go. Don't let anyone tell you any different,' he said.

Ray seemed to open up when Martha wasn't around. His eyes came alive and his hands waved in the air when he debated. Otherwise, he was a man of few words. In looks, too, he appeared as two separate people. A dishevelled bottom half: flared trousers and cheap market shoes below a torso of Black Panther-cool; black polo-neck jumper, black leather jacket and a short afro on top. Whenever Auntie Martha worked weekends we'd fire up his sound system: a silver mix of Technics and Pioneer models with a double cassette deck and an eight-track player, tucked neatly in a corner of the living room. Uncle Ray played DJ, pumping up the music to full volume while I skanked my heart out. Every now and then he'd remember where he was. 'Careful Stanley! Don't break her stuff dem!' Snapping a limb off a plant was a sin, and if Uncle Ray ever got anxious, he'd dart from his armchair beside the stereo and hurriedly move an ornament or an item of furniture out of my way, just in case.

On weekends he taught me how to fix things. He'd lie under his bright yellow Datsun car, propped up on bricks, while I passed him a spanner and he'd fiddle around with the brake pads. It was a running joke with the neighbours, who would always ask him when he was going to sell that tin can because he was always fixing it. He also taught me how to build a kite made from bamboo sticks cut in half, and a long roll of red cellophane brought from his workplace, stuck down with electrical tape. We flew it regularly in the nearby park. Uncle Ray acted as a balm to soothe the pain of separation. I soaked it all up and was grateful, but, in truth, I never got used to the feeling of dislocation from my home.

At Douglas primary, I stumbled around trying to find my feet. On one occasion, when I played Thick the thief in the school production of *Ali Baba and the Forty Thieves*, I thought I found another way to fit in. I played the part of the gullible rogue down to a T and had parents and teachers in stitches during the performance. 'You're going to be a great actor one day, Stanley,' a teacher told me afterwards, but I was only doing what came naturally and reminding myself of the shows I use to put on for my family.

It must have been a few months after I arrived. I was leaning on the railing outside school with friends when I caught sight of a woman and her kids trundling up the opposite side of the road. From a distance, I could see the kids' afros bouncing up and down as they walked. Out front was a pram.

'Look at this Brady Bunch,' I pointed and laughed. The sort of thing that ten-year-olds say to puff themselves up in front of mates. But as the bunch got closer, I had to do a double take. Nah, it can't be. It was Mum with Angie and Mini, and Huggy in the pram. They didn't see me. Without a second thought, I jumped over the railing and bombed it across the road. 'Mum! Mum!' *Was it really her? In Nottingham?* I couldn't believe it.

'Come, let's go pick up your tings. We're going home,' she announced. I could see in her eyes that she wasn't well, but my mind was filled with how brilliant it was that Mum had come to rescue me and we could all be back together again. I hugged Angie and Mini, and baby Huggy, but Mum didn't respond. She kept walking at a hundred miles an hour.

'Mum, let's just go now! Let's just go!' I said. I knew that if we went to Ray and Martha's they might try and stop her, but Mum was insistent.

'No Stanley, we're going to get your tings,' she replied. I relented, not wanting a scene, so I ran in front and showed her the way. But as I'd feared, Martha was home, and my prediction played out. Mum refused to go inside their house. Instead, she sent me to grab my stuff. Martha begged for her to come in and talk, but Mum ended up yelling and cussing her out on the street.

'This is my fucking son! You don't come and take my fucking son, Martha. If you want a son, then go get your own fucking son. You don't fucking take my kid!' she screamed.

Then, she marched us down the road. 'Let's get on a bus, Mum,' I pleaded. I knew if we walked together someone would find us, but if we got on a bus, we could disappear. Mum refused. Maybe she wasn't thinking straight? Maybe she wanted to be caught? Maybe she wasn't serious about taking me back to London with her after all? When a police car finally pulled up, the officers jumped out and stopped Mum on the pavement. The officer made it clear: Mum had to apply to a court if she wanted to take me, otherwise they would have to arrest her. Even if I wanted to go with her, I couldn't. Auntie Martha and Uncle Ray were my legal guardians, and I got put in the car and taken back to their house. So close, but yet so far. I had no more tears left, I felt my heart harden.

After that, whenever Alan Mackie came to pick me up to take me to London for a couple of weeks during school holidays, I stayed with Angie, Mini and Huggy at Forest Road Children's Home, where they were taken into long term care themselves, following Mum being sectioned again. Alan said I had been made a ward of the court and only when I was 18 would I be free to live where I wanted. From then on, if ever I saw Mum in London it would be at the care home.

Chapter 16

Sex, Drugs and Reggae Music

I am 12 years old. Tonight, I'm at T's house. I know him because he roller skates and does breakdancing and body-popping with a crew in the city centre. I can't skate to save my life. I struggle with wheels under my feet, but I love hanging out and learning the dance moves: the windmill, the crab, electric boogaloo, and locking while the music pumps. We walk around with a big piece of rolled-up lino and breakdance on the streets or in the shopping mall until the security guards tell us to leave.

I also hang out with older boys now. The boys that I've met at the local youth club called the Red-Y. It's a big converted church and we listen to dancehall reggae and play table tennis or pool. When we don't have money, we hit the white ball around the green-felt table. I've chosen them because they're hardcore. I'm younger, but as daring with less inhibitions, and they've put me on a pedestal, made me feel special. They're 'ragamuffins', bored of school, drifting, selling weed, stealing and shooting pool. I fitted right in, they're my new tribe.

Even Carlton has been banned from hanging out with me. We had a paper round together, but I lost the job when I persuaded him to dump the papers in a skip but still collect our wages after. When we got found out, the newsagent sacked me on the spot. Any hint of trouble and his dad is round at Auntie Martha and Uncle Ray's. And not long ago, he told them straight, 'Mi noh want him come knock mi door again for Carlton, you hear mi?' Since then, Carlton and I walk on the opposite sides of the road when we turn the corner into our avenue. That way no one suspects we're still best friends. We have a special signal: an owl whistle that we use when Carlton's parents are out. Then he can sneak me into his living room to play records with his older brothers, dancing and singing the evening away, imitating Michael Jackson's moonwalk.

I never stay at Carlton's house but sometimes I sleep on T's sofa. His place is where kids go to smoke and drink when his mum is at work. Often, he stands in the doorway in tight jeans and leg-warmers and decides who's in and who's out, as if he's presiding over a guest list. I like that he's wise and he doesn't seem as aggressive as some of the others.

His mum is a nurse, and I've never seen his dad, so when she's on night shift, that's when he lets me in. He lives too far away from Martha and Ray's for me to get home. Besides, I hate staying there these days. Occasionally he forgets I'm coming and falls asleep, leaving me out on my arse, so I improvise. One time, I curled up under a lorry on a piece of cardboard because the engine was still warm. Otherwise, I sleep in the shed up the alleyway at the side of his house.

Tonight, T's girlfriend Donna is here, and T's stolen vodka and whisky from his mum's drinks cabinet. I feel embarrassed for him sometimes when his mum gets drunk. She's an alcoholic and even tried to kiss me once and told me she wanted to adopt me. She was always singing my praises because I was polite and had a London accent.

Donna isn't that pretty. She's plump, with spots and ginger hair. I'm surprised T has chosen her as his girl, he's a good-looking guy, a ladies' man, but, she's brought her friend Virginia, whose name makes me giggle because it reminds me of the word vagina. She's here especially for me. Knowing that he will disappear with Donna, T asked her to bring her friend. 'Just say you're 14,' T told me before they arrived. As I look older, I know I will pass for 14, but Virginia doesn't even ask. She's 15 and not long come out of hospital after having a baby. She seems horny as hell.

Hard liquor makes my head spin, so instead of spirits, I sip Tennent's lager from a can, but I don't even enjoy its bitter taste. I do it to be part of the crew and also to feel less nervous. T's definitely had sex with Donna, but I don't know what proper sex feels like, even though I fantasise about it. Tonight, curiosity leads me, so I follow when Virginia pulls me into T's little brother's room and asks me to take my clothes off. At first, I'm not sure whether she's for real, so I sit on the bed and pull the duvet over me while I slide my trousers down around my knees. 'Don't be shy,' she says. Then Virginia tells me I have a good body, and that I should be proud of it, so I take everything off and leave my underpants and socks on. 'Take them off,' she laughs. 'Only if you get naked first,' I say.

Part of me is shocked at the speed at which Virginia strips off butt-naked in front of me with no inhibitions, but I'm also excited by her. She is super-confident with almond eyes that dance around, and after her trousers and T-shirt hit the floor, she unhooks her bra and slides off her knickers. Her boobs are enormous, swollen by pregnancy. When she strides over, her pubic hair meets my eye line and she takes my hand and motions for me to stroke her. I can't help thinking it feels similar to stroking a cat's fur. Then, she sweeps her long, dark hair aside and climbs in under the covers beside me. Placing my hands on her breasts, she kisses me and pulls me on top of her. I fall between her legs and start grinding up against her, gradually getting harder.

This is not my first experience, but it does feel different. Mostly,

I am clueless, but I know that grinding gives a person pleasure. In the past, when Uncle Ray was at work and Auntie Martha was back from her night shifts early in the mornings, she called for me from my bed to come into her room. 'Oh, Lamb of God, here I come, I'm going to lie down. Come, lie down, and rest with me Stanley,' she would say before guiding me onto her bed in my brief and vest, and start tickling me and playfully nuzzling my neck with her teeth. On those times when she invited me in she was warm and open. Martha stripped off her uniform, down to her petticoat, to reveal her large breasts straining against the material and deep cleavage that I couldn't help catching sight of. Then, she flicked back the sheets and cuddled me into her, and rubbed my back which felt comforting. I melted into her belly folds of fat wanting to be held and loved. 'Oh, I'm so tired Stanley,' she said, and the first time it happened, her legs fell open. My body slid in between to enjoy the warmth but, instinctively, I began slowly rubbing up against her. I kept looking up to her face to check whether she would tell me off, or stop me, but she didn't. Instead, her head tilted back and her eyes closed tight, and she started moaning faintly and moving her hips, creating a rhythm before rolling her head from side to side until we both fell asleep, with me on top of her.

Virginia is now telling me to put it in. I am confused, but I want to please her, so I keep doing what I know: grinding against her harder until she loses patience and grabs hold of my cock. She places me inside her. Her power feels exhilarating, but none of this makes sense. Although she is warm and wet, I have little sensation in my body. It doesn't feel like me. Then, she keeps asking if I've come. I don't know what that is. I've only ever kissed and felt up girls before, rubbing my erection up on them or my mattress or against Auntie Martha in her petticoat.

Ever since I was fostered with Martha and Uncle Ray, all they do is argue. The word divorce, which I didn't fully understand, has even been mentioned on occasions, but nothing has happened. It's one of the reasons why I've started running away and staying at T's a lot. Sometimes I stay at Brian's grandmother's too. I hate the arguments at the house, it's never felt like my home and listening to them makes me feel more homeless.

It all came to a head one morning when Ray returned to the house after forgetting something. The next thing, he's leaning on the bedroom door frame, hand on his hip, looking down at me grinding on top of Martha. The look on Ray's face told me something was wrong.

'Martha. What yu tink yu doing? Stanley, get up out of the bed,' he said, before ushering me out.

Instead of going straight to my room, I hung around at the top of the stairs, enough to hear Uncle Ray tell Auntie Martha that if he caught her again doing anything like that he would call the social services. 'Yu know what yu was doing. Call yourself a Christian?' he kept repeating. And I knew it was serious because he raised his voice and Uncle Ray never raised his voice unless he was *really* pissed.

When he was done, he came and spoke to me in earshot of Martha. 'Never yu go back into her bed again, yu hear me son,' he said, adding that none of this was my fault, and that 'yu auntie' should know better. But it didn't feel that way. I sensed it was wrong, even though Martha didn't say anything. But I feel confused around Martha, so I avoid her. Mostly, I can't help feeling that I've let Uncle Ray down because he tries so hard with me. It's never been spoken of since, but it hangs between the three of us as a lead-weight secret.

Virginia keeps repeating the question: 'Have you come?' I don't know what to say, so I say, 'Yes.' I am out of breath and sweating and she seems high and giggly. Afterwards, T tells me how he could hear us having sex. *Was that sex?* I'm thinking. If that was actually it, I'm not in much of a hurry to do it again. It felt strange and awkward. I prefer getting high, which I do a lot instead.

I've started going to Hyson Green with the ragamuffins from the youth club—a criss-crossed concrete maze of five-storey council flats and overhead walkways. On a weekend, I bounce from one party to the next along its landings. Sometimes I don't go home at all and hide my school uniform in a bush so I can change before first bell on Monday. For the rest of the day, I sit at the back of the classroom trying not to get caught by the teacher for sleeping.

When I started staying out, Martha and Ray called the police, but they've turned up so many times to no effect that they've lost interest. Then they called the social services, and Alan has to drive up to see me, yet another meeting with no action. We sat in the front room and I told him how I don't want to be here with Martha and Ray anymore. I hate the way Martha tells Ray what to do, and how she wants to control me, although I haven't told him about me being in her bedroom. I've buried that, I've buried that so deeply I won't talk about it for more than 30 years during therapy. Also, I know that Martha listens in at the door in between topping up his coffee. It doesn't seem that Alan fully understands me, no matter what I say to him. I keep reminding him that he promised I would only be here temporarily, but that hasn't happened. I get angry and tell him to fuck off. I feel he's let me down and walk out of the living room. 'What a waste of fucking time,' I shout. 'I'll have to find my own way.' I want to be back in London more than anything else right now, so I hope that by staying out I'll get sent home. But my Nottingham crew feel familiar, too. I'm drawn to them. They're invincible and broken, the same as me. Other than Uncle Ray, they feel like the only family I have right now.

On the council estate landings in Hyson Green, I'm like a kid in a sweet shop. There, you can move from one blues party to the next, like an open house, buzzing from drink and ganja and pulled by every kind of sound system with DJ's toasting on the mic. There's a choice of reggae and dancehall, soul and rare groove, and when it gets late, lovers rock drifts out the windows. Bodies squeeze past each other on the narrow hallways. Men and women are pinned up against the stairs, hands roaming all over each other. Ratchet knives peek out from back pockets, some with flannels hanging out too. I carry mine everywhere. I love the sound it makes when it flies out of its casing with a quick flick of my wrist. I have cuts and slices on my hands from practising and play-fighting with the brothers, pretending to cut and stab each other, seeing who can draw and flick their blade out the fastest, like the gunslingers in Western movies.

In the kitchens, the air is soaked with ganja mist and bottles are lined up on the side next to a row of mixers. Brandy, whisky, vodka and Guinness litter the worktops and, in the ashtrays, long, cone-shaped spliffs burn like incense sticks. Spliffs are passed through hands and fingers or dangle from lips. The smell feels welcoming, and as one is passed, I take it between my fingers and take a long, slow draw. I love the feeling as the smoke strokes the back of my throat and I take it deep into my lungs, and feel my body soften and my head start to spin. In my mind, I am still that five-year-old boy, home again, skanking for my tribe.

On the makeshift dance floors, dreadlocks swing out from under Kangol hats, perched above Fila tracksuits, and Adidas trainers that shimmer brilliant white. Short dresses, fake fur and leg warmers move around, while high-heeled boots beat out a rhythm on the floor. Mixed in with the smell of weed is the smell of sweat and excitement, and I weave my way in and take my place, right in centre of the action. The hypnotic tune echoes out, rising

and falling with the melody of the 'Sleng Teng' riddim. I'm skanking now. My hips are twisting down and I close my eyes, feeling
the heavy bass vibrate through me. My movements are deliberate,
exaggerated. I'm on one foot now, arms outstretched on either
side. My body rises and drops as I move from foot to foot. It feels
like slow motion. It feels like flying.

In the early hours, when the lovers rock starts, I find a woman
to rub down with. All the men do. It's as good as winning a trophy
for the night. Because I'm young, most women ignore me, but
there are always one or two who are willing to oblige and high
enough to want to bump and grind with me on the dance floor. I
know how to grind and they love it as much as I do. To bump and
grind is a skill and takes practise, a lot of practise. A woman can
just walk away from you and dance with another man if you don't
know how to do it properly. It's erotic and sensual. As a man,
you must know how to control yourself too. We press our bodies
tightly up against each other as we gently, and ever so slowly, wind
our hips, going up and down, with the man leading, moving in
circular motions, as warm droplets of condensation drip from the
ceiling and onto our faces from the heat. It can get so hot it feels
like a sauna at times, and a man makes sure he always has his
flannel on hand to wipe away the sweat and fan the ladies, the sign
of a true professional. I lose sense of time, of existence.

On weekends I toast on the mic. I've joined the Prophecy
High Power sound system and we play music all over Nottingham
in dance halls and youth clubs, parks and blues parties. We lug
bass speakers up narrow flights of stairs and tweeter boxes through
windows, careful not to get dust on our outfits, in case there's a
woman to pull later.

Toasting, the reggae version of rapping, started in the 1950s
when disk jockeys would talk over the music, toasting the occasion
of that hit record. We listen to the hits before they are hits. As the

dubplates, sent straight from Jamaica and recorded by big-name artists, moved into the sound systems, they eventually influenced the creation of MCing and hip-hop culture in America and later grime in the UK. Reggae gods like Dennis Brown and Gregory Isaacs would light up the dance hall with their voices, impressing the revellers by mentioning the crew.

'Das right: Yu listening to the massive Prophecy High Power, straight outta Nottingham! Big up yourselves!' Then Brown starts singing his hit song 'Here I Come', which sends the crowds so wild we stop and start the record to the shouts of 'Rewind!' This can go on for a long time before we are able to play the whole record through to the end. It's all about pleasing the crowd.

I go by the name of Stan-up Iric, to hold on to my roots and to remind me of where I came from. Irie is a term used by the Rastafarian community as a greeting; everything is nice, blessed, good vibes. And Auntie Beryl called me Stan-up from my early skanking days back home, a name that followed me to Nottingham. When the mic first got handed to me, I was buzzing. I'd been practising in my room before I ever toasted with a sound system, mainly in front of Carlton, who's my biggest fan.

'Give the yut man the mic,' they said, when I hung round the mixing deck long enough and kept reaching for the microphone. When they asked me back I couldn't believe it. They wanted me? *Me*? Now I grab the mic as if it were my life: I'm the urban Shakespeare, rhyming in couplets, all my rage right there, I'm being heard for the first time, I bounce up and down in the darkness behind the sound system, except for the spotlight from the small lamp used to find records glowing in my face. The people go wild. I am a superstar:

> *'Now yu in tune to the hit 'bout champion sound as I man do say,*

When we come ah dancehall Prophecy don't play,
In an outta national we don't partial,
Listen dem ya tune and lick wood to mek yu feel good,
Yeahhhhmannnnnn. It's I man Stan-up Irie pon di
microphone stand,
Mek yu move and groove to the champion sound,
PROPHECY HIGH POWER!'

The sound clashes are the best, though: system against system; mic against mic; man against man. Sound systems arrive from London or Birmingham, Leeds or Manchester, sometimes even Jamaica. Then, we clash at the Marcus Garvey Centre, a notorious venue for dancehall music. We bowl in, set up our speakers and eye-up our dance-floor rivals. We're heavyweight, moving together in an army in case things go south. Sometimes it can get heated and violence breaks out, similar to football matches when the fans kick off. Mostly it's a good, clean fight, but we have our toolbox on standby: swords, axes, baseball bats and chair legs. We know when to stand firm and when to run before the police sirens start wailing. We play dub roots dancehall and spread the message of righteous living, unity and love. But if shit goes down, we're tooled up. We're ready.

Chapter 17

The Black Waltons

In the summer of 1983 I got arrested for a crime I didn't commit. The police found that hard to believe, too. Apparently, I'd stolen a handbag and hidden it behind the bins in a block of flats. Of all the things I had done, this wasn't one.

The main man in my crew from the Red-Y youth club was called Danny Jones, Jonesy for short. He was a dark skinned, slim, don't-fuck-with-me guy who always wore a red beret slanted on the side of his head. Someone who knew his own power but never abused it, always keeping cool, calm and collected. A voice of reason. I looked up to him for that and we often had deep reasonings about life. I'm not sure why, but he seemed to have a soft spot for me, always defending me if one of the bigger brothers tried to put me down and wanting his younger brother Mark to be more like me. One of his sidekicks was Courtney: a guy who pretended to be tough, but who hadn't learned his lines. Anyone could see he was harmless. I befriended him and he even came round to Auntie Martha and Uncle Ray's on occasions. Martha even commented on what a polite young man he was. 'He got manners, you should try to be more like him, Stanley,' she said. So it came as a shock when he stitched me up.

The first I knew about it was when two officers turned up at Martha and Ray's door on an evening I was there. They handcuffed me in front of the neighbours and lowered my head into the back of a panda car. Martha was beside herself with shame, smiling at every one as if nothing serious was happening. It was bad enough when they came when I'd gone missing, but to be arrested for an actual crime was another thing. Uncle Ray protested my innocence from the outset. He and Martha followed behind in his Datsun and confronted the desk sergeant, demanding to be present during my interview. When Uncle Ray explained my alibi—that I'd been at home watching TV—the officer ignored him and continued to harass me into a confession.

'Tell us the truth, Stanley. You stole the bag. What did you do with it?' he repeated.

'That is the truth!' I shouted back.

'We know you did it. Someone's told us it was you. Admit it, Stanley.'

I've always heard of brothers being framed for crimes. And back home, Uncle Winston had always told stories, but the injustice of it actually happening to me felt surreal, as if the ground was being pulled from under me. They weren't asking me if I did it, they were telling me I did it, just like how the brothers said it would happen when I was warned about police corruption. Worse still, they treated me as if I were a grown man, not a 13-year-old teenager. In the end, Uncle Ray stepped in.

'Bring us the person who claims Stanley did this, and let him say it to his face,' he said. Moments after the detectives agreed, the door flung open. Courtney stood there, wrists cuffed behind his back and head bowed. He was flanked by two officers. Blood stained his mouth and chin from a busted-up lip and nose, his eyes were swollen and bloodshot. I stared at him in disbelief.

'Well go on then. Tell them what you told us!' one of the detectives shouted. Courtney couldn't look at me. Then, he whispered, 'It wasn't him. I made it up.' I could hear him crying out in pain when the officers dragged him back down the corridor and into a cell.

After a week or so, I bumped into Courtney in the street. I wasn't half as angry with him as I should have been. Seeing the bruises on his face that he'd received at the hands of the police stopped me from wanting to hurt him any further. Had it not been for Uncle Ray following in his Datsun, that could have been me. His injuries hadn't yet fully healed and I felt an empathy towards him. Whatever he'd done, he was still a brother. We bonded over a shared victimhood, maybe the realisation that whatever troublemakers we were, we were also the targets. And the police were above the law. Courtney still couldn't look me in the eyes and I could see that the humiliation was eating him up. He apologised and begged me not to say anything to the crew. He didn't want to be known as a grass. We agreed it wouldn't get mentioned again.

That year Uncle Ray got made redundant. He said the country was going to the dogs and that a man couldn't even rely on a job for life anymore. The cloud that hung over us in the house got darker and he talked of nothing else but going back to Jamaica. As far as I was concerned, I had had enough of Martha. Apparently, she instructed Uncle Ray to lock the doors at night and strip me of my house key because she was worried that I'd steal something from them. She even started locking her bedroom door while she was at work. Not that I went back there much. On the sly, Ray often left the back door open, or my room window unlocked at night, so if I did return I could climb up into it. And on the nights Martha was on a night shift, I would sleep there and leave in morning before she came home. He said that when he went back to Jamaica he would take me with him if I wanted to go. 'Jamaica is no place to play up. Over there the police are tougher and shoot to kill. No teachers will put up with any foolishness,' he warned me.

Whilst I was living with Auntie Martha and Uncle Ray, the pair of them had been called up to my secondary school on so many occasions: me bunking off; me fighting; me telling a teacher to fuck off. The headmaster, a burly Irishman, told them how fortunate I was to have been taken in the first place. The Trinity School, with a similar name as the primary school I went to while at the children's home in London, was a Catholic secondary and I wasn't even Catholic. *And this was how I repaid him?*

One time, I got hauled up to his office with Danny Jones's little brother Mark after disrupting class.

'We're going to get caned,' Mark predicted as we lined up outside.

'What's that?' I asked.

'Haven't you been caned before? It's a long piece of stick that the headmaster uses, you have to bend over and feel the licks on your arse,' he laughed, adding that if he knew he was due for a caning he shoved some extra clothes down the back of his trousers to cushion the impact. I'd been doing that since the age of four, I thought, incredulous that he was willing to be caned.

'I'm not letting anyone cane me, bro! I don't care who they are!' I said, and when it was eventually my turn, I refused to bend over.

'No, that's not happening,' I said flatly, shaking my head.

Finally, Ray and Martha got called up. In my amazement, Martha said she didn't agree with caning and that if there was any disciplining to be done, it should be done by them. I don't know if her intention was kind, or whether she wanted to save her own face. If it was kindness, it was the only time Martha ever offered me a get-out-of-jail-free card.

At one point, I ran away so many times that Alan was called up from London and a decision was made that I be placed with another set of temporary foster parents. 'So move me,' I shrugged. 'Like I give a shit.' Except that I did give a shit. I didn't want to be moved around Nottingham. All I wanted was to go back home to London to my family. In the end I was moved, but this time it was a revelation Alan hadn't mentioned that the family I'd be shipped out to were Black. More than that, this Black family was whole and complete. There were four brothers and two sisters from the same mum and a dad. Plus they all looked alike as though they belonged to each other. It was as if I had landed in an episode of *The Waltons*, Caribbean style. That's how it felt, anyhow. I loved watching *The Waltons*, and often dreamed about having a huge family like that myself one day.

Immediately, it was the smell of the house that drew me in. I became a sniffer dog. The mum baked bread the same as my mum used to. There was rice and peas, curried goat, jerk chicken and fried dumpling. In the morning there was mint tea on the cooker and cornmeal porridge served with condensed milk, sprinkled with nutmeg and vanilla essence.

In the bathroom, there was Palmer's cocoa butter cream for my body and Vosene shampoo and coconut oil for my hair. I unscrewed the containers and breathed in their scent. The stair railings were painted brown, and the doors a burned Caribbean orange—colours that reminded me of Alkham Road and the bright colours Mum used to remind her of Jamaica, before she was sick. The photographs on the wall were of Black faces smiling down. Strangely, there was no sign of Jesus hanging around! And, at the weekends we played football and basketball in the garden and in the evenings we played board games—Snakes and Ladders, Monopoly, dominoes and draughts. I didn't need to be persuaded. In a split second of seeing them, I went from being silent and sullen to being part of the family. They welcomed me with open arms and I dove in. Then, I realised. Everything made sense. I'd been born to the wrong parents at the wrong time in the wrong place. The luck of the draw. As much as I missed Angie and Mini and Huggy and Mum, this was it. I'd made it. This was where I was supposed to be all along. 'Night Ma. Night Pa. Night brothers and sisters. Night Stanley.'

My dreamtime with this family, though, was short-lived. It turned out the parents weren't my mother and father. These weren't my brothers and sisters. I wasn't their long-lost son. And when social services wanted to place me back with Martha and Ray, I had to face the truth. I begged for them to let me stay, but I was told it had always been temporary until things stabilised. The whole family stood on the doorstep to say goodbye to me. The whole family. Heartbroken, I flung my arms around the mum and dad with my head sandwiched between them, not wanting to let go, holding on for dear life. The pain I felt was immense. Once again, my emotions betrayed me, overwhelmed, I bawled my eyes out, not letting go of my grip. Alan sat waiting in his VW. Engine running. Forms ticked. I was returned. I buried that pain so deep; I can't even remember the names of any of the family members.

More than ever now, I wanted out of Nottingham. I wanted out of Martha and Ray's and wanted out of whatever merry-go-round system I was in. I stayed out more, bunked off more, and escaped with my crew at the Red-Y. I kept pushing, pushing, pushing at the boundaries. Sooner or later something would break. It probably wouldn't have been quite so quick had I not been getting into fights at school. One was with the headmaster's son, who was in my year and the youngest of the Granger brothers. No matter how many times we got pulled apart, the feud snowballed. We forgot how it even started. But whenever a fight got picked, he fetched his older brother who was stronger than me and had a name for himself. Then, I got a lucky break. One afternoon, I was bunking off school when I met a brother called Andrey skulking around the streets doing the same. He was a really tall, thin, light-skinned, sixth former, four years older than me. When I told him about the

Granger brothers, it energised him. 'Don't worry, man. I'll deal with the older one. You concentrate on the younger,' he said. We made a pact. The following day, we'd sort them out.

During next day's lunch break, Andrey chased down the older Granger brother, manhandled him then restrained him in front of everyone. Meanwhile, I cornered the younger brother, but he didn't want to fight me and tried to walk off, not so tough without his brother. One phone call later followed by a meeting with Martha and Ray, and I was out. The headmaster said he had done everything he could for me, but this wasn't working. Ray had a man to man talk with me and warned that if I carried on like this, one day I was going to end up in jail. But that he also understood how tough things were for me.

'Why can't I just go back home?' I thought. 'I just want to go home.'

This time around, expulsion felt suffocating. I didn't want to hang around at Martha and Ray's, nor could I sofa-surf every night, but I headed to T's when I could. The journey was one I had repeated many times throughout my time in Nottingham: bus from Ray and Martha's into town and then a connection from near the train station to St Ann's, where he lived. That week, I set off. In the city centre I kicked around and waited for the number 41 connection. Then, I saw it: my ticket to freedom. Parked up on the side was a National Express bus. The luggage holdall was wide open and the driver was piling in cases and rucksacks. Above the front window was a sign: LONDON VICTORIA in bright white capitals. It stopped me in my tracks. All this time I'd been in Nottingham drifting around the streets, going from house to house, hating school, desperate to go home and begging Alan Mackie to take me, and I never thought of it. I never thought that I could just get on a bus, destination London. Home. I could have kicked myself. I ran over and interrupted the driver.

'Excuse me. Is this bus going to London?'

'That's what it says, lad,' the driver smiled.

'What time does it leave?'

'Every other hour on the hour.'

'What!? Every other hour on the hour?' I asked the driver to repeat it, in case I'd misheard. There and then, my trip to T's got cancelled. Instead, I headed straight back to Ray and Martha's, and found with relief that Uncle Ray was home alone. I ran upstairs and piled trousers, T-shirts, trainers as fast as my hands could move—as much as I could scoop up from my room—into a holdall. Downstairs, I made myself a sandwich for the journey, while Uncle Ray sat in the living room, patiently smoking his Rothmans.

'So, yu leaving?' he said quietly, as if talking to himself, as I was on my way out of the kitchen. I nodded silently. We just looked at each other. There was no need for words. I never would have told him if I thought he would stop me, but there was something resigned about Ray, as if he'd given up on England and his life, and maybe on me.

'Don't blame you, son. Knew you would figure it out one day.' It was as if he knew that if you keep chipping away at a kid, then bit by bit they fracture. Then, they break. He'd watched me break, powerless to stop it.

'You have money?' he asked.

'A little,' I replied, not even thinking about how much it would cost to get to London. He reached into his pocket, pulled out his wallet and slid four crisp £10 notes from it as if he'd been saving them up.

'You're going to need it, son. Make sure you make it last. Yu have cigarettes?' Uncle Ray often passed me the odd Rothmans. Now, he opened up a fresh box, slid a couple out for himself, and handed me the rest of the packet.

'Take care of yourself, son. You're a bright young lad full of potential. Do something positive with your life, Stanley. Stay out of trouble, yu hear?'

I hugged Uncle Ray as if it would be the last time I ever saw him. I hugged the warmth, the love, and the father figure this man was to me. I hugged him to say thank you and to tell him I was sorry. Sorry that things hadn't worked out better for us all. I never did say goodbye to T, or Paul or any of the brothers I moved with at the Red-Y or in the Prophecy High Power sound system. I didn't say goodbye to my best friend Carlton either, though he risked seeing me even when his dad forbid it.

All I could think about was that I was going home, although I didn't know what I was going home to. Would I even remember the way home? Who would be there? Could I make it to the children's home to see Angie and Mini and Huggy? Huggy was four years old now. Whenever I saw him in the holidays he'd grown, crawled, walked, and talked, but he'd never truly known me as his brother. We got pulled apart before he could even say my name.

Fields of countryside and service stations rolled by, while tears of rage and frustration rolled down my cheeks, and I tried to hide my anguish from the passenger sitting next to me. Leaning my head against the window with my hood up, I buried my face in the scenery that flashed before my eyes, triggering flashbacks from all I had been through since that night I was taken to the children's hospital at the age of nine. I was alone and vulnerable. Yet, at the same time, I felt an exhilarating sense of freedom, as if a huge weight had been lifted off my shoulders

Chapter 18

The Prodigal Son

I cross over Cazenove Road and break into a sprint, sweat soaking through my tracksuit top. I'm picking up speed. *Run. Fucking run*, I repeat in my head. If I don't make it home quickly the Old Bill are sure to nick me. What the fuck was I thinking? I ran head-first into their trap.

I've been thieving ever since I arrived back from Nottingham: car radios, handbags, anything I can get my hands on. There's one line I won't cross, though. Old ladies. I don't rob the elderly, but anyone else is fair game. Today, I had a sixth sense about that woman, even before I snatched her bag. She was standing casually, dangling it out to one side. Not even on her shoulder. She was asking for it. Yet when I grabbed it, she didn't say a word. Usually they scream 'Thief!' or 'Get him!' or something. But nothing. Fuck! I knew it. Undercover police. When I glanced back she was on her radio. *My next move?* Scan the streets. Look for accomplices. Undercover police always come with backup.

Today I'm flying solo, but most of the time I work with Jamie. Not long after I got home, I bumped into him walking up Cazenove where he lived. I hadn't seen him since primary school. It's not as if we were close or anything but, like me, he was a troublemaker. I recognised him straight away: same pasty white skin;

146

same snotty nose; same streaks of eggy food on his jumper. Now he's what we call a proper tea leaf—a thief. Like me, he doesn't go to school either.

'Stanley? Staaaaanley Brawnnn?' he asks in a thick cockney accent. He couldn't believe it. He said everyone at school had wondered where I'd gone.

'You disappeared, bruv. No one thought we'd see you again!'

I told him about the four years in Nottingham, and how I'd come back for good. Since then, Jamie and I have made a good team. He's taught me a lot. If its cars we're robbing, we use a wire coat hanger bent into a hook and shove it down the side of the door edge to lever up the lock, and if all else fails, I wrap up a brick in my tracky top to dull the noise, smash the window, while he pops the latch and jimmies out the cassette player. We get good money for it—maybe as much as £80 from the mechanic in the alleyway by Stoke Newington station.

I think it's funny that I've come from Nottingham. I say I'm Robin Hood and Stoke Newington is my Sherwood Forest. I'm robbing the rich to give to the poor—the poor being my mum. I know we can get Angie, Mini and Huggy back from the children's home, and I keep telling Mum not to give up, but there's no way social services will let it happen, not with the house in the state it is and with Mum still recovering from her sickness.

Angie, Mini and Huggy haven't lived with Mum for the whole time I've been away. When I got home, it didn't look as if anyone had been there, either. I jumped off the National Express at Victoria and found my way straight onto the number 73 by asking all the conductors I saw where I could find the bus. I couldn't believe my luck that the 73 actually terminated in Victoria and took me all the way to Stoke Newington.

London felt foreign, yet familiar. The red route-master; the friendly conductor; Marble Arch; King's Cross station; then we passed Stoke Newington Town Hall—and the memory of Bill and Molly came flooding back, but I didn't let it settle, I wanted to forget. And when the bus turned the corner into Stoke Newington Common, I saw Alkham Road. The trees still kissed in the middle. But the green door on our house had been changed to dark blue, and it looked different. Maybe it was a new door the council put in after that night. I knocked but there was no answer, so I sat on the side slope of the steps, bathing in the sunshine, soaking up the street and the memories. I couldn't believe I had made it back.

It felt surreal sitting there as if it had all been just a bad dream. Everything seemed smaller. The road, the walls, the pavements, even the houses. A good 20 minutes passed before I heard a faint rustling and the door slowly creaked open. At first, I thought it had swung open by itself. I got up and moved towards the gap. When I looked behind the door I was face to face with Mum. I was lost for words. 'Mum? Mummy?' I said. I hadn't seen her for a good part of two years. The medication made her face so bloated and expressionless. Her eyes could barely open, and she shuffled rather than strode like she used to. 'Staaaanley?' she kept repeating in a monotone, drawled voice. I hugged her tightly, as if she was the long-lost child, my throat choking up with sorrow. But I was also angry. *How can this be allowed? How can this be allowed to happen to my Mum?*

It was the smell that got me. The damp. And the rubbish. The stench of rotting food. The stench of my Mum left to rot. When I made my way through the passageway, black bags were piled upon black bags, some of them moving with vermin. Mum said she hadn't the strength to move them down to the bins outside. In the hallway I see the evidence of Mum's sickness, a plethora of equations etched into the wallpaper, some scrawled in pen ink, as if it's her secret language.

I've not been near a school or the social services since my

escape. I won't see Alan Mackie, and I hide if anyone like Andrea comes to the house. Alan let me down big time not getting me out of Martha and Ray's sooner. Fuck him and fuck the social services. At least if I'm home, I can make a getaway through a back window if they come.

I've cleared our hallway, lugged out all Mum's rubbish. I've washed the dishes piled high in the kitchen sink and drained out the bath full of clothes. They stunk as if they'd been left there soaking for years. I've bought new wallpaper for the kitchen and got her a new dining table and chairs from the high street. Plus, I've removed the beads from the kitchen doorway—the beads that rattled like a maraca shaker—and put them on top of Mum's wardrobe. I didn't have the heart to throw them away, but the sound of them hitting against each other vexed me so badly that one night I ripped them all down. I've ripped up the red and yellow lino in the hallway and kitchen too. And started painting and papering the other walls. At first, it was trial and error fumbling my way through, trying to line up the wallpaper patterns. I've painted the ceilings brilliant white, but it's taken several coats. Mum's cigarettes have stained the whole house a burnished yellow that keeps peeking through. I want my sisters and brother back home and what I steal with Jamie is paying for the redecoration. I can't afford to get caught now.

Fuck! There's a guy strolling towards me. Casual type: early 30s, jeans, pale waist-length jacket and trainers. There's something about the way he's moving, looking at me. I'm sure this guy is Old Bill. He's reaching out, trying to get my attention. Thank fuck the bag isn't on me anymore. As soon as I realised it was an empty decoy, I lobbed it into a garden. He's asking me a question, now.

'Sorry, 'scuse me mate, have you got the...' Bang! I barge straight into him with my shoulder and send him over the low fence at the edge of the pavement. Within seconds he's up on his feet, shouting into his radio, giving chase.

Sirens sound in the distance now. I'm sprinting down Kyverdale Road. I'm not going to make it home. Instead, I look around for cover. Porches are too risky. So is crouching behind walls or hedges. I'm scanning every house and alleyway, gate and window, like a laser beam. Fuck! The rotor blades of a helicopter are in the distance. Rat-a-tat. Rat-a-tat. Helicopters fly round here all the time, so I don't know if it's for me, but the sound is getting closer and closer. Rat-a-tat. Rat-a-tat.

There's a basement flat door that's slightly ajar, behind an overgrown hedge and I throw myself down the steps. I creep in, locking it quietly behind me, listening for any movement. Nothing, but the faint murmur of a TV. Straight ahead I can see the kitchen and a clear route out to the back garden. Someone from the household must have briefly popped out to the corner shop and left me the front door open. Can I make it out without being seen? Slowly, I ease my way down the passageway. I peek through the crack of the living room door. There's an old couple, sat on the sofa, engrossed in daytime TV. If I time it right, I can step through the hallway the second the volume gets louder. Now. Here's my moment. The credits are rolling. A few beats in and I've crossed the kitchen and bolted out through the rear door and across the garden.

The helicopter is still there. Rat-a-tat. Rat-a-tat. I jump the wall and sprint into Alkham Road, key in hand, determined to make it to my front door. I run at breakneck speed as if my life depends on it. If the police have Alkham Road covered, I'm done for. Only a couple of hundred yards to go and I can slam our front door shut. The second I'm in, I'm doubled over in the hallway,

Me and my siblings with their partners at Mum's funeral

Mum before her diagnosis.

Mum on medication.

Me and my foster dad in Jamaica

Great-great-great-Grandma
Harriet

Mum with my nephew Kyle

Mum after she got a job and won
my siblings back from the courts

Douglas Primary School photo
age 10, Nottingham

Me outside my foster parents' house, Nottingham, age 9

Me in my mum's kitchen at Alkham
Road, Stoke Newington—14 years old

Me before I cut my dreadlocks

Me (bottom right) and older sister (top right), Angela, at Holy Trinity Primary School opposite the Children's Home in Hackney, London.

Me and my two sisters with our cat, Timothy
(original version of the cover photo)

Me and my siblings on a Butlins holiday with
the Children's Home.

Me and my baby brother, Huggy, on the same holiday

Me (third from left, top row) at summer camp with the boys as a camp counselor.

Me at summer camp with my campers

These are some of the pieces from my portfolio that were assembled as part of my GCE O Level while at Warren Hill Young Offenders Prison. I received 98% for my work.

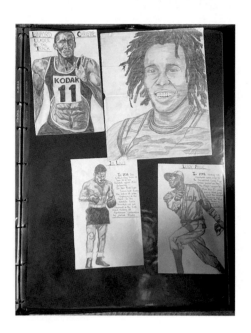

Self-portrait
Warren Hill Young Offenders
Prison

Self-portrait I did while
smoking crack-cocaine

Me after completing my
Personal Training (PT) course at
Warren Hill Young Offenders Prison

Self-portrait, Brixton Prison

Me and my friend Tom in the hospital during
his recovery

Me working as an addictions counselor at Coldingly Prison
with my colleagues

My first oil painting,
Pentonville Prison

My first watercolour painting,
Brixton Prison

Warren Hill Young Offenders Prison

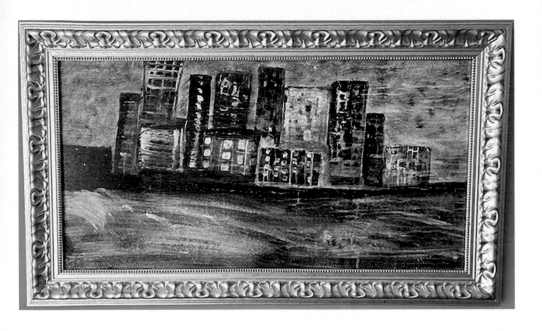

Some of Mum's paintings

One of my first headshots

The cover of my first album.

This is the cover of my current album *"Simply Stanley"*, available on Spotify and iTunes.

lungs burning. Fuck! Thank. Fuck! My chest is rising and falling. I'm wheezing while I catch my breath, rolling on the floor. I clumsily run upstairs to peek from the kitchen window to make sure I haven't been followed. Unsatisfied, I stumble into the living room to check from that window too, just in case.

I can't stay in these clothes. If the police come knocking they'll recognise them straight away. Using the strength I have left in my legs, I run upstairs to the third floor, peel off my tracky bottoms and T-shirt, shove them under my bed, and throw on the overalls I've been using to paint the house. They're covered in gloss and emulsion, and I take the paint brush and daub parts of my hands and my face with paint, then get my paint-splattered woolly hat and place it on my head. When I go back downstairs to look out the kitchen window, police are combing the street. A van has pulled up further down. Alsatian dogs are pulling on leads. Neighbours' doors are knocked on.

Casually, I step outside. Our next-door neighbour is on her porch now and the helicopter is still sounding overhead. Rat-a-tat. Rat-a-tat.

'Wha gwan wid the police, man?' I ask coolly.

'I don't know mi love, must be a Black man dem looking for with all di police dem have out here.' Her eyes raise to the heavens.

'Yeah, makes sense,' I nod, looking resigned. One of the dogs is sniffing round Mum's bins, so I ask the officer what's happened for all these police to be here. He just sees a teenager and tells me to mind my own business but admits that they're looking for someone. After that, I sit on the stoop and watch them move up the street and disappear round the corner onto Northwold Road towards the common. The neighbours are tutting and shaking their heads and I join in too, before everyone drifts back inside. Even if they find the bag, the Old Bill don't have my fingerprints on file. I'm safe, for now.

Chapter 19

Ragamuffin Soldier

After a few months of being at home, Mum's health started to improve. I persuaded Dr Egbonwon to alter her medication, to take her off her injections and start her on pills. She was so drugged up that, at times, she could hardly lift her feet to walk, and sometimes she couldn't make it to the toilet in time. Occasionally, she soiled her bed, and I made a habit of checking and stripping the sheets to take to the laundrette. And I washed Mum when she couldn't wash herself. That felt weird. Undressing Mum, seeing her nakedness and wiping the soapy flannel across her skin. She let me do it, but I wonder now how she must have felt. I'd not long turned 14, an unnatural age for a kid to be caring for a parent. Still, that little big man, trying to take responsibility the only way I knew, even when my own life was collapsing around me.

I cooked for Mum in the way that Rasta Mark and Simeon had taught me all those years back and took Mum off the white bread, butter and sugar she had been living on. Simple, healthy Ital food: vegetables, fruits, nuts and brown rice that I bought with the money I earned from thieving. As soon as her adjusted medication took effect, I bought her a tracksuit and trainers and walked her round the block every morning to gain back her strength, until eventually, we built up into a little trot with me egging Mum on as if I was training her for the Olympics. Mum had always walked and had good lungs on her. She could walk for miles. It seemed to calm the voices in her head, the rhythm its own kind of music. But the years of medication caused side effects, especially weight gain, a huge, bloated stomach and a swollen face. (I noticed the same disfigurement in others who were unwell and received medication for schizophrenia whenever I had to take Mum to the hospital.) Mum had gone from being a terrifying physical presence, to a husk of a person. I even found Roots among her piles of rubbish and took a Stanley knife to him, cutting his leather fingers to smithereens, all the time thinking how ironic it was that the knife was called Stanley.

By now, however, I had a new enemy: Hackney Council. Its workmen had been due to make repairs on Mum's house, but no one turned up. As fast as I was giving it a makeover, everything underpinning it was disintegrating. The rain still leaked through the upstairs roof and ran down the bannister. The sash window frames had wood rot and crumbled in your fingers. And the panes of glass had massive gaps around the edges where there was no longer any putty. You could see outside through these gaps, and they leaked what little warmth there was from the new electric heaters I had bought. In the spur of the moment, I kicked off in the council office one day when no one took my complaints seriously. I just lost it and acted like a madman, threatening the staff behind their desks. Soon, I got known as a troublemaker: the teenager who turned up and held the office hostage with his mouth. Only one woman, a light-skinned African sister, seemed to appreciate what I was trying to do. She took me aside, slipped me a piece of paper with a number on it and told me in a hushed voice that if I rang the manager and made a polite, formal complaint, the repairs might get done quicker. It worked. The woman became my ally and I was surprised to learn much later that her name was Joy. Whenever I called the council office from the red telephone box in Cazenove Road, I realised that if I spoke in my own way, the manager was unavailable, but when I put on a posh English accent saying, 'May I speak to the manager please?', like magic, he was in the office available to speak. When workmen did appear, I always slipped them a tenner and asked the guys to carry out extra repairs after hours, off the books. Soon, I got to know them on first-name terms and had a few I could turn to without having to go down to the office and fill out forms to get things fixed.

Now I know that in 1984 Hackney Council was at the centre of a report by the Commission for Racial Equality, the first formal investigation into racial discrimination when it came to the allocation of public housing in London. The Commission found that Black people had been disproportionately pushed down the list for council properties, and its report paved the way for the racial monitoring of housing. But housing discrimination didn't only happen in Hackney, but across several London boroughs, and it had been going on for years. Now I'm surprised we had a house at all, even if it was falling apart. All I remember was that council repairs were as rare as gold dust, even more so if you were from a Black or ethnic minority family. I was just a juvenile working the system trying to help his mum.

Subconsciously, I looked around for a stabilising force, which led me to Grant Davis's door. I had an urge to go there. Like Jamie, I hadn't seen him since primary school but I'd often thought about him.

'Stanley Brown with an E? I can't believe it's you, man!'

He looked gobsmacked. His gangly frame had filled out and he now stood as a broad-chested teenager. He and his family welcomed me as if I was a hero. After I filled them in about my disappearance, they empathised with my situation and took me under their wing. Grant's parents said they knew something wasn't right with Mum and remembered how rough we looked, and, had they known, they would have taken me and my sisters in. I was touched by the gesture, knowing this family, who wasn't even our blood, would have been willing to help us. That said, I hid my street exploits from Grant and never told him about how I earned a living, mainly, not wanting to get him involved, and partly, because I already felt like a fraud sitting at their dinner table whenever I was invited. And when his dad offered me some work, I accepted.

Grant's dad ran his own TV and video repair business in a tiny shop at the back of Dalston train station. He was a short man, barely reaching the steering wheel of his white van. He looked in fact like a black Danny DeVito from the TV series *Taxi*. I helped him with some errands—mainly picking up broken TVs or delivering repairs. He always kept a can of Tennent's brew in the van door pocket for himself. It was kept in a brown paper bag. He told me I could be anything I wanted to be and slipped me £20 at the end of the day: chicken feed compared to what I could earn on the street. Slowly, I stopped turning up, and eventually, I stopped seeing Grant altogether.

After a while our social worker Andrea got wind that I was back home. For starters, it was obvious the house had been cleaned and decorated; there was only so long I could hide. Andrea had always treated Mum sympathetically, although she had her limits, and a job to do. One memory of her always stuck with me. Mum had gone missing for two days and Andrea found us home alone. I told her I think I might know where our mum is, so she piled us into her car and I showed her the way to Holly Street, a rundown council estate in Dalston. Here Mum's friend Sheila had a flat, two miles from where we lived. I don't know how I manage to remember the way. Andrea pleaded with her: 'You can't just leave your kids, Joy.' On that occasion, she didn't report Mum, and I got a deafening box to the side of my face after Andrea left for bringing social services to her friend's door, while they were in the flat smoking weed. I couldn't hear properly out of my left ear for days. Now, I asked to be transferred from Alan's care into hers. On one condition, she negotiated: that I went back to school. I agreed because it was easier: I had no intention of staying in school. I was the man of the house and had bills to pay.

* * *

I walked into fourth year of Homerton House secondary to start the Autumn term of 1984. Long since bulldozed, it was a 1960s pre-fab monstrosity for boys. The place was a hellhole. I fitted right in. Black leather jacket, baggy jeans turned up at the ankles, white Reebok trainers, and an uncombed, picky hair. I cruised along the corridors to the headmaster's office, eyeballing anyone in sight. 'We have lots to offer boys like you, Stanley, if you put your mind to it,' the headmaster told me at my induction meeting. His lips were moving, but I was somewhere else. I couldn't see the use in me being there. I wasn't listening. 'Expel me on the spot,' I thought. 'It was bound to happen sooner or later.'

'Did you get any of that, son?'

'I ain't your son, but, yeah, yeah, all good, man,' I mumbled, getting up ready to leave for my lesson.

If I hadn't gone to Nottingham, Homerton would have been the secondary school I'd have graduated to from Fountayne Road primary. This meant most kids there had been together since first year. Suddenly, I was the newcomer again, the nomad in search of a tribe. In class, the teacher introduced me. 'This is Stanley, please make him feel welcome. Also, he'll be turning up in school uniform tomorrow.' The comment was intended to restore class order when the kids clocked that I wasn't wearing it and started complaining, but for the rebel in me, it had the opposite effect: I vowed never to wear the school uniform, period.

On my first day, two boys sidled up to me. 'I'm Jason, but you can call me JJ and this is William, he goes by the nickname Wrighty,' they introduced themselves, before showing me the dining hall and telling me about the teachers I needed to watch out for.

'Who's the baddest fighter in the school?' I asked them over lunch. That's all I wanted to know, nothing else. They looked surprised at the question.

'Speak of the devil, see that guy there?' they whispered, pointing him out in the dinner queue. 'He's trouble, that's Duvall. Stay away from him, man. He's crazy.'

Duvall was a sixth former. Stocky and fair-skinned. Face as angry as an open wound, but a puppy compared to what I've witnessed and done to grown men on the streets. I sized him up. It was all about the eyes. The eyes never lied. And his were a front. My reasoning was simple: show the whole school that no one fucks with me by taking out the best fighter. I watched as he pulled rank on the younger kids, shoving them out of the way to get to the front of the line. It was all the licence I needed: a red rag to a raging bull. I had zero respect for bullies and guys who abused their power.

'So he's the baddest in the school? Yeah, well watch this,' I said, and slowly bounced over to him. I balled up my fist and stood in front of Duvall's face at arm's length. 'Get to the fucking back,' I said through gritted teeth, looking him dead in the eyes. I wanted him to fight me. I was thinking, *Come on, fight me*. He stared back as if reading my thoughts. The sound of knives and forks hitting plates and teenage chatter subsided. The teacher on duty acted as if he didn't see a thing and left us to it. I stared back even harder, willing him on, I wanted to bruck him up so badly. Then I saw the glint in his eyes, the realisation that he was out of his depth. I smelt his fear. He turned around abruptly and joined the back of the queue while I stood there, just watching him.

'What the fuck, man!?' JJ and Wrighty sat open-mouthed, now cautious of me, as if I was the madman.

'What's the next lesson?' I asked casually, as I took my seat.

'History, man, boring as houses,' said JJ, cupping his mouth. 'But man, what the fuck!? OH MY DAYS! I can't believe you just did that.'

'For real man!' said Wrighty. 'But he had it coming to him, big time, bro, you're a hero man!'

'I'm out of here,' I announced, pushing my chair back and leaving the dining room, before walking out the school gates.

After that, no one messed with me, but I bunked off most of the time anyway. Wrighty introduced me to the Myer's pool café in Clapton, where he sometimes worked after school. It was small and had a barbershop upstairs overlooking the guys shooting pool on the two tables downstairs. Myer's was on a stretch of road called 'Murder Mile', where many a man had lost their lives to knife or gun crime and not far from the hospital I'd been born in. The café had a frosted glass door with an iron gate behind it to slow down police raids, Ragamuffin rude boys like me who were all from the streets, a heavy smell of weed, and the juggling of stolen goods and drugs. I acclimatised quickly. Briefly, I joined a sound system, giving myself the name MC Trigger Bandit and turning up for sound clashes at the Wally Foster Community Centre, off Hackney Marshes. I lasted all of two clashes before I stopped going to rehearsals. My only real aspiration was to earn money: money for Mum; money for status; money to stop me from losing control.

Of all the brothers I started to move with at that time, only one or two are still alive. We were Natty, Big Man, BB, Wayney, Sticks, Mad T and me. And known as the Stokey Massive, but part of a much bigger crew who were from our ends. We threatened and robbed taxi drivers and men on the street. We robbed tube trains on the August Bank holiday weekends when hordes of revellers made their way to the Notting Hill Carnival. We formed a line and steamed through at speed: faces covered with bandanas, picky hair, black leather jackets, baggy jeans and white trainers, kicking it down carriages, sticking up passengers for their gold chains, wallets, watches and handbags as we swept through. Anyone who tried to stop us got dealt with. We did the same when we got into the carnival and worked our way through the crowds, robbing at will. On the news they called us 'Steamers'.

I got a taste for violence, the sheer power of it, and the rush. And among us, the tension that it sparked. We weren't the Windrush generation—the generation of some who kowtowed and said please and thank you to the white master and spoke the Queen's English, ashamed of their roots. We parleyed in patois, or what we call 'Jamerican', a mixture of Jamaican and American ghetto slang. We'd rather die than lick the boots of the white man or the police who rolled up in their SPGs. If people feared us, we gave them good reason to. Payback. We were fearless. A racial storm of rebellion was brewing in the underbelly of the poor and downtrodden, who had enough of the system and their equal opportunity policies, the brutality and inhumane treatment, the smell of death and the stench of degradation that plagued us. Inevitably, as the years rolled by, this would hit the UK in waves, with force.

Black attitudes towards the system were changing, and so was mine. Whereas before I'd taken Mum's beatings and felt helpless as a kid, now, as a juvenile delinquent, I had authority. Purpose. Even Mad T didn't faze me. Out of us all, he was the guy who we deemed the most 'off-key', the guy who took no prisoners. I had the utmost respect for him. A loner, like me, raised by his gran. If we robbed a man on the street, we worked in pairs. We took it in turns to tap the guy on the shoulder while the other smashed a fist in his face. It was a competition to see who could knock the guy out with one punch.

Then, we would drag him around a corner, empty his pockets, and prop him up by bins to make it look as if he was drunk.

Years later, Mad T was executed, receiving gunshots to the head inside a nightclub in Hackney. Apparently a Yardie had beef with him, and he refused to lay low.

'I ain't afraid of dem, let dem come, man,' he told me when I bumped into him on the street. 'They're gonna have to kill me bro, but trust, I will take one of them with me.' A week later he was brown bread—dead. I was crushed when I got the news. As crazy as he was, I still missed seeing him. Death was closer than ever before. It could have been me.

On Cazenove Road, I hung outside The Bronx nightclub, shrouded in the vibes and energy, feeling the weight of the bass that would literally vibrate and shake the windows of nearby houses. We watched and learned, observing our role models, gangsters who descended into the basement after coasting out of their Porsches and BMs, in their silk suits, dripping in gold. The Bronx was a sleazy late-night shebeen, crawling with prostitutes—a last stop in the early hours when clubs like the Four Aces on Dalston Lane or All Nations in the wastelands of London Fields were shut. As we were underage, Muscle-Head, the bouncer, rarely let us in, so we stood around on the street talking about our lives, our hopes, our dreams and our fears, witnessing raw street life with no apology. A prostitute smashing the head of a punter, limping around after him on one bare foot while using the high heel of the other shoe to knock him unconscious for not paying her, then rifling through his pockets while he lay helpless, with everyone sitting on their cars, watching in stitches, as if it was an Off West End comedy theatre show. A man, slashed for something trivial, staggering from the club, holding the flesh of his face together while blood poured down his arm. There was always action of some kind and it didn't take long for it to show up. One of the brothers, Cheese, had also been fostered with his auntie, but had no contact with his parents. He earned his nickname because he was always eating cheese and onion crisps. We built up a strong bond. Anyone could see he was a gentler soul than the rest of us. He laughed and talked and reasoned—fighting came last.

'What's the worst way you could die?' he asked me one night.

'I guess being burned alive,' I reckoned.

'Ahh man. For me, it would be a man jooking me up. Can you imagine a man letting rip, stabbing you over and over,' he said, oblivious to the fact that one day, that would be his own fate. Less than a year later, Cheese died: stabbed 18 times in the local basketball court by a brother he'd grown up with. I was devastated and in shock at the same time. It felt eerie after what he had shared with me.

Instinct became everything on the streets, and I was primed. The threat came from two directions: the police, and my own people. Around the inner cities of London, mainly Hackney, Tottenham and Brixton, 'Black-on-Black' crime was at a record high. Didn't matter if you were street or not, the innocent often got caught in the crossfire. If you robbed or harmed a white person, though, you would be hunted down like a dog. But if you harmed a Black man or a Black woman, you could, quite literally, get away with murder. And we did. It had been the same for more than 30 years. Black crimes went undetected and ignored, so we were left to our own devices, to police our own communities and take the law into our own hands. Along with the other gangsters, my main role model was Uncle Winston and the men he moved with. I aspired to hold up dance halls and shebeens, just like he did I had witnessed the atrocities of brothers getting cut or stabbed just for accidentally stepping on another man's shoes. The stakes were high and I knew all too well the risks of crossing a packed dancefloor especially when intoxicated. Now, it was my turn. *The way to stay alive?* Move up the ranks. Become the baddest of the bad. A street man. A sticks man. A Ragamuffin. Coarse. No smiling. Wear a deep frown and fit in to this family who might protect you, but also wouldn't flinch to take your life.

The walk from Alkham Road through the tree-lined streets of Stoke Newington, or through the backstreets of Hackney, was now fraught with danger. Revenge attacks from crews crossing from Tottenham or landing from Brixton were common. We were east, but dem man come from north, south and the west. A blinkered viewpoint that kept us chained in mental slavery, and tribal warfare, divided into titles, borders and checkpoints—all the data we needed for survival. Yet, we owned none of it. Not one thing. No shops. No houses. No businesses. Nothing. So we had nothing to lose fighting over turf, a preconception, an illusion borne out of need. The need to belong. The need to be a part of something bigger than ourselves. I hugged in close to houses on residential streets and, on the high street, close to shop entrances to avoid being ambushed. More than ever, my ratchet knife became my best friend. At every sound of every step drawing nearer, I slotted my finger in the keyring holder dangling from my jeans pocket. It attached to the ratchet, and I was poised to use it. Eyes clocked eyes. Bodies got located, dissected and ranked in order of threat: an item of clothing, a hat, a scar. Within seconds, I knew if a brother was friend or foe. A simple nod of acknowledgement from a brother on the street, a complete stranger, was enough to put us both at ease. To this day, that simple nod continues, leaving my white friends confused and in awe of how two unacquainted Black men can greet each other as if they were long-lost brothers.

*** *** ***

At home, Mum was slowly improving. According to Andrea, she could begin a court process to win Angie, Mini and Huggy back. Papers would have to be filled out and she'd also need to be assessed. To help her, I replied to an advert in the *Hackney Gazette* for the job of caretaker at the nearby public toilets. After speaking with the manager there, and telling him about Mum's situation, he agreed to give her a chance. It wasn't the type of job I really wanted Mum doing, but under the medication she needed to take, it was a start. If Mum could show that she could hold down a job then the courts might look on her more favourably. Plus, her having a routine and a reason to get up every morning would be good for her emotional well-being. To help sharpen her mind, I played board games with her in the evenings: draughts, cards, dominoes or chess—all the games Mum enjoyed with us when we'd been kids before her sickness.

During the time I'd been away I realised how invisible Mum had become. Without us there, other kids didn't knock, and neither did parents. Only the authorities came. She dissolved into nothingness: not useful to anyone, not in the way society judges usefulness. Because of the medication, she wasn't even useful to herself. And as everyone retreated, everything got sucked out of Alkham Road. But with a lick of paint and Mum slowly regaining her health, I pictured it coming to life again.

Over the time I was back in London, I sought out the people from my past who had been part of *our* life. I became like a detective, asking questions whenever I bumped into someone on the street who knew or reminded me of some of Mum's old friends. I found Uncle Ashley who told me he'd been to see Mum so many times, but when he knocked, no one answered the door. Uncle Winston was the easiest to find, always hustling on the frontlines in Brixton or Hackney; it was just a matter of catching him at the right times. He, too, had tried to make contact. Then one day on Ridley Road Market, I bumped into Sister Isacher, Simeon's queen. At first she didn't recognise me, but when she did, she hugged me, overwhelmed with joy. She'd moved house, she told me, and that she and Simeon weren't together anymore, but he came and visited the kids regularly, doing the rounds from one queen to the next. All my sprawling, extended family that I'd missed so much back together again. Now I was back.

My last stop was Auntie Beryl. I hadn't been to her flat on the Downham Road Estate since I was five or six, but I reckoned I could find my way from Kingsland Road Fire Station, my landmark, because Mum had walked us there so many times. One afternoon I found myself on the 149 bus headed in that direction. I made my way up Downham Road, and into her block, unsure of the number, or which floor she lived on, knocking on doors to ask if they knew the family.

When it came to Beryl's door, anticipation tore through me. Seeing it brought back memories. Of how Mum used to frequent her flat, leaving us to play with Beryl's kids, especially her son Nicky. Of how we'd stay over for weekends and how she'd cook for us. Of how Beryl was a constant presence at our house. Of how life was before Mum got sick.

'Yes?' There stood an older, wearier Beryl in the doorway, but those eyes that trespassed on your soul were unmistakable.

'If you're looking for Nicky, he's not in…' she said, looking at me quizzically.

'Auntie Beryl? It's me. Stanley.' Had I changed that much? She had no idea who I was. She looked a little closer.

'Stanley? Stanley! Stanley!'

She burst into joyful tears and pulled me into her chest, hugging the life out of me and repeating my name over and over in disbelief. For the next few hours we sat at her kitchen table. I told her about Nottingham and about how Angie, Mini and Huggy were all still in care and how I planned to get them back. She'd told me also that she had tried so many times to make contact with Mum.

'Stanley, mi goh round dere, and mi knock di door, but no answer! Nobody don't know nuttin and nobody tell me anytin! Mi leave rock, mi leave stone, fi mek her know seh me did visit, but mi noh hear nottin.' Leaving a rock or a stone outside someone's house was not uncommon, something people did back home in Jamaica and the Caribbean islands to let that person know you had called while they were out.

'Mum was always in, but because of the drugs she couldn't reach the door in time to answer it,' I said.

'What yu saying? Whaaaat? All this time she inna di house!?' Auntie Beryl looked horrified.

Later, she prepared food. Halfway through the conversation, she leaned in when I asked for Nicky. 'Nicky isn't the person you remember, Stanley. He's my son and I love him, but he's not a person for you to be friends and hang around with.' He'd lost his way, she continued. He was always in trouble with police. Feigning surprise, I listened. Not once did I let slip that the person she was describing was also me. I'd only just found her, my long-lost family. I couldn't destroy the fantasy: hers or mine. Yet, I wanted to see Nicky even more now: a moth to a flame. Not long after, his key turned in the lock.

'Nicky? Come! Come! I've something to show you,' Auntie Beryl shouted. 'Come here noh Bwoy!?' she shouted again, impatient for us to meet.

Just like Beryl, Nicky didn't recognise me, but when he did, he couldn't believe it. He had the same round face that I remembered, but he now had a chunkier build and his accent was more cockney than patois. After the welcoming fanfare, we slipped away from the kitchen, leaving Auntie Beryl on the phone in the living room to tell everyone she could think of that the prodigal son had returned. She also told me she was now a churchgoer. 'Wow, things had changed,' I thought to myself. I could never have imagined hardcore Auntie Beryl going to praise the Lord. Not in a month of Sundays!

'Come!' he said. 'Let's catch up, bro!' And with that I followed him into his bedroom. That afternoon a whole new world opened up to me. We smoked weed and chatted and compared stories. Instinctively, we knew the path we were on, as if we'd subconsciously sought each other out.

Then Nicky secured the door with a chair, putting his fingers to his lips to shhhh me. He reached under his bed and pulled out a shoebox. In it was a small cellophane bag with brown powder, a couple of lighters and some other bits. He stretched under again, bringing out a roll of tin foil in his hand. It was as if I was watching a magician reveal his box of tricks. Absorbed in the drama of it all, my eyes followed as he placed a pinch of powder along a foil crease and heated it up until a black wax bubbled. Reaching into the shoebox again he brought out a cheap biro pen which he carefully wrapped the foil around to make a funnel that looked like a short straw. As the powder melted, he took the funnel into his mouth and drew up the whispers of tarry smoke into his lungs, chasing the beads as they moved across the sheet of foil.

'What is it?' I asked, but he didn't answer. Instead, he held his breath, letting the smoke fill him up. He filled himself to the brim until he couldn't hold it in any longer. When he finally exhaled, a tranquillity washed over him.

'Shhhh,' not so loud, he whispered. Then, he leaned over. 'It's heroin, Stan,' he mouthed before closing his eyes.

'Heroin?'

'Heroin. Do you wanna try some?'

Before he passed it over, he chased one more time. In my 14-year-old head, there was no debate, nothing to stop me. I was so engrossed I was almost salivating. It looked like slow motion. It looked like flying.

Chapter 20

Keep Coming Black

It is 1997 and I am 26 years old. I am in St Louis, Missouri, at the world convention of Narcotics Anonymous. I am in my third year of recovery and here under my own steam. It's Saturday, but it was only last Tuesday when I saw the flyer at an NA meeting in the UK headed: 'Show Me How to Live'. The organisers are taken aback that I've travelled all this way without a reservation. I tell them I've hit a wall and I'm afraid of using again.

The Americans are evangelical. If I closed my eyes, I'd think I was listening to a gospel service, not an NA meeting. Some have been clean 30 years or more, others have been clean for one whole day. They are 'loud and proud' and I am in awe of them. It's the first time I've been to a world convention of recovering addicts who look the same as me: a sea of Black faces. 'If you're not carrying a message, then you need to shut the fuck up until you do!' they say. I love how they talk. They don't take any prisoners or sugar coat a damn thing. Just like Jamaicans, they tell it how it is

By the end of the first day, I've made a friend called Sadie and she introduces me to her people. 'Getting clean is one thing, but staying clean is another,' she says, and everyone agrees. They nod and say 'Uh-hum' and 'Amen!' and 'Yes sireee. Speak that truth sister.' I only know partial truths. I've spent so many years hiding

167

from my truth, it's painful for me to untangle it all. I'm trying, though. I'm really trying.

On the last night, I went to the Marathon meeting. It's a meeting that runs for 24 hours throughout the convention and participants are free to drop in and out. I've shared versions of my story among familiar faces, but never in a crowd as big as this. The place is jam-packed. It's 2 AM and the room stretches so far back, sometimes you can't see who's talking, so I shut my eyes and listen. It's raised-hand sharing, and unexpectedly, I am picked, which has caught me off guard and I need to gather my thoughts. I stand up to share. Feeling fragile, I try to avoid the sea of gazes I've attracted as they hear my UK accent. Once I do open my mouth, I surprise myself. I can't stop talking. I tell the crowd how I'm scared of relapsing and while I feel this way, I can't be near my family. How I love them but I need to be in a stronger place. That I'm not sure what's going on with them, that I've arrived at a place in my recovery where I feel I don't belong in the meetings anymore. My mind is a mess and I know I will use if I don't tell on myself. 'You're only as sick as your secrets' is another saying they use in the fellowship, and I have to be brave and go for it.

I let go, and blubbering my way through the snot and salty tears, share all my fears and reservations. The crowd is patient. When I eventually sit down, I feel an overwhelming sense of surrender. I surrender to the moment and surrender to the reason I started this journey in the first place—to continue with my recovery.

One by one, a line of strangers appears. One person taps me on the shoulder then moves to hug me. Another taps me, their arms wide open, and along the line it goes, hug after wordless hug. It makes me sob even more. I cave into the warmth of this tribe, this family. Maybe I'll make it through one more day. When I get back to the UK, I'm re-energised and hit recovery with force, sharing at every opportunity the message of hope. In meetings they start to call me 'Stan the Man with the 12-Step Plan', referring to the 12 Steps of the NA programme. I laugh and take it as a compliment. I even help form a group called Keep Coming Black, a play on the NA mantra, Keep Coming Back, which attendees say at the end of every meeting. For the first time in my life I feel that using drugs is not an option.

Chapter 21

Road-Man-Dem

Mum stares and looks vacant when on pills, but on heroin I'm different. My head drops, nodding out as if I'm wrestling sleep. Then that warm feeling. I love that warm feeling, when responsibility evaporates, slips from me and I bathe in the womb-like peace of it all. I don't care about the itching, though it drives me crazy. I can't keep up with the places where my skin prickles: neck, arms, in my back where I can't reach. Even the vomit. The vomit that's become a part of my existence. When I first chased the dragon, I puked my guts up, but it's less now. In any case, we keep poly bags beside us, and share if there aren't enough. We fill them up with spit and puke and disappointment, then lean back against our bedroom walls and think of England.

When I'm not on the gear I go to work. Nicky's introduced me to his crew: white guys. Some wear fake, snide Cartiers and Rolexes and polo shirts and bright white trainers with straight-legged jeans. They say things like, 'On your fucking bike, you daft cunt.' I don't speak their language and, at first, I'm wary of them. So I hang in the shadows. They remind me of the loud-mouth NF back in the day, but if Nicky trusts them, then it's good enough for me. Besides, moving with them keeps me with gear and cash. He's introduced me as his cousin.

Nicky and I creep all the time now—robbing people's houses

in the dead of night, after heads hit the pillows and folks are deep in sleep. It's not my crime of choice. I prefer street robbery or drumming empty houses during the day. Everyone knows you risk more time for an 'aggy'. (The Queen's English: aggravated burglary.) But Nicky's a skilled operator. If I'm going to creep, I'd rather creep with him.

Weeks ago, I went drumming with two brothers. I barely knew them. Big mistake. Apparently, the homeowners were away on holiday, so we jimmied open the ground-floor window on the Victorian terrace and hoisted ourselves in with an aim to look only for tom: tomfoolery being cockney slang gold jewellery. We get more for it and it's easier to move. But tom is always trickier if doing a creep. It means going upstairs to the bedrooms, searching through drawers while the occupants sleep, expecting the unex-pected: the comfort of the sound of a snore suddenly stopping, or them stirring and waking. I was on my way to the upstairs landing when one of our guys came flying past me, heading down the stairs. He didn't say a word. To the right of the landing, the main light was shining from one of the bedrooms. So I walked straight in thinking he had searched the room already and didn't find anything, so I thought I would double-check; sometimes it's a knack of knowing where to look for hidden tom.

'Call the police!' this white woman started screaming. She and her old man were sat bolt upright in bed, dazed and confused, squinting against the bright bulb that had been left on. I spun around and sprinted down the stairs taking two steps at a time, heading back into the living room towards the window. I saw the gap, ran towards it and pushed myself through, managing to get my upper body dangling halfway on the other side. Then I felt the owner's hands grabbing my jeans waistband as I tried to wriggle free. Him pulling me, and dragging me back into the darkness, like the monsters on Mum's stairs when I was a kid. The noise of a table crashing to the floor. Ornaments and chairs flying. The flashes of the guy's contorted face.

I was alone: that's what I was thinking while fighting with this burly man. How fucking alone I was—just me and the owner. We both put up a fight, both of us out of breath, me trying to slip through the window, and him wrestling me back to the floor, time and time again. I was driven by sheer panic and fear because I thought I was definitely going to be nicked and get a serious beating from the Old Bill. If one of the guys hadn't jogged back during my last attempt to escape, my torso hanging out of the window, and stabbed the guy in the arm with a screwdriver, I'd certainly be facing down a long sentence. The minute I was released from the owner's grasp and fell to the ground head-first, I ran like the wind.

A crew of us meet at the flats in Holly Street and pair off to go to work after a quick debrief, of what to watch out for, or what latest unmarked cars the undercover Old Bill are driving, and sometimes, we even had their number plates too. We take our jobs seriously and get up early like were going to a nine-to-five. Ronnie's wiry and ginger-haired and we work well together, robbing houses in rich neighbourhoods like Sloane Square, and Kensington, where the posh Georgian townhouses are. As a Black man, I'd stick out like a sore thumb by myself in a place like that, but with Ronnie I'm safe: we role play, pretending to be window cleaners. And at times we travel out to Essex because they wear a lot of tom there. Depending on the day, sometimes we come back to the manor empty handed, but sometimes the gods smile down on us and give us a little helping hand—like not long ago, when me and Ronnie were coming out of Dalston Kingsland Station.

Immediately, I clocked him: coming out of the bank, the African brother bowling down the street as though he was just out for a stroll, a fat pouch clasped under his armpit. I could smell the money from across the road. Black taxi drivers carry them too, and keep their earnings in there, so we knew there was cash for sure when we robbed those. We followed him up Kingsland High Street before we moved to him in broad daylight. Me coming up from behind, and Ronnie distracting him on his left side. My hand got tangled in the pouch when I ran past to snatch it. This stopped me dead in my tracks with the weight of the man, arm outstretched, prostrate on the pavement, refusing to let it go. I pulled and tugged but the strap wouldn't break. Ronnie stepped in, and started stamping on his arm over and over and the guy still wouldn't let go! 'Fucking let go, you cunt,' Ronnie was screaming until the handle finally snapped. Now we know why he didn't want to give it up. Five and half grand. Five and a half thousand pounds in crisp £50 notes, divided into wads with the binder from the bank still on it. Only Ronnie and I keep the amount we got to ourselves, otherwise the crew would ask for endless handouts.

Sometimes we had bad days, though. For every high, there's a low. We headed off to buy gear with the money, and we planned to juggle it in Hoxton, on the frontline, and there we can double or triple our investment. We must have looked hot—five teenagers packed in a car and just come from the dealer. Then we saw them. The undercover drug squad had been tailing us. Soon as we clocked they were following, I popped the eighth of gear in my mouth. Gone. Just like that. When the Old Bill searched every inch of the motor, they couldn't find a thing, nothing more satisfying than those smug bastards leaving empty-handed. I felt I had saved the day.

It took forever, though. When the Old Bill eventually let us go and we pulled off with a warning, Ronnie's brother Keith asked where the gear had gone? 'I swallowed it!' I said, cockily. Then, sheer panic erupted in the car.'You'll die, Stan. If it bursts inside you, you'll fucking die!'

Honestly, I hadn't thought that far ahead. I thought that by swallowing it I could puke it up later because it was wrapped in cellophane. All of a sudden the reality of it hits me, and I feel the blood drain from my face the more the guys panic and keep saying the word OD every two minutes. They spun the car around, and drove back to the dealer's place, banging down the door until they rushed me into the toilet, as if I was being rushed into hospital. I can still feel the bruise on my back where Ronnie kept pounding me, forcing me to vomit it up. It took us for ages and we almost gave up, me bent over the bowl tickling the back of my throat, retching dryness. Nothing. Until a flood of vomit hit the basin. Then searching around in the bile to pull out the eighth, still perfectly wrapped in cling film.

'Thank fuck for that!' Ronnie said, crouching down on the toilet floor. 'What the fuck were you thinking, Stan!? We could have lost you mate, for fuck's sake, don't you ever pull a stunt like that on me again mate!' I didn't know Ronnie cared until that incident. I could see by the way he had gone pale like he'd seen a ghost that he was freaked out by it. I had his back from then on.

Thank fuck the gear is in one piece, I finally thought.

Selling more gear means robbing less houses. I prefer it that way. We've got pagers now, too, so we're professionals. The money can't come in fast enough. Who needs a regular job? It's keeping me topped up with gear but it's also keeping things running smoothly at home. Mum's court application got okayed and we've got Mini and Huggy back from the children's home. Mini came first and I've given her my old room. She's 14 now, and I reckon she needs her own space.

Up in hers and Angie's old attic room, I've divided the space for me and Huggy. On my side I've placed my bed by the alcove and papered the wall in blue and grey striped wallpaper—it looks modern and grown up. Huggy's half is decorated in Disney character wallpaper. Snow White and the Seven Dwarves, Mickey and Mini Mouse, Daffy Duck, Dumbo and Cinderella all smiling out at him. And I've had grey carpet laid in all the bedrooms, including Mum's. It's as spongy as Martha and Ray's.

But Huggy cramps my style. If I have mates round in the evening I bribe him with sweets to go and sleep in Mum's or Mini's room. And I feel bad for Mum sometimes when I see the relationship she has with Huggy. When we picked Huggy up from Forest Road, he cried his eyes out, said he didn't want to leave. He clung on to Josie and Dean as if his life depended on it. 'I'm not going! I want to stay here! You're not my mummy!' he shouted. I saw how Mum's face remained placid and she just took whatever he threw at her in front of these people. Secretly, I think he's a spoiled little brat. He doesn't know what a good licking is. Yet, he's innocent and so cute, with his fair-skinned complexion, same as Mum's, and looking more like a girl, especially now Angie has braided his long, bronze, curly hair in corn-rows, and all the staff mollycoddle him. At the same time, I also understand his pain. He reminded me of my own trauma and wanting to be with a different family. He's five and half years old, torn, and he doesn't know where to belong.

Not long after he came home, he kicked Mum in the shin during one of his tantrums. Mum just took the blow, but I could see he hurt her when she rubbed her leg and tried to hide the pain. She had been bending over backwards to accommodate him, buying him sweets, and letting him watch cartoons to win him over, while I stood back and observed. Enough was enough, so I grabbed hold of him and kicked him right back on the shin. The shock of it brought him down to earth.

'You're not allowed to do that,' he said matter-of-factly, with tears streaming down his face,

'That's right little man. And you're not allowed to kick my mummy. Welcome home!' Then I made him apologise.

Angie hasn't come home with the others. She's 16 now and she's chosen to live in an independent unit. It's a wing shut off from the dormitories at Forest Road. She's got her own bedroom with a shared kitchen, TV room and bathroom. I loved going there and drinking and smoking weed with the other teenagers. Sometimes I go out raving with them, but mainly we just hang out. At times I wish I was there, too. It's been my dream to have everyone back in Alkham Road, but now I can't stop worrying. I feel a pressure on me that I've never felt before. I'm scared Mum will relapse and go off-key again, and Mini and Huggy will hate me for bringing them back home. I try not to think about it, so taking and juggling gear helps. It fills my day, every day. And it fills me up, too. Easing the stress.

When Mum is well enough, she takes Huggy on the bus to school. He still attends Holy Trinity opposite the children's home, the same one me, Angie and Mini went to when we were there. At the start, I accompanied her. I'm anxious because Andrea is always coming around to the house with her clipboard, ticking off lists and asking questions, so I make sure Mum is dressed and that she's taken her pills. I make sure Huggy is in school and the fridge is filled with food; more than anything, that says we are coping. On the days when Mum stays in bed, I take Huggy in myself. After I drop him off, the day is mine before I pick him back up again.

My bedroom is now my office. I meet with the crew early doors. We check how much gear we have left to sell and work out if we need to buy more. With Mum in her room most of the day, I can bring the guys back and we cut the gear with razor blades on my mirror on top of the dresser. Then, we bag it up. This takes forever. We cut rectangles out from white paper and fold the powder neatly into each sheet: less for the £10 bags and more for the £20, which we cut with baking soda or flour so it goes further. We do it methodically, carefully, as if I'm handling one of Mum's records. We bag, then we have a toot, chasing the gear around on foil. It's our reward. Later, we head to Hoxton frontline to juggle it, all of us out of our nuts.

Hoxton's changed since the dealers moved in. The narrow market strip with the fruit and vegetable stalls and cheap nylon dresses are fewer now. Traders say they're afraid to open because there's too much beef. Plus, it's crawling with the Old Bill, sometimes under-cover trying to catch us out. You need eyes in the back of your head: police, rival dealers, junkies slipping you a few notes short.

Mainly, we deal through car windows. The motor pulls up, the window winds down and palms touch palms, quick as a flash. We grease palms, too, in the shops on either side, or with the remain-ing stall traders. From time to time, they stash our gear for us, but on the road we keep it in tin cans and bottles: near, but not too near. It means if the police try to nick us we've got nothing on our person, though they sometimes stitch us up and plant gear on us to get an arrest.

Lunchtimes are the best. Then, it's like Piccadilly Circus: cars pulling up, junkies crawling out from every corner. Sometimes we catch the odd one trying to sell bagged-up brick dust, just so they can get the money to score themselves, and we give them a good kicking to teach them a lesson for ripping off our punters. Then, we give the muppet they sold it to a freebie of gear, to make sure he buys from us next time. If junkies don't have money for gear, they bring us TVs or videos which we exchange for a bag or two depending on its worth, then we take it down to Sandringham Road, frontline in Hackney There's times we've been caught out when goods don't work: a dodgy wire, a dead TV, a busted belt on a VHS recorder, but the junkies eventually always come back to score, so we take whatever they have as compensation. It's a dog-eat-dog, concrete-jungle world were living in. Like crabs in a bucket, someone's always getting hurt.

I prefer staying in Hackney than being in Hoxton, but that's where the money is and where we have to go to juggle gear. The frontline in Hackney is always more colourful. Often, it's where I find Uncle Winston. At the bottom end of Sandringham Road, there's Johnson's cafe, and further up, where he usually stands, there's the Lord Stanley pub on the junction of Montague Road. In summer especially, it's bustling with people: dealers, the same as us, and the herbs-men on the street, barber shops with their doors flung open, hair clippers humming like dynamos, and reggae music belting out from different windows, cars, shops, houses and the pub. It's like a mini version of Kingston, Jamaica. You can get anything you want there, except heroin, which they see as the white man's devil drug, and anyone who comes asking for it is run out off the frontline, with beer bottles exploding at their feet. Here they juggle everything else: weed, coke, TVs and stereos, and you can even get a bucky—a gun.

I realise I can be an asset to my crew when we visit. Because they're white, it's not easy for them to buy or try to offload any of the goods we have for fear of being robbed or ripped off. Frontline was strictly a Black-owned business. But through Uncle Winston, I'm known by the bigger man dem and can move around freely. I stand with him and watch the gangsters, understated in their sharp suits, and the hustlers loud and proud in their string vests, dripping in gold. Mainly, they drive BMWs, which we nick name Black Man's Wheels or Bob Marley and the Wailers. The vibes in the air are palpable, you can cut them with a knife. It can kick off at any moment for no reason. You know not to mess with the gangsters, or anyone there for that matter. And I know better than to mess with any of the women: tight jeans, high heels, denim jackets and jewellery sparkling off them like Christmas trees. Faces fierce as fuck, some even adorning battle scars like the men.

My crew wait round the corner in the car ready to pop the

boot, while I walk back with Uncle Winston and some of his crew following. He's always asking me who's in the car. He hates that I bring white guys to the frontline.

'Ah wah di bumbleclart, Stanley?' he asks. 'Mi seh, mi noh want to see no fucking white man bout ya! Yu ere mi?'

'Just cool noh uncle,' I tell him. 'They're safe. We got goods to sell, man.'

I couldn't get away with doing this on the Brixton frontline: that line runs from Railton Road right the way down Atlantic Road, near the tube station. There, you're stepping into the Wild West. And the brothers are super-sensitive to strangers, especially white people. They look you up and down as if you owe them money. But sometimes I go because I know I can find Uncle Winston there, and I would always pop in to see his mum, our Great-Auntie Hattie, and her husband Uncle Wally, both alcoholics, who live close by to the frontline and used to take us kids to Brixton Market to eat Jamaican beef patties when Mum visited. But I hate crossing the river south. It has a different vibe altogether, and sometimes I'm paranoid that a street man might recognise that I'm not from the manor and try to whet me up because I'm from Hackney. Since the riots a few years ago, everyone standing on the frontline suspects a stranger is undercover police—regardless of whether you're a brother or not. Whenever I ask for Uncle Winston, I have to always go through an interrogation until I see a familiar face. 'Who is yu? How yu know Winston? Where yu from? Yu better mind yuself round here yut man...' If the guys don't recognise me, I see their hands reach for their ratchet knives, as if something is going down. 'Jus cool man, is Winston cousin, 'im alright, cool yuself,' I hear one of them say. At least on Sandringham Road, I know who's who, and they know who I am.

Chapter 22

Secrets and Lies

I've come to find Uncle Winston on the frontline in his usual spot, outside the Lord Stanley pub. He's leaning up against the wall, one foot against it, arms folded, chewing on a tooth pick. I'm here to get some weed, but often when I come, I chill with him for a while and chew the fat.

'Wha gwan couz? Wha yu bring fi mi? Gimme something noh? Wha yu a look fa? Wah yu want, weed?'

'Wahpen Uncle, let me get some ting noh?'

'How much you 'ave?'

'Twenty.'

'Alright, gimme di money.'

I slip Uncle Winston a £20 note. Because of undercover police, we never hand over money or drugs openly. I turn my back to him with my hands behind me, and allow him to brush pass, taking the money with him before he disappears for a while.

When he returns with my parcel, we build a spliff and smoke together. He always wants to know how Mum is, and he often tells me stories about when they were back in Jamaica. I enjoy talking to Uncle Winston. He gives me clues—clues to who Mum is; reasons for why she is sick; more pieces to the puzzle of mum. I know about Great-Great-Grandma Harriet, and that when Mum was sent for by her real mum, Grandma Greta, that's when she came to England. Mum always calls Grandma Greta a wicked woman. When she arrived, Mum discovered she had six brothers and sisters. She was made to cook and clean, wash, iron and sew and she says the lickings we get are nothing compared to the beatings Grandma Greta gave her. I know she got sent to a nunnery, but I also know that Mum keeps secrets. She never wants to talk about Greta for long. Nobody does. And I've never asked Uncle Winston why until today.

'So, how's di family dem? Joy, Angie, Mini, Huggy?'

'Everyone alright. Mum still the same. Taking her pills, but the doctors say they can't do nuthin else.'

'Bwoy, mi sorry fi hear dat my yut. Is her mudder dat mess up her head like dat.'

'Yeah. What really happened?' I ask.

'Oh bwoy. Greta use to give her some serious licks and mistreat her when she com over ere.'

'She always say she was wicked.'

'Oh bwoy, she was.'

'Why she handle Mum dem way?'

'She never told you? Bwoy... Joy, she did get malless by di husband, all dem ting dere is what mek Joy di way dat she is.'

'Mum was molested?'

'Yeah man. She never tell you? Greta's husband take after her one of di time. Yu mudder was a pretty, pretty, woman yu know! Everybody want to he wid Joy and fancy Joy, but dat dirty fucker old dog put im han pon her. And di one Greta, instead of she stick up for she pikney, she run Joy out of di house. All dem ting dere is what I believe mek yu mudder get sick inah she head.'

'Rasss, I never know dat!'

'Trust me, dere is a lot of tings yu don't know! After Greta run er outta di yard, yu mudder end up in ah one ah dem nunnery, where di nuns and all dem somting dere look after ere. Mi tink she was wid dem fi ah good while still, she tell di courts straight dat she not going back to Greta and she never feel at home dere. Mi can't wrong her wid everyting dat take place, she stay dere for ah while until when di council give her she own place fi live.'

'Yeah, Mum tell us dat she did get sent to one nunnery, strange because Mum's not religious, so maybe dem just take her in?'

'Must be dat, because Joy never go to no church! None ah di family follow dem foolishness deh. Only time was in Jamaica as a likkle bwoy mi use to get force to go, but even den, we never go more dan so, juss once in ah while.'

'So mum was molested? Dat is serious, and what yu say mek sense why mum end up losing her mind.'

'Mi and Joy was close. Mi use to look out fi Joy dem time there. Nobody could mess wid mi cousin, nobody. Me just sorry for yu pikney dat ave to suffer. What unno go tru is no joke. Mi sorry mi couldn't help unno. If mi did ave ah better set up, tings could ah did different for unno. But, mi ah soldier and mi roam all bout, so mi couldn't take on any pikney, mi just about see mi own pikney dem!'

'It's ok. I understand, you noh ave fi seh dat.'

'I know mi noh ave to seh dat, but mi just ah tell yu di trut.'

Chapter 23

Nicked

'**B**east,' Nicky is whispering loudly to me. 'Beast! Beast!' His eyes are wide now and he looks panicked. I'm panicked, too. It's slang. It means the Old Bill. We haven't got much time, so I help him wriggle out through the sash window and hold his legs while he jumps.

It's around 3am, the early hours of Saturday morning and we're on Kyverdale Road looking for a drum. We've stayed up all night smoking gear and free-basing cocaine while Huggy's asleep in Mini's room. After smoking the small rocks, we're alert, pumped up, ready to work. We don't need cash or gear. Now, it's the white-knuckle adrenaline shot we crave. Burgling houses, drumming, as we call it, is like playing the lotto—you never know what you're going to win. We'd almost given up, then I saw a window peeking open on the second floor of a terrace. Nicky climbed up while I kept a look-out. He must have been in there for less than ten minutes. Someone also up late must have spotted us and called the police.

As soon as Nicky is down, we jump from garden to garden. We're running blind. Like ninjas, scaling back walls and broken fences. Above one of the street walls we can see blue lights flashing. Silent sirens. It's the tactic the Old Bill use when they don't want to alert thieves, but we can see their whereabouts because it's pitch black, and the lights are bright against the darkness. Out of nowhere, there's beams from torches criss-crossing the gardens. And when we stop still, we can make out the crackle of their radios. We're surrounded. They've got Osbaldeston and Kyverdale roads covered and they've got us trapped in the strip of gardens in between the two roads.

Blood is pounding through my body. I've spotted a drainpipe we can scale. So we creep tentatively across a garden and make our way up. Me first, with Nicky pushing me from under my trainers and him following on. I stop myself from looking down as I climb higher and higher, staying focused upwards towards the roof. Just a bit further and I can lever myself up using the guttering. Then, we low-crawl along the slates and lie there for a while watching the drama from above. There are more police vans pulling up now, more beams being thrown behind walls and through bushes. All the action, right there underneath us. We have front row seats.

Nicky's determined not to get caught. He's already on bail after being done for another burglary. He's got a court date hanging over his head and he doesn't want to get banged up in a detention centre, even though there known as Butlin's, the holiday camp, but none of us want our liberty taken. So far, I've managed not to get nicked, but I'm always balancing on the tight rope of the law. I walk a knife-edge between two worlds. I live the thug life, for cash and gear and the excitement, but I know I can't leave Mini and Huggy alone with Mum. And what with everything that's pulsating around these streets at the moment, I don't want to get arrested either. Police claim that brothers are hanging themselves in their cells, that they take their own lives with their belts or shoe-laces, but we know the truth. Stoke Newington Police Station has become the most notorious for fatalities of Black men dying whilst in custody. And it's got worse since the recent riots in Brixton and Tottenham.

My my mind flashes back to that night. I was chatting outside Grant Davis's house with him and his brother, when word got to us about what was going down in Tottenham. We couldn't believe what we were hearing that another Black woman called Cynthis Jarret, had suffered heart failure while her house was being raided by the police. They say she collapsed and died after being pushed by one of the officers. She was only forty-nine. It was just a week prior that the police had shot Cherry Groce, during a raid on her home in Brixton. She was left paralysed.

The Black community were once again enraged at this latest news. Brothers and sisters started throwing stones and petrol bombs, lighting up the autumn sky like it was Guy Fawkes Night. I felt overwhelmed by sheer anger and frustration by the liberties the police were taking with our people and wanted to vent my rage with everyone else, but Grant wasn't sure. He reckoned it was too dangerous, and Grant's never been one for trouble. 'Let's go up there man!' I pressured. I was pumped and ready to fight!

When the first Brixton riots happened in 1981, I was in Nottingham. I remember being at Martha and Ray's when it came on the news. I listened with interest because Auntie Hattie and Uncle Winston lived in Brixton. I watched the images of cars alight and the police in their helmets clutching shields and edging closer to the barricades. Back then, Uncle Ray said it had been a long time coming, what with the way the police treated Black people. And it spread like a contagion, to Liverpool and Birmingham and Manchester and to Hyson Green in Nottingham, up the road from Martha and Ray's. I missed out on both of those Brixton riots and wanted to make sure I didn't miss out on this one. Uncle Ray said that it was time for us as Black people to let our voices be heard, even though he wasn't a man of violence and barley raised his own voice. And I had plenty to say. I was fed up and vexed with the Babylon system.

In Tottenham we got close. As soon as we reached the main junction on Stamford Hill there were cars shooting in all directions. As we moved down towards St Annes Road, and then walked forever up West green road, using the back streets, we got nearer to the Farm and hit a wall of flashing blue lights.

'You think we should turn back?' David asked.

'Nah man, let's keep going ' I said, desperate to push on. The Farm is the Broadwater Farm Estate, but none of us had been there before or knew the way. Then, when we turned one corner two SPG vans sat nose-to-nose like rhinos with locked horns, blocking the street.

'Let's just cut round the back,' I urged, breaking into a trot to get closer to the source. But everywhere we turned, vans or lines of police blockaded the route. We doubled back on ourselves so many times we got lost. 'Enough man, let's just go back, now!' the others said. Mutiny divided us and we finally made the decision to head home after arguing it out. I was so pissed off and deflated, but maybe it was a good thing. The next day we heard about PC Keith Blakelock, the police officer who got hacked to death and the rumour going round he was beheaded. Until I saw it on the news, I didn't believe it. Now we were really at war. I knew the repercussions were going to be heavy, they started arresting Black people left right and centre trying to stitch them up for the riots, even if they weren't there. The police will beat the shit out of any brother that moved, after dark. And I've seen their SPGs cruising around, waiting to snatch us from the side streets. The payback was brutal.

We've been on this roof forever, and the police are still down below. It's October and it's freezing and instead of giving up, they're relentless. When I hear the helicopter blades in the distance building to a crescendo, I know that if we stay up here we're gonna get spotted. I shut my eyes tight and curl my head in so its beam can't illuminate my face when it sweeps across.

There's only one way down. The same way we came up. Running along the roof would be too risky. We slide along the slates to the roof's edge. Now I'm shitting myself. When I peer over, we're far higher up than I remember. My head spins, and I fight to control the fear and adrenaline. The noise of the blades overhead is now deafening. The beam so intense that's it's blinded me and I can't make out where the drainpipe is. One wrong move, one slip, and we are both goners. Nicky panics and I see him slide his body further down towards the edge of the roof; he's upside down with his feet facing towards me, flat against the slates, his hand desperately moving along the guttering to find the pipe. He turns his body around and starts lowering himself over the edge. My heart is in my mouth. No way am I doing that. *No way man*. But I inhale and fill my lungs to calm me down and copy everything he does, not wanting to miss a beat. I follow to the roof edge in the same manner, lowering my legs over and clinging on to the gutter for dear life, terrified my weight will bring the whole lot crashing down with me. As the wind buffets us around, I also inch my way onto the pipe, whispering to myself that I can do this in between sharp breaths. I shimmy down. By the time I reach the bottom, Nicky's already gone, but I play it safe and crawl into a bush, hoping that I can shake the helicopter beam and that it will shine elsewhere.

'You! Come out now!' I hear an officer shouting, but there's no way I'm giving up that easily, so I push myself further into the foliage, and wait.

'If you do not come out now, I'll release the dog!' the voice shouts again. There's no escaping this. I'm nicked. I stand and make my way out, hands raised. No one is there. When I glance around, there's a crowd of police surrounding the wrong bush. But it's too late to run. They're on me, and as they pull my wrists back to handcuff me, I feel a blow to my face. A dead weight.

In the back of the van I sit, legs open with my head bowed, the cuffs cutting into my skin. Already, my cheek is swelling and feel the blood in my mouth. Now, two more blows to the back of my head make me lurch forward and roll onto the van floor, huddled in a foetal position for protection.

'Where's your mate?' they keep asking, but I'll never grass Nicky up.

'I don't know him. I don't fucking know him!' I say. A boot lands in my back before they yank me up by the cuffs and sit me back on the bench. There's little dignity to stop and search, but nothing feels like this. I'm scared, but mostly I'm embarrassed for being caught, and the Old Bill know it. They take delight in it.

'Guess what, sunshine?' one of the officers asks, leaning in as he gets off his radio. I don't answer.

'We've got your mate now. What do you think of that, eh?' he gloats as he slaps me across the head.

Nicky and I are taken separately to Stoke Newington Police Station. It hasn't changed from the time Mum marched me down the high street for stealing dinner money. Names, pictures and fingerprints are taken, and we're placed in separate cells. Nicky's given them an alias. I heard him at the desk, and I'm kicking myself for not doing the same. The police have my real name, and as I am 15 a parent has to come to the station. I explain that my mum is mentally ill so there's no point in contacting her and I don't have a guardian, so we're shoved back in our cells. After another couple of hours, we're both thrown in the back of the SPG van, this time uncuffed. Apparently they're taking us to our homes to verify where we live.

Nicky can't look at me in the back of the van. As well as a false name, he's also given them a bogus address. Now we're driving around an estate in Hoxton I've never seen before. When the van pulls up Nicky is dragged out and he takes the detectives up a set of stairs to a second-floor landing. I'm watching through the rear doors when suddenly I hear shouts and see Nicky hurtling over the balcony, hitting the ground and having it away on his toes.

'Where the fuck does he live?' the officer is shouting. Moments later, two more officers arrive back, breathless.

'Fucking show us, you black bastard,' they are shouting, pulling me to the floor, blows raining down on me. One half of me hates Nicky for ditching me, but the other half is in awe of the stunt he's just pulled. I take the kicking for him, until the pain is too much to bare.

'Alright! Alright!' I shout. 'I'll show you the estate.' But I lie and say I've only been there once so I'm unsure if I can remember right. As the van crawls around the streets, they become impatient.

'Listen you fucking coon, which estate is it?' one officer shouts, spit pelting my face. I'm buying time, working out how not to take them to Auntie Beryl's door, but time is running out. On the edge of the Downham Road Estate, I tell the officers it looks familiar. I have them knocking on all the doors I know aren't hers. I'm slammed against the wall, my head and nose bleeding, with one officer's arm in my throat.

'Tell us now, which fucking door?' he shouts, but I say nothing. As we get closer and reach Auntie Beryl's, half the landing is awake and she answers in her dressing gown. At first, I can't raise my head, so I gaze at the floor feeling like a rat just crawled out from a sewer. When I do look up, Beryl glances at me, then looks away, and I'm hoping she's clocked on to my game.

'Never heard of him,' she says, as the police deliver Nicky's alias. I exhale, as her door shuts and they carry on knocking until the Old Bill call it a day and take me back to the station where I'm locked in a cell. By the time I am pulled out again, the sun is coming up. The buzz of the gear is long gone with the madness of it all. Their questions are exhausting. 'Who is he? How do we know each other? Who are his friends? Who is his family?' I stand firm: I've only met him once. I have no idea.

It's around 6 AM when I'm eventually charged with attempted burglary and released. I hobble up the high street, my body aching from my wounds, one of my teeth is wobbly, I spit out the blood and cut across Stoke Newington Common towards Alkham Road. Back in my bedroom, Huggy is in his own bed, and I scrabble around under mine for the pinch of gear I keep for emergencies. I crouch under the open window and smoke it while he sleeps, blowing the fumes out the window. When I finally nestle under my duvet, the heroin's warmth and relief curls up through me and eases the pain of my injuries. I can feel the blood drying up on my head and face. I know I have only a few hours before I need to get Huggy up and ready for school.

Chapter 24

Her Majesty's Pleasure

There's good reason a prison van is called a sweat box. Each cell is three feet wide and three feet deep, with a reflective and rectangular one-way window, no air conditioning and only the stench of stale sweat as company. At five foot nine, my teenage knees hit off the metal wall, with just enough width for my shoulders to sit flush against the casing behind. Destination: Hollesley Bay Detention Centre.

By the end of 1985, my life was documented through a series of four walls. After the concrete cell at Stoke Newington Police Station on the night of my arrest, there were the four walls of the stagnant youth court at Highbury Corner Magistrates', looking more like a church, covered in dark wooden panelling, with pews running in the middle and down the sides. This was where my case was heard.

'Who's your legal representative?' the district judge asked when I stood anxiously before him. When I replied I had none, my hearing got adjourned until later that day. I was told to see the duty solicitor. Instead, I found Marianne Willis in the corridor: slim, silver haired, and with an accent that could cut glass. She had 'I can get anyone off' written all over her. Except on this occasion, she couldn't. Because I'd given a signed statement to the police on the night of my arrest admitting I was on look-out. I'd written my ending before I'd even begun. 'Never make a statement without an adult or legal representative present,' Marianne warned. It was as if she had a sixth sense that our paths would cross again, and she wasn't wrong. From then on I only ever said, 'No comment'. As this was my first offence, she was confident that if I pleaded guilty, I'd get probation or a community service order.

The next four walls were the youth court holding cell: short and narrow, with glossy white tiles, like a butcher's shop, where I was placed until my name got called and a sentencing date handed to me. A few weeks later and I was back in the same cell waiting to hear my fate. The district judge had no choice, he said. Because I refused to tell the police the name of my accomplice, he wouldn't let me off lightly. As the words 'six months' and 'detention centre' echoed out, I could feel my insides folding in. 'With good behaviour you can be released in three,' he continued, as if he was sending me to the shops. It was no comfort. I stood stunned. I'd made no plans. I hadn't even told Mum where I was, and I had no way of contacting home. The only thought spinning around my head: who's going to pick Huggy up from school?

Back in the cell, Marianne loaded it with apologies. She was shocked, she admitted. She didn't think the judge would come down that hard, make such an example of me, and that she felt responsible. She stopped short of mentioning my colour, but the unspoken fact hung between us. I could hardly speak.

'My brother... I... I... I collect my brother from school. Who's going to collect my brother?' I stuttered.

'Oh right, I see,' Marianne looked puzzled.

It was one thing telling people I had a mentally ill mum, but quite another, them understanding all of what that entailed day-to-day. Before I was escorted out to the armoured van, Marianne gave me her word that Huggy would be taken care of. She then handed me her card in case I needed to call her. My brother entrusted to another stranger. I couldn't forgive myself?

In the van, I could hear shouts from the other guys, 'Governor. Can you loosen the cuffs for fuck's sake!' But I stayed quiet, looking out at the traffic and the cyclists with whom I was almost cheek-to-cheek. I thought it odd the way they couldn't see me looking out from behind the tinted glass, envying their freedom. I was the invisible man again, like I'd been throughout my childhood.

When the urban sprawl gave way to fields and trees, I tried to erase from my mind the vision of Huggy's face at the school gates, eager to see me, and Mum and Mini's faces after they found out where I'd been sent. And when I looked down at my handcuffs, I again imagined myself as Kunta Kinte from *Roots*, transported to an unforgiving world. I could feel my core harden. They could put chains on my body, but never chains on my mind.

Soon after we arrived, we were ordered to file out of the van, and were taken through a series of doors to a wooden counter. It reminded me of Larry Grayson's *Generation Game,* an endless conveyor belt of items being passed through the hands of inmates and soon-to-be fellow workers that needed to be checked off, but there we're no prizes to be won in this game.

'What size are you mate?' one said, but before I could answer I was handed: 2 x shirts, 2 x vests, 2 x underwear, 1 x boots, 1 x best shoes, 2 x socks, 1 x jumper, 1 x jacket, 1 x sheet, 1 x blanket, 1 x pillow, 1 x pillowcase, 1 x toothbrush, 1 x tube of toothpaste, 1 x comb and a bar of soap with the HMP logo stamped on it, all this piled high onto my outstretched forearms, as precarious as the Leaning Tower of Pisa.

I'd heard about the detention centres, but I wasn't prepared for the professional pleasure that the screws took in humiliation. Mum threatened and beat me, but she stopped short of humili-ation. The Old Bill loved it when we got stopped and searched, but we didn't have to live with them. But these men were with us 24/7. Before I got taken to my cell, I was escorted outside to an open field surrounded by miles of rolling Suffolk countryside, my tower of belongings teetering. In the distance, I could see a screw standing and some of the guys I'd arrived with running and balancing their towers, like a cruel twist on an egg-and-spoon race. The officers pissed themselves laughing.

'See that officer at the other end of the field, sunshine?' one screw barked at me. 'When I say run, run towards him as fast as you can. Do not look back.' But I'd already made up my mind. I wasn't running for no one. I started strolling, casually. When he called me back, I looked him dead in his eyes. He stepped so close to my face I could smell his breath and feel the heat from his chest.

'RUN!' he yelled, so I turned and strolled again. Seconds later his footsteps were behind me and I lurched forwards as his fist smashed into the back of my head, my tower toppling to the ground. My urge was to slam my fist into his face but I decided it would be more satisfying to fuck with him. 'My mum can hit harder than that,' I murmured, and picked up my belongings and started strolling again. Another pause and I was sandwiched between two screws. 'RUN! RUN! RUN!' they shouted, as if they were sergeant majors in the army, but I kept on strolling, as if I was taking a slow walk in a big-arse park.

By the time I got dragged into the main building, I was grinning on purpose, which pissed them off even more. 'Right. You're going down the block!' one announced. Like I gave a fuck, whatever that was. The block was a prison within the prison, a large garage-type building with thick breeze blocks and a flat roof—the solitary wing.

A heavy metal door. A dark passageway. A strip light flickered to life. Then, I was inside the tiniest of four walls: no window, only a mattress and a bunk with what remained of my belongings, thrown into the cell with me. If I stretched myself out, my feet and hands could almost touch the opposite walls. As soon as the door banged shut, I used my jumbled-up kit to pad myself out. Ready. Jumper under my vest, pillow shoved down my back. Boots on and jeans tucked into my socks. Next, I checked if the bed could be dismantled and its parts used as weapons. But nothing budged, the bed was even bolted to the floor. The screws would return to try and teach me a lesson. I was sure of it.

That night I refused sleep. Instead, I propped myself up against the back wall facing the door and waited. And waited. Nothing. Whenever I heard footsteps along the corridor, I readied myself in a fighting stance, but no one entered. Instead, the spy hole slid open two or three times and I watched an eyeball peer in before it was slammed shut again. It took me a while to figure out what their game was. They were waiting until I fell asleep before they ambushed. Sneaky fuckers. The paranoia ate into me. Eventually, when they did enter, I was positioned up against the wall, fists clenched.

'Come on, then! Come on, then!' I growled, but the screws didn't rush me. Instead, they looked dishevelled, ties loosened below their collars, shirts hanging out of their trousers, alcohol breath stinking. I peered in closer. They were tipsy!

'Lisssten Browneeee,' one said in a thick, country bumpkin, East Anglian accent, while swaying and slurring his words. 'Calm down boy. We're not going to hurt you.'

'If you're going to get on here, you have to drop the attitude,' the other chipped in, adding that if I played ball, they would let me join the other boys the next day.

'Can you play ball, Browneeee. Can you do that?' he repeated. I didn't answer. Eventually, when they did back out, I still didn't trust them, so I stayed poised ready to fight for a while afterwards, and slept upright, facing the door for the rest of the night.

* * *

Bosmere Unit was a dormitory of 12 boys—built like a garden shed with a pitched roof and fluorescent lighting suspended from it. There were showers with toilet cubicles next door that had the world's thinnest toilet paper, tracing paper really, which made it hard to wipe your arse. Whilst sitting on the throne one morning, doing 'one for the Queen' (a phrase we used whenever we needed to take a number two, because we were here, At Her Majesty's pleasure), I noticed a quote etched on the back of the toilet door: 'This loo roll is so rough and tough, just like John Wayne, it don't take shit from nobody!' Not only did I have a new a home, but I had a new name and number too: A345 Browne. When I got taken there, my roommates were on work detail but it wasn't long before their chatter filled the room as they streamed in. Immediately, I did a double take. One guy, Colin Matthews, was a brother I knew from Stoke Newington and I'm surprised to see him here. Colin's family were known as hardcore, functioning alcoholics. They were not street people, but they knew everyone. His two older twin brothers are built like brick shithouses, dark-skinned, bald-headed, big gold-looped earrings dangling from their lobes, looking everything like genies in a bottle. You could see them walking to work in their British Rail uniforms, each with one hand slung over his shoulder carrying a work bag, and the other carrying a can of brew wrapped in a brown paper bag—no matter what time of day it was. Colin is the youngest, with a shorter, wiry frame. A softy, he was known as a bit of a clown, but not a thief. But it turned out he got done for shoplifting. I felt a little sorry for him. Colin didn't have a bad bone in his body. Selfishly, I was relieved to see a familiar face, and someone who could show me the ropes. On seeing me, he wrapped his arms around my shoulders like a long-lost brother, and bigged me up to the other boys, who welcomed me into the unit.

Hollesley Bay reminded me of the children's homes: that same stifling routine of up early, breakfast, work, dinner, TV time, showers and lights out. And the same bland, lifeless canteen food slopped out on plates. Whereas in Forest Road there'd been some effort to nurture us, here it was all about falling in line. No sooner had the boys come back from their break than a whistle blew and we all filed out and stood in a line. We lined up along the corridor, named the M1. And we marched in line everywhere; to work details, to gym, to church, or any time we left the unit to go to any other part of the DC: a life led in lines. Colin told me the Jam Factory detail was the best place to work, piss easy and loads of jam to scoff. I made a mental note of this. The Servery detail back on the unit, working in the kitchen, was also a cushy number with the same benefit of leftovers.

'Hands by your side and place your thumbs along the crease of your jeans,' Colin whispered as soon as we were outside. And I followed the others when the screw shouted, 'Attention!' and the boys' backs straightened like egg soldiers. Now I felt like I was definitely in the army.

On my first day, I was assigned the strawberry field. 'By the left! Quick march! Left! Left! Left! Left!' And when my group reached the field on the edge of the complex, the order changed. We were bent, doubled over at the waist, looking at the endless rows of strawberries stretching for miles and miles as far as the eye could see. 'Miss one, pick one, miss one, pick one.' It was difficult to take the screw seriously, dressed in a pair of brown dungarees and wellies up to his knees, his officer's belt attached to his chain and keys dangling from his midriff. It was literally backbreaking, hardcore work. The only consolation was in feeling the spring sun on our faces, but when the wind blew, it bit into me and the coarseness of my prison clothes rubbed against my skin. I made a vow to get to the Jam Factory as fast as possible.

That evening, Colin sorted me out with a shiv. A razor blade is lodged into the heated melting plastic of a toothbrush head, with its brush singed off until cooled and moulded to the razor. I put my shiv inside an empty folded toilet-roll holder and lodged it down the side of my boots for easy access. Sometimes razor blades also got broken up into little pieces and mixed into someone's porridge or custard if a boy had beef with you. For the whole time I was at Hollesley Bay, I never took my eyes off my food.

'Don't have porridge on PE mornings, bro,' Colin warned me. Apparently, this mattered, especially when it came to circuit training which almost killed you. And then there was the bleep test.

'The bleep test!?' I repeated, dumbfounded, before the room erupted with laughter.

'You'll find out soon enough, bruv,' one of the boys interrupted, but Colin already started to demonstrate by running up and down the dorm walkway shouting 'bleep!' whenever he touched his hand to the floor at either end.

'The recorded bleep goes faster and faster, so you have to pace yourself,' he said, breathless.

'Alright Matthews, you're making me fucking dizzy for fuck's sake!' the same boy shouted. I found it strange that boys addressed each other by their surnames like the way the screws did.

The boys hadn't been wrong about the bleep test. As I was a fast runner and had good lungs on me, I always made it down to the last three boys but sacrificed winning to save my energy for the dreaded circuit training, which was bone crushing. Red. Black. Green. A colour chart hung over each exercise with a number on it: 10, 15, 18. You started on green and went three times around as fast as you could, before moving on to the next colour, black, then red, which was the toughest. Two sick buckets sat at each end of the gym, which was just a massive empty barn yard with training equipment in it. When the whistle blew, we moved from exercise to exercise as if our life depended on it. Medicine balls: weights lined out like a xylophone; a long wooden bench, as heavy as lead, hooked into the top of the wall at an angle, that you had to balance above your head, with arms outstretched, before dropping down into a squat. Faces strained, muscles trembled, screws barked more orders and if a boy's vomit missed the bucket, he was forced to get down on his hands and knees to clean up his mess. I often felt dizzy enough to puke, but I shook my head like a wet dog to fight it off. Sometimes the screws made the boys sick on purpose. Another bucket filled with water got passed around, and each boy was made to drink from it with a ladle. They watched gleefully as exhausted, thirsty boys vomited up that morning's porridge.

We rejoiced whenever we got one up on the screws, but more than that, we longed to be teenagers. On one occasion we crept out of our beds and tiptoed down the M1 to the office where night-duty kept watch. We stuck Rizla papers all over the screw's face while he snored drunkenly. Then, Colin set them alight one by one and we legged it back to bed pissing ourselves with laughter, all to the sound of the screw slapping his face, as if he was swotting flies. Next thing we know, every single dorm got woken up, even though they had nothing to do with it. We were made to put on our PE kits and marched outside to stand at attention, before being sent off to do laps around the field in the freezing cold because we couldn't control the smirks and giggles. In the pitch darkness, on the cusp of the woods, one guy had the foresight to bring a spliff, and halfway round we stopped and passed it to each other while standing in a huddle. The night air under the blanket of stars felt like magic. I don't recall ever in my life seeing the sky so vast. I felt exhilarated. I felt like a little boy in his element allowed to play. Happy. Joyous, and free. No stress, and no pressure. Although word got round that our dorm was responsible, no one ever grassed us up. And it was worth it, just for that moment. Instead, everyone endured the punishment of no TV.

Mostly, though, I tried to keep my nose clean. And, like they do in the military, I folded my clothing into a perfect box shape with seams running along the sides, just as they taught us to do, ready for inspection; and I made my bed with perfect hospital corners as well. Oversleeping was not an option. My insides crumpled when I watched the screws creep in and tip up the bed of a boy who was still fast asleep, creasing the mattress around him. Now stuck upside down against the wall, his arms and legs flailing like an upturned beetle while another drenched him in cold water. Their contempt for us boys triggered me. Thankfully, it only happened to me once. I was in the sweetest of dreams, back on the streets, smoking heroin with the crew, passing the foil around and gouching when all of a sudden I was upside down, my face and body dripping. As I came to, the whole room was laughing. 'Got ya Browneeee,' one screw smirked. I laughed and joined in too, attempting to ease my growing tension, but I was secretly seething and vowing revenge.

Every boy had his own coping mechanism. Mainly, mine was to keep my head down and see out my sentence, but that didn't last. I noticed that Colin's got involved as the screws's pet, and prefers to move with the white boys, speaking in a cockney accent. He lets them say things like, 'Come here you black bastard.' Instead of challenging them, he stands to attention and plays along, saluting, 'Yes! Sir!' I cringed. The Black man with the jazz hands.

'How you mek them call you dem names, bro?' I said, taking him aside one day.

'Ah it's nutin, man,' he said, brushing it off.

'Don't you see it looks bad on all of us?'

'You can't let em get to you mate. You've got to play em at their own game, innit?'

'Nah man, I'm not making no white man call me black bastard as any joke, I don't business who they are' I told him, firmly.

From then on, I had Colin marked as a coconut—black on the outside, but white on the inside. Seared into my brain was what Rasta Mark had taught me all those years ago. 'Always stand up strong and keep yu integrity. Don't mek anybody talk to yu like that again.' One time, I was forced to clean the M1 with a toothbrush after I refused to polish a screw's boots. It was a way for boys to earn extra canteen; screws would get them to do personal errands for them. I didn't mind hustling and doing most things, but never that. The screw put me on M1 detail for three whole days, but I took a perverse pleasure in each tiny circular motion, knowing that I'd not caved in. The M1 looked like it was a hundred miles long—hence the name, with a bright, faded green, mirror-polished lino floor running the full length of it.

Our work detail got shifted around, usually based on crime and punishment. Everything got measured in degrees of behaviour. If you were a persistent offender, you'd get stuck in the block or sent to the fields forever.

'Browneeee. Jam Factory!' I couldn't believe my luck when my name got called. I felt like Charlie Bucket in Willy Wonka's chocolate factory waving my golden ticket. Ages ago and with Colin's guidance, I'd filled out the slip requesting to work in the Jam Factory but forgot all about it. It was everything he had promised: Holiday Bay, not Hollesley Bay.

The factory itself was cavernous with three giant vats of jam looking like giant cement mixers. They had mini stairs running up the sides so we could lean in and pour in the ingredients. Along the sides were conveyor belts moving massive tins around, waiting to be filled and sealed and labelled. Apparently, the factory supplied other prisons plus the whole of Suffolk, and the managers we worked with were locals rather than prison officers. They didn't have keys that jangled and they spoke to us like equals. Other than the white overalls and hairnets that gave us the appearance of old women, it was as close as I got to being on the outside. And lunchtime was the best: gooey strawberry jam sandwiched between two hunks of white prison-baked bread. Oh man, I was in heaven.

Another time I requested to be sent to the education wing, which also had a lightness to it. In art classes we drew and painted, and one teacher who came in from the outside was a woman. I noticed how we all acted differently, including me, making an effort to behave like gentlemen. There was something pleasing about having a woman there to punctuate the testosterone-fuelled air, the smell of perfume, the softness of her voice, the shape of her figure, and during her lessons we had deep conversations about life. She bothered to ask us what we would do when we were released.

'Big spliff, couple of lines of Charlie, and a brew, Miss,' one of the lads called out. All of us giggled at his audacity. But the question played on my mind. I'd written letters home to Mini, but I'd not sent any visiting orders. I didn't want anyone travelling that distance, I told her, but the truth was, I didn't want my family to see me in a detention centre. I wanted to protect them from the world I was living in. I'd left without saying goodbye, best to keep it that way. But when Sunday rolled around and the other boys got dressed up to receive their people, that's when it cut me up. Then, they brought their parcels of toiletries or food back to the dorm, and I'd ask how their families were, like tuning into a running soap opera—a voyeur of other boys' happiness. Now, as my sentence progressed, I worried about what family I was going back to.

I did my full sentence of six months after getting nicked a few times for disobeying orders and ending up in the block again. I got out on my LDR, my latest date of release.

'You'll be back, Browneeee,' said the screw I had a vendetta with. I'd pissed him off for not cleaning his boots and showing him up in front of the boys.

'Maybe you're right, *Sir!*' I shouted back over my shoulder on my way out the gate. 'And you'll be waiting for me, *Sir! Doing your own life sentence, paying off that mortgage *Sir!*'

I was given a brown envelope containing £46, a discharge grant courtesy of Her Majesty, before I and another inmate got dropped off at the Melton train station. Before we'd even boarded, we made a beeline for the off-licence. As the carriages rumbled towards Ipswich and then on to London Liverpool Street, it didn't take us long to get wasted before we arrived.

Chapter 25

"Fix My Mum Man!"

The waiting room at Dr Egbonwon's is filled with coughs and sniffles and old people. I know that people are sick, but they can't feel like me. They can't. I'm not ill, at least not in the 'normal' way. But a madness has descended over me. I'm desperate. I'm here to get him to make everything stop. Before I'd reached Alkham Road, I knew what I'd find, though I tried not to think about it. I think it's why I got so pissed on the train back from Hollesley Bay. Nerves jangling the whole time. The grinding in my belly whenever I thought of Mum and Mini and Huggy.

That afternoon, I listened for the sound of the TV, then the blaze of a cartoon as I made my way up the stairs. As I turned the corner, I could see Huggy cross-legged and glued to the screen. Mini was on the sofa. I hovered in the doorway for a moment, then left them to take in the kitchen, the sadness welling up in me. Plates filled the sink. Mum's living creations covered the work-tops and windowsills—plastic bottles chopped in half and filled with water, some with seedlings sprouting, others with eggshells or string or food left to rot floating on the surface. A film of dust covered the table. I sat there for a while. All the work I'd put into making the house livable, all down the drain in six short months.

'Where's Mum?' I finally interrupted Mini and Huggy, who looked up, half-pleased to see me.

'In bed,' Mini replied.

I looked around the living room, items of clothes and toys lay scattered about.

'Why isn't he at school?'

'We woke up too late,' Mini said.

'The place is a mess, man. Start tidying up!' I ordered her, but she stared at me, disbelieving. The kind of look that says: who the fuck are you? You're not my dad. Since then, I haven't felt like the man of the house. However much I try, I can't pick up where I left off. I'm a stranger, not only to my family, but to myself. Disconnected, like a severed phone line.

I climbed up to my room and sat on my bed to take a moment to work out how I could fix everything. Then it hit me: that over-whelming desire to escape from it all. Next minute I'd thrown on my tracky top and slammed the front door shut. Time to reconnect with the crew and smoke some gear, until I could figure it out.

When I finally get to see Dr Egbonwon, his same moon face is looking down on me. He's been Mum's doctor for all these years, yet he remains calm and matter-of-fact, as if nothing is an emergency. This always puzzles me because after everything that's happened, I think it's all an emergency. I don't understand why Mum isn't a priority. I don't understand why nobody seems to care. Dr Egbonwon tells me Mum's prescription of pills is on repeat, and there's nothing more he can do. 'It's not the point,' I tell him. Doesn't he understand that Mum is mentally unwell? That she doesn't do things in the way normal people do? That she plays by her own rules?

Apparently, after I'd left for the detention centre, Mum kept up her job caretaking and cleaning the toilets, but not for long. One day she stopped turning up and retreated to her bedroom. But that's not what's brought me here. I'm here to see Dr Egbonwon about my discovery. Not long after I arrived home, I was stood on the kitchen table reaching up for a tin from the overhead cupboard, when I saw it. It stopped me dead in my tracks. The tidal wave of Mum's medication piled high on top of each other like mini mountains. Some pills were smashed and squashy as if she'd chewed them first, spat them out, and thrown them up there still wet. I must have run my hands through hundreds, and hundreds, which meant she had not been taking them from the start, all that time. At that moment, I felt like I had received a blow to the stomach. I started getting dizzy and lightheaded. I felt like a fool and felt completely powerless to control anything. Mum had played me. And she played me good. But there's a part of me that understands her not wanting to take her pills. The drugs rule her life, they trap her. They stop her from being free.

I'm still buzzing off the memory of my first hit after coming back from Hollensey Bay. That sharp acid vinegar smell of heroin burning was like an old friend. The feeling of pure warmth that wrapped itself around me was the warmest of welcome-home hugs. The shock of finding Mum's pills and the guilt of being away vanished. It's given me a renewed energy, but I want more. I don't want to stop smoking; I want to lose myself. And now that I've done bird, I feel more invincible than a superhero. All of the crew—Nicky, Ronnie, Keith—think it's great that I've served a sentence. 'Welcome home, son!' they said, patting me on the back. 'Got your first bird under your belt.' Some guys are so proud of it that they tattoo themselves with pen and ink while they're inside. A little bird peeks out of the fleshy part of their hand, between their thumb and their index finger. It's like a secret 'in' to an exclusive club. 'It was a piece of piss,' I told them before they took me out to celebrate with weed and gear and a few lines of Charlie. The day after my release I went straight out with Ronnie, drumming houses.

I tell Dr Egbonwon that since I've been home, I've started

losing my hair. One morning, I woke up and felt a small, shiny bald patch right in the middle of my head, smooth to the touch. At first, I thought Mum had shaved me while I'd been asleep—the sort of crazy thing she might do. Then, I thought I was imagining it, but whenever I look in the mirror the patch is still there, smiling right back at me. I'm well embarrassed by it, so I've started wearing hats. Dr Egbonwon says stress is the most likely cause, but I am not joining the dots at first until he explains how it can affect the body as well as the mind. I'm in denial, and still not fully getting it, but I agree with him anyway.

I want to tell him how I've taken Huggy to school every single day and picked him up. How, with Mum not working, I need to earn money but I've too much to think about. I want to tell him that I'm scared for Mini. I've caught her bunking off school, hanging out with the sisters of some of the street brothers I know who juggle heroin and weed. She and I have had serious fights. Not long ago I pinned her down on her bed to stop her from going out that night and held her firm while she kicked out like a mule. 'You're not my dad! I can see whoever I want!' she shouted. I've tried to talk to her about those girls and how they'll be pregnant soon and throwing their lives away breeding for some brother. 'Trust me,' I said to her when she calmed down. 'I'm getting us out of this one way or the other. You have a better life ahead of you sis.' I know it's what Mini needs to hear, but I feel like such a hypocrite saying it. I can hardly lead by example. I want to say all of this to Dr Egbonwon, but I can't. I don't trust him.

I will never confess to him about my drug use, although I follow his eyes as they roam all over me. I'm unsure whether he suspects it. I don't know whether doctors can diagnose you without you opening your mouth. I shuffle self-consciously if he stares too long, but I decide he can't know. It's none of his business, anyhow.

I've been to see my dad Anthony, in Edmonton. I know I shouldn't expect much of him, but I need him to step up, to see what I'm going through. *To see me.* I didn't hear from him the whole time I was at Hollesley Bay and I didn't write to him either, but he says he knew where I was. He says I'm out of control and I'm too big for him to have any influence over my life. I'm like a beggar, begging for his attention, begging for his love, begging for his acceptance. His girlfriend, who I call Auntie Olivia out of respect, sticks up for me. She's kind, and motherly, and I've always felt love towards her. She tells my dad that he should take me out somewhere. I like that she tells him off, but I feel embarrassed that she has to do it. 'Cha, man, he's alright,' is always the response, and he says it kissing his teeth.

The last time I visited he sat watching the cricket. He'd promised to give me money for a new pair of jeans. And even though I had a wad of cash on me, I wanted to test him, to see if he'd remembered.

'Any chance I can get the money for those jeans?' I said.

'I don't have any money for you this week,' he said, dismissing me. 'Car needs fixed. Come try me after that.'

Auntie Beryl says he always was tight, and he never paid for anything when he and Mum were going out. But it's not about the money. It's the principle. I'm testing what I mean to him. The last thing I wanted to do was disrespect Auntie Olivia, but I lost it. Without hesitating, I pulled out my ratchet knife and slammed my wad of notes on the table.

'Hey! You know what!?' I shouted. 'Fuck you Anthony! Fuck you and your bloodclart money.' He raised himself up from the sofa, his worked-out chest on display like a peacock, but I saw his eyes. It's all about the eyes. I saw the fear. Inside that big, muscle-bound gym chest, was a mouse.

'You think I need you, Anthony? I can get my own money

using this.' I took a step towards him, clutching the blade, wanting him to do something so I could whet him up, until Auntie Olivia rushed in from the kitchen and stood between us.

'Please Stanley, for the love of God,' she pleaded. 'I'm begging you. Please put away the knife. Please!'

'You're fucking lucky to have Olivia,' I shouted in his face as I flicked the blade back in its place and shoved the cash back in my pocket. He stood there, like a little boy, looking lost, gripped by fear, as if I was a stranger. I felt like I had truly seen my dad for who he was for the very first time.

'Aunt Olivia, he don't deserve you,' I shouted before leaving. I walked up the row of houses on their road and found a ladder in an alleyway and drummed his neighbour's house, just to spite him.

Dr Egbonwon nods poker-faced at the revelation that Mum's not taking her pills, but the more he nods, the more vexed I'm getting.

'Mum will end up in the psychiatric hospital!' I tell him.

'From what you are telling me, and our most recent assessment, your mum isn't a danger to herself or anyone around her at the moment,' he says.

'Hold on bro, what do you mean a 'danger'? So you're saying my mum has to hurt herself or somebody else before you can do anything? Can't you see what will happen?' My voice is raised now, more urgent.

'We can't intervene here,' he says calmly.

'But it will be too late! You're meant to be her Dr; can't you do something?' I argue. I can feel the fury rising in me.

'Can't you give me a medication that I put in her tea? You can give her the drugs that way?'

Dr Egbonwon looks at me with a pained, emotionless expression that makes me boil over. I'm angry, then furious, then livid. I yell that if he doesn't do something now, I'll smash up his fucking office.

'Can't you see what's going to happen?' I roar. 'Can't you see it? She'll be sectioned and lose all her kids again!'

'We cannot put drugs in someone's tea,' he says in a thick Nigerian accent. 'People have human rights! Your mum has her own free will and I cannot force her. She will either take it or not take it.' But I've had enough of him smugly rocking back and forth on his office chair, elbows resting on his desk, with his palms together, looking like some Buddha. I am possessed, and I can't leave without a way out of this mess, even though I know Dr Egbonwon isn't budging.

'Don't you fucking care? Don't you fucking care about anything?' I smash my hands across the table, sending his files and coffee cup flying. Then I point straight at him.

'One day you'll get your comeuppance,' I threaten before storming out.

My fury lasts for days. I decide that if Dr Egbonwon won't do something about Mum's mountain of pills, then I'll have to confront her myself. I know to choose my moment carefully, so I do it while Mum is relaxed, smoking her cigarette in front of the TV. Instead of accusing her, I manoeuvre around.

'Time for your medication, Mum,' I say in an upbeat tone.

'Leave them on the side, I'll take them later.' She doesn't look up.

'Okay, cool. But I think you need to take one now, though?'

'I'll take it when I'm ready.' I can hear the irritation in her voice, but I can't hold it in any longer. I lose control and blurt out the one thing I wasn't supposed to say.

'I found the pills on the top of the cupboard, Mum.'

There's silence in the room as Mum continues to smoke her roll-up.

'Mum? Did you hear me?' As I push further, I can feel her tension rise. Mum lifts herself up, gathers her smokes and leaves the room.

'Mum, talk to me about it, man?'

'Fuck off and leave me alone. You're not mi bloodclart doctor!'
I trail behind Mum to the kitchen telling her that if she doesn't
take her medication, she'll lose everything again. I remind her
how hard it was to get Mini and Huggy back in the first place. She
cuts me off mid-flow.

'There's nothing wrong with me, okay? I don't need to take
medication anymore. They give me a headache. There's nothing
wrong with me, alright?'

Over the next few weeks, I will try again and again, but she will
refuse and cuss me out. I don't show it, but everything is slipping
from me, slipping from us. And my head is spinning in a whirl of
questions: *Why, man!? Why? Why us? Why me? How am I going to
fix my mum now?*

Chapter 26

Zero

It's 2012 and I am 41 years old. I am attending a self-development course. Everyone is here because they want answers to the questions in their own jumbled-up heads. Our search for meaning is the thread that connects us.

In the introductory session, one question stands out. It stands out because no one can answer it: what is the meaning of life? At first, all the participants think it's an easy question, but when we start debating, it becomes impossible. How can such a simple question cause us so much pain? When nobody in the room can answer, our facilitator takes the microphone, and we lean in and listen.

'The answer to the question is that life has no meaning. Life means nothing. The meaning of life is a big fat zero.'

He says it is human beings who add meaning to life and everything in it: we attach a meaning to our past, to our present and to our future. We attach meaning to it even when meaning isn't there. We are labelled to create meaning and we label ourselves. We spend lifetimes trying to find answers to why something has happened to us, or why it hasn't.

I have an *eureka moment* and totally embrace this concept. Immediately, a burden of blame and expectation lifts from me. I realise that for all these years I've been searching for answers that don't exist. *Why did Mum become ill? Why did I get separated from my siblings? Why have I put myself through so much suffering? Why me?* I've been torturing myself, asking questions for which there are no real answers. Maybe the only answer is to reframe the question. *Why not me?*

Chapter 27

Bucky

'Walk,' I say to Jamie under my breath. 'Turn around and walk out. Now.' He's just got home after a stretch in Brixton Prison for burglary and we're shifting stolen goods.

'Just walk,' I repeat, but Jamie's rooted to the spot hugging a video recorder to his chest, brow crumpled as if he doesn't know which way to turn. I know which way. I'm outta here. If it wasn't for the cross-patchwork of scars covering that Yardie's face, I wouldn't have recognised him, but I've seen him as clear as a bell and he's clocked me, eyes dissecting me like a blade. My instinct tells me he's carrying a bucky.

It was Jamie's bright idea. 'Let's shift the recorder at the pawn shop on the corner of Stoke Newington Common,' he said. It was just around the corner from where I lived, but I wanted to show off, too. I've bought myself a green Renault 5 so we drove there instead. When the buzzer sounded on the shop door and we bowled in, everyone turned. Just my luck. The Yardie propping up the counter is the same scar-faced motherfucker who tried to rob a gold ring from me weeks ago.

If Jamie doesn't clock on, I'm gonna leave him behind. He doesn't know the danger I'm in, but I know he'll understand when I run. It's good to have Jamie's back, though. Everyone else has disappeared. Auntie Beryl has sent Nicky to Jamaica for a few months to get him off the gear, stop him from falling into an abyss. And Ronnie's been shipped off to Spain, along with his brother Keith, to do the same. It happened not long after one of their older brothers hanged himself in his cell in Pentonville Prison and was bang on the gear. Their mother's terrified of losing another son.

No one's shipped me anywhere. Mainly, my dad Anthony has washed his hands of me. Not long after I had the run-in with him at Aunt Olivia's, I bumped into him on Stoke Newington High Street as he was driving by. I was still smarting from our row, but when we sat in his Volvo estate he apologised for not being there for me more and asked me to keep out of trouble. It was as if for the first time ever, he saw me and talked to me like a man. He said he's thinking of moving to America, and if I keep my nose clean he'll take me with him. I don't have the heart to tell him I'm in way over my head, far deeper than the burglary that got me sent to Hollesley Bay.

And Mum? She's in no state to do anything. Maybe she knows what I'm caught up in, but I doubt she understands. Mostly, she exists in her own world: her and the voices in her head and the invisible rivals she squares up to and cusses out. So long as I'm buying food and looking after Mini and Huggy, that conversation is never on the menu. Besides, at home I cover up. Even the smell of gear burning is masked by the smell of weed from my room, or I chase by an open window.

You could call me a one-man band of crime. I'm a drug user and a drug dealer. I'm a burglar shifting stolen goods and tom I'm a fraudster, signing false signatures on stolen cheque books. Bun and cheese, we call it, slang for book and card. And, since I've started hanging out with a new crew from Stamford Hill, who dabble in armed robbery, mainly robbing other drug dealers. I've stepped up the food chain. The crew have a gun stashed round the back of their estate. It's that crabs in a bucket thing: we're so far in the shit, we crawl across each other's backs, desperate to find a way out. But I keep sliding back further and further.

* * *

I slip past Jamie, palming off my car keys into his hand. I don't have time to get in my car. I can feel him on me. I'm out of the shop now, bombing it across the common towards Stamford Hill, picking up speed. Don't look back, Stan. Come on, Stan. Faster. Faster. My lungs burn in my chest but I won't stop. I'm safe for now, but this guy wants me dead, I can feel it. If that Yardie grabs Jamie, he might interrogate him and want to know where I live. I need protection. I need my crew and I need a bucky.

The Stamford Hill crew are the most hardcore I've moved with and aside from smoking gear, making money is their second habit. Skanker, Des, Bruck-up and Sticks. Skanker's the thinker, the skinny brother with the Bob Marley dreads. And Des is the loose cannon—there's always one who goes that extra mile, who wants to rip shit up. Bruck-up and Sticks tag along, and then there's me. I graduated to respected crew member after I snatched a gold chain from a guy's neck and left him unconscious on the pavement in Stamford Hill. In their eyes I'm fearless. It was a hot move to make in broad daylight, but I had to show them who I was and what I was capable of doing.

I move with them all the time now, especially since the front-line in Hoxton's been shut down by police. Not long after, we shifted ten minutes away to Haggerston and formed another, like migrating swallows. Haggerston's better, anyway: the open square there is flanked by shops and low-rise blocks, better to run and hide in when the Old Bill turns up. We can juggle gear there from midday to around 8 PM. And we've raised the stakes. Recently, we ripped off one dealer who came from the south coast to buy heroin. We gave him good gear to sample, he handed over the cash, then we cut his final order with baking powder, and kept the good half for ourselves. It was win-win when we pulled it off.

The cash has rolled in. It's how I've bought my Renault 5, even though I haven't passed my driving test yet. I couldn't even drive when I bought it. Instead, I got Skanker to drive it back to my house and he's been giving me lessons in the car park behind Alkham Road. I can manoeuvre in first and second gear, enough to cruise around and hope I don't get a pull by the Bill.

Fuck! Jamie's got my car keys. Why did I pass them to him before I ran? I panicked. Oh man, if that Yardie finds them on Jamie, my car's gone too. I'm nearing Skanker's now and enter onto Stamford Hill Estate. I'm panting for breath by the time Des answers the door.

'What's up man?'

'Need a bucky. Now. Skanker in?'

'Come in, bruv.'

I sit with Des and Skanker and recount the whole story. I tell them how I'd been with a brother called Mikey weeks ago. How I'd been offloading tom at the jewellers by Stoke Newington train station, and how this Yardie disrespected me—just strolled up, picked up one of the chains I'd laid out on the countertop and ran it through his hands, without even asking.

'Ow much?' he said.

'That piece ain't for sale,' I told him. Then, he went ahead and picked up a ring.

'Ow much fi dis piece, bwoy?'

'You never ere what mi bloodclart say bro, it's not for sale,' I said in a low, deliberate voice.

But can you believe, the bredder took it and walked out? So I followed. No way he's getting away, walking out wid my tings, I tell Des and Skanker and continue with the story.

'Give me back my tings, bro!' I called after him. He spun round and reached out to try and feel the outside of my pockets. 'What yu ave for mi, bwoy? Gimme what you av!' he said.

Can you fucking believe dis bredder!? I say to Des and Skanker. No way I was going to let him dis me like that! Yardie or no fucking Yardie! But the bredder was quick. Before I know it, he pulled his dulle out on me, a ratchet, man, his blade hovering just above my face before I grabbed and held onto his wrist and pulled him down on the dirt ground in the alleyway. The blade swiped past my cheek bone, bro! I held him back for as long as I could, but inch by inch I could feel my strength giving way, the ratchet getting closer and closer to my face. Thank fuck for Mikey, man. When I looked up, he was stood over us brandishing a piece of wood and telling him, 'Just 'llow it sceen! 'llow it man!' The Yardie raised himself up as calm as anything, brushed the dirt off his strides, and pointed at me.

'Yu is one lucky bwoy! Yu hear mi? Next time mi see yu, mi ah go do yu sumting! Memember dat! Mi ah go kill yu! Yu life done!' He then dropped the ring on the ground. I've never seen the brother before, but Mikey says he's a bad-man fresh from yard and has a rep.

Skanker agrees to get the bucky. Des disappears. The crew's 9mm handgun is kept round the back of the flats, buried by the bins, wrapped in a black plastic bag. When he returns, it's lodged down the back of his trousers. I've never handled a 9mm before, only a sawn-off shotgun that one brother taught me how to dismantle and clean when he use to come over to my house in Alkham Road. The sawn-off was black with a mahogany handle. Smooth to the touch and beautiful. I turned it over in my hands one night while it was loaded and practised aiming it in front of the mirror, desensitised to its power. It went off deafening me for a while and putting a massive hole in the wall just above Huggy's bed. The room was filled with clouds of gun smoke and dust from the plasterboard. I was shaking like a leaf thinking what would have happened had Huggy been there and me accidentally shooting my own brother. I made sure I treated that gun with much more respect and never handled it with live rounds again.

But I need to find this Yardie before he finds me.

We pile into Skanker's car. We're screeching down Stamford Hill. Skanker and Des understand my fear. If Jamie's caved in and told the brother where I live, my family will be in danger. What if Mum's answered the door? What if Huggy answered? What if? What if?

Skanker's car is pulling up now and I'm scanning the street. Everything I fear is confirmed. My fucking car is sitting there right outside our house. What the fuck, man! I can hear my heart beating in my ears, I start to break out into a sweat. The crew is talking to me but I can't hear them, I just want to bolt from the car and run inside Mum's and have it out with this fucking Yardie. 'Let me out,' I say. 'Let me out, man!' Skanker tries to calm me down. Des shifts the 9mm to his front and shields it with his jacket as we step out and move towards our door, which is ajar. *The door is open? Fuck!* Now the blood is pounding around my body and I feel the adrenaline kick in. This is war! I draw my knife out and we make our way inside, slowly creeping up the stairs with me leading. Afternoon light is brushing the stairwell and I watch for the slightest shadow. Nothing. I listen for voices. Nothing. Suddenly, someone moves slowly across the upstairs landing.

'Who dat!?' I shout, signalling for Des to ready the gun.

'That you Stanley?' It's Mum's voice.

'Mum!? You okay!? Who's in the house?'

'Course I'm okay, silly billy!' Mum looks as if she's about to cuss me out, but I cut her dead.

'Mum! Is there anyone in the house!?' Mum looks puzzled,

and looks at the crew behind me, who all greet her politely, while Des masks the bucky. Then she pushes past as Mini comes down the stairs from her room.

'Mini! You okay!? The door was open. Who's here!?'

'Just Mum and me and Huggy,' Mini says, casually. 'The door's open because we let the dog out. Oh, and Jamie dropped your car keys off earlier.'

'Jamie? Who was he with?'

'No one! Says he'll pass round later.' Mini is frowning now.

By the time Des and Skanker leave, my head is thumping. The many worlds I inhabit are blurring at speed, like a runaway train. This time, I'm safe. But what about next time? Can I protect my family then?

When Jamie does pass around, I listen closely at what he tells me. The Yardie and his friend caught hold of him, took the car keys and forced him into my car before holding a gun to his head. He demanded Jamie show him my address. Jamie drove down every other street but Alkham Road to buy him some time to think. Then, in a moment of genius, he announced the car was stolen.

'Pull over,' the Yardie demanded. The trick seemed to work. They both started wiping their fingerprints from the door handles and disappeared into the back streets.

Jamie's energised by the incident, not angry. I owe him big time.

'Fuck Stan!' Jamie says. 'Mate, you're bang in trouble. He was well mad Stan! Said you're a dead man! Just kept repeating it to me, mate. He wants you gone! What did you do to him, bruv?'

We smoke gear and I fill Jamie in on the details. For weeks after I check every street and every alleyway whenever I step out, paranoid at every sound, and every movement.

Chapter 28

The White Lady

Nicky's back from Jamaica. 'Once an addict, always an addict.' It's what people say. I didn't believe it before I saw him. Back from three months in the Jamaican sunshine and the fresh food, he's gone from glowing and putting on weight, to looking like me: eyes sunken, rough and ready. It's a shame he's back to being bang on the gear. But it's good to have him around again. Even though I'm envious that he's been to Jamaica, lucky fucker. I wish I had parents who could send me away to recover. He tells me about it while we're smoking, gouching out: the sea that sparkles like sapphires, the fit-looking women, the sound systems and the dance halls. The endless amounts of seafood and coconuts. I dream of this world where I wanna escape to someday.

Mostly, we hang out in my room, but now I even chase in the living room while watching TV. If I hear anyone coming, I shove my paraphernalia under the cushion and light a smoke to cover the smell. I've started sending Huggy to the corner shop to buy KitKats for me. He's over-the-moon because I let him keep all the chocolate. I just need the foil it's wrapped in because I've run out.

It's late and Nicky's brought some gear, but I'm out of foil again and it's too late for the shops to still be open, so it will mean a trek to the petrol garage on Stamford Hill, and I can't be arsed. I think of which neighbour's door I can knock to hustle some foil, and suddenly remember that I've seen people coming in and out of the Hawthorn's old basement flat below. It's been empty since Mr Hawthorn died and Mrs Hawthorn disappeared with relatives, but maybe I can knock and pretend Mum's baking a cake? 'I'll be back,' I tell Nicky. The flat's shrouded in darkness, but footsteps sound in the hall.

'Yes?' A short, wiry, white guy with a pencil-thin black moustache and a Hawaiian shirt, peers out the crack of the door opening. Straight away I notice his knuckles are tattooed with the words 'love' on one fist and 'hate' on the other, and he has a jail-bird tat on the fleshy part between his thumb and index finger. An ex con. I deliver my monologue about living above, and the late-night cake baking, and I'm surprised when a smirk spreads across his face.

'What, d' you wan it for, a bit of gear, mate?' he laughs. As it's the first time we've met, I feign ignorance.

'I'm Trevor,' he says, moving to shake my hand. 'Relax. It's all kushti, mate, safe as houses, come in, bruv.'

Trevor leads me through the tight passage into the house and tells me he's seen me around. Everything looks dull and dated and smells damp. The wallpaper's peeling, untouched from when the Hawthorns lived there. Then it hits me. That familiar acid smell. When I turn the corner, I can't believe what I'm seeing. What. The. Fuck! There must be at least a dozen or so people camped on the living room floor with the windows blacked out. More bodies lurk in the kitchen. I'm stepping over arms and legs and used tin foil scraps, and tablespoons burnt and bent out of shape, scorched black from the lighters used to heat them up; used syringes, and beer cans and various bottles of alcohol all add to the litter that's everywhere. It is literally everywhere. In every corner, and in every part of the flat, a plethora of drug paraphernalia as if these guys have been partying for months and have never cleaned up.

'Maria—bring the foil?' Trevor shouts, and an African sister appears from the kitchen, skin so smooth and black she's shining, a shiny blue-black. And tall and really thin, with a pregnant belly swollen out in front of her that somehow looks unnatural, and disfigured, because she is so skinny.

'Hey, you live upstairs, right?' she asks. Maria's also seen me, and she's seen Mum talking to herself outside on the steps and asks if Mum's okay.

'Nahh, she ain't well,' I tell her, trying to cut the conversation. It makes me uncomfortable talking to a stranger about my affairs, standing in a place that feels like it could be Sodom and Gomorra.

'Get the foil for him, will ya, for fucks sake...?!' Trevor presses her. Maria attacks back before he has time to finish his sentence. 'Fuck off Trevor! I'm just have a fucking conversation, so fucking what if I'm taking my time, it's my life, don't be so fucking rude, I'm talking thank you very much, I'll give him the foil in a fucking minute! Jeezsuskryst!' She says this with a thick African accent mingling in the air with his thick cockney accent. There is no way I would have paired them as a couple. I watch as they go at each other in front of me with no shame, no inhibitions, and listen to the way their words furiously chase round each other. It reminds me of Tom and Jerry, relentless.

When I get back upstairs to Nicky I'm smiling like a fool. I fill him in on what I've found, an oasis below, begging for us to juggle gear there—until the cows come home and go back out again. Junkies lined up waiting to be served. 'Forget hustling in Haggerston, bro!' I tell him. This wide and vast universe is busy carrying out humble duties for all of mankind. We have landed on our feet.

Over the next few weeks we juggle exclusively in Maria's flat, first starting off with an eighth, and working our way up to a half ounce of smack which we don't cut; we want to keep the punters sweet, and make sure they come back. We became the main suppliers from that night forward. Maria and Trevor love me in the way that only junkies can. So long as I'm delivering good, quality gear direct to their living room, they talk to me like I'm a king, bending over backwards to please my every need. The place is filthy, and nasty and it makes my skin crawl. I serve everyone standing up, as I'm too squeamish to sit down on one of the dirty armchairs.

Most of the junkies who visit there inject, and wear long, red-raw track marks up and down their arms, legs and necks, and some inject into their toes or groin when all the other veins elsewhere have collapsed and they can't get a hit. I watch as junkies breakdown and cry in sheer panic and frustration because they can't find a vein, while the other junkies operates on them, stripping off layers and layers of their clothing, searching for a vein they can use, until they're almost naked on the ground. I have no respect for them and judge them for being hardcore junkies, but after a few months, I start to get to know them on another level and am surprised to find out who they are as people and not just as junkies.

Some have regular jobs: nurses, doctors, teachers, even solicitors come. They mix with the prostitutes and the pimps, and I'm unsure what to make of them. At first, I'm shocked that these people with needles in their arms and their dribbling mouths and hang-dog faces hold down normal jobs. I couldn't even imagine working full time, having a proper job, and being bang on the gear at the same time. I've never injected. It's bad enough that I smoke heroin—the white man's drug—but fixing up is the lowest of the low. I'm not even curious. I smoke weed and chase gear and snort Charlie, and now I freebase cocaine with Skanker and his crew, but I'm no junkie.

At Maria's I make money hand over fist. For someone who abandoned school, I'm good at arithmetic. I do it in my head. I know who owes me what, and I rarely forget. I'm especially motivated because there's a motor I want to buy: a new Mini—and it's easier to zip through the streets if the police take chase. My green Renault 5 got sold on after the tussle with the Yardie, because I can't risk him recognising my car. I replaced it with a light blue Mini, but that got written off within two months of me having it. Ronnie was not long back from Spain when we were chasing gear while driving around looking for a house to drum. I braked. He dropped the foil with the powder balancing on top. We panicked, trying to save what we could. I leaned over to help pick up the gear, but with my right hand still gripping the steering wheel while the car was in motion, I unwittingly turned the car in the same direction I was leaning. BANG! Straight into the back of a parked car. I had to leave it and run. Luckily, the car wasn't registered to me.

I see Skanker and the crew more now that I've started freebasing with them. It's a purer hit. Powerful. I can't get enough of it. Skanker always brings out his long, slim, glass pipe, shaped like a mermaid, that he calls the 'The White Lady'. When he mixes the coke with the baking soda and water in a test tube, I feel hypnotised watching it dissolve and go gooey at the hiss and heat of the Bunsen burner with the glowing, raw-blue flame. Then, to see the way it clings to the coat-hanger wire after Skanker inserts it into the tube stirring it around. And how, when cooled, the gooey blob hardens into a solid white rock at the tip of the wire, and is chipped into smaller pieces on a mirror, which we light and burn on the Lady, inhaling deeply until she fills with thick, white clouds of smoke, and us holding it in for the longest time. It's not warm like heroin. It's loud and fiery, like a grenade going off in my lungs. The hit is instant. Like a shot from a gun. My head explodes with bright lights. I'm overwhelmed and have to keep blinking my eyelids to stop the feeling of blacking out. My pupils expand and my eyes widen, taking on a life of their own. I feel like I'm wrapped in a massive sheet of bubble wrap and can walk into anything and not feel the pain. It leaves me wanting more: right there, right now.

The downside is that the comedown and the paranoia are brutal—the prang, we call it. And after a session, it leaves us all on our knees, searching the floor for anything white that we think might be a rock that escaped the mirror. It's not long before I'm freebasing alone, having learnt the tricks of the trade of washing-up coke. Freebasing burns through my money like a man placing bets at the bookie. And it's crossed my mind whether I have a habit, but at this point I just don't' care. I want to smoke every day and stay up late into the early hours, getting high. So many times I've forgotten to pick up Huggy from school, and Mini's fetched him instead. And in the mornings, when he's shaking me after I've just fallen asleep and he's telling me he's dressed and it's time to go, I get up—but I curse him. It's not his fault, but I can't stand that Huggy needs me, and feel that he loves and resents me at the same time. When I do get up, at least I know I can score some gear on the way to school to bring me down from the coke. I leave him waiting outside Maria's or in a stairwell in Haggerston and disappear, then try to straighten myself out before we reach the school gates. He knows better not to ask me where I go.

* * *

It's December 1986 and it's the night of my 16th birthday. I've spent most of the evening at Maria's. I have now grown accustomed to the filth and make myself comfortable on one of the sofas. My Mini's parked outside but I rarely drive it. I spend so much money on using, I don't have the cash to put petrol in it half the time.

'Hey mate, can you do me a favour and take my wife to work?' Dave, one of the junkies is asking me. He's often there and his wife, Denise, comes with him. She's short with dark hair and olive skin and her breasts and hips curve like treacle. I secretly fancy her. Dave is pallid and his skin looks battered and weather-beaten. They don't look like husband and wife.

'Sure,' I say. 'If you're happy to put something in the tank. What hospital you work at?' As it's late, I assume Denise is a nurse and needs dropping off at her night shift. When she doesn't answer, Dave smiles and talks for her. 'She works on the Hill,' he says. I'm still not clocking on to what he is saying exactly.

'So, what do you do?' I ask again when she and I are alone in the car.

'I'm a brass,' Denise says, while fixing her hair. I can't quite process that this beautiful woman uses heroin and is married, and, at the same time, sells her body for sex. Other prostitutes come to Maria's, but never with a husband or as well-kept as Denise.

'Doesn't your old man mind?' I ask.

'Course not, silly!' Denise replies. I keep driving. Now I'm confused; there is no way if I had a woman like her, I could ever have her on the game fucking other men and then coming home into my bed, no way. But at the same time, I'm turned on by her. Denise has the sexiest lips that I really want to kiss. My first true romance was with Michelle, a girl I met while juggling gear. She lived in Haggerston. She's drop-dead gorgeous, and I loved kissing her, but she didn't let me past first base. She is mixed-race and has long black hair and a slim body and she's so shy, I just melted into her whenever she spoke. I want to look after her still. I like that she doesn't do drugs, even though her brother was a known smack-head and died after having a hit. He collapsed on the pavement when I sold him a bit of gear. No one wanted to touch him, including me, in case the Old Bill came, so everyone just watched him twitching on the ground. He was gone by the time the ambulance arrived. I felt bad that I couldn't reach out to help him because he was Michelle's brother, but I can't let the guilt of that in, I had enough on my plate to contend with at the time. It wasn't an overdose that killed him. He was an epileptic and swallowed his tongue during the seizure. Michelle wouldn't see me after that, on the strict instructions of her mother, who marched to the frontline afterwards to cuss out all the dealers for not doing something and blaming them for her son's heroin addiction. I miss Michelle, and now I look for her whenever I'm over there. Sometimes, I pass her house on purpose.

'So what do you charge?' I ask Denise.

'You want business?' she asks. Before giving it a thought, I say yeah, alright. Plus, it's my birthday, I tell her, thinking she might give me a freebie.

'It's £20 for straight, £15 for a blow, £10 for a hand job,› she replies, but now my insides are squirming. I've never been with a brass before. It feels so wrong, but I'm also curious.

'Let's do straight,' I decide. Denise is happy to go round the back of a block of flats at the top of Stamford Hill, but it would be too smelly and exposed for me. Instead, I offer to take her back to my bedroom in Alkham Road and turn the car around.

When we tiptoe upstairs and past Mum's room, it's well past midnight. Huggy is asleep, so I scoop him up and carry him down to Mini's room. Back upstairs, I stand excitedly beside the bed in front of Denise and reach to undress her. In the half-light I can see the ruby red of Denise's lips and I lean in to kiss her. A tingle spreads across my skin.

'Uh, uh! No kissing,' she says firmly. 'And money first.'

The rejection wounds me. She's as business-like as I am on the streets. I have £15 in my pocket, but no other notes to pay the remaining £5.

'Do you mind the rest in change?' I say, embarrassedly. She shrugs her shoulders. 'Money's money.' So I get my emergency glass bottle full of change that I throw 2ps and 1ps into, and tip that out onto the bed and start counting. She watches. When it takes forever, she helps me count the 2ps. Two, four, six, eight, ten...Two, four, six, eight, ten. Until we arrive at £5. Then I empty the deadweight of change into a poly bag along with the notes and pull back the covers as she slides off her skirt and her knickers. Her blouse is still on and I slip my hand underneath to cup her breasts which are velvety soft. I have an urge to brush my lips over her nipples.

'No tits. No kissing,' she says, peeling off my hands and pushing my face away. She reaches into her handbag and pulls out a condom which she struggles to roll onto me before letting me inside of her. I want to wrap myself in her, to feel the same warmth that I do from heroin, but every time my fingers and lips move towards her breasts, she slaps my hand.

'Let me know when you're finished,' she says, and when I look up, her face is turned away and I can hear her mouth smacking as she steadily chews her gum. Just like in the movies.

'I'm done,' I say after grinding into her for a while, but I haven't come and I don't want to go on. I don't know if it's the gear, or her, or the misshapenness of it all. It just feels too clinical, and void. Instead, I pull my trousers on and lead her back downstairs. 'Can you still give me a lift up the Hill?' she asks.

* * *

I'm withdrawing so badly now. I've seen the junkies clucking like this outside Maria's with their eyes watering and their mad panic, but I've never felt this before. I'm sick, and I stink. There's mornings I get dressed when I can smell myself. Then, I roll out of bed and zip up my tracksuit jacket right to the top, under my chin. And then I tuck my socks into my trousers to stop the smell from seeping out. I lie awake at night and shiver so badly that I never want to go downstairs to the toilet. Instead, I shit in newspapers and throw the parcels out the back window, into the gardens of the derelict houses.

Every fibre of my muscles ache, and the pain gnaws into the marrow of my bones. There's an alarm bell in my chest that comes in waves, like a stabbing. It's before sunrise. The sleeplessness is like a pneumatic drill in my brain. I lie in bed, fully clothed, teeth clenched, sweat pouring off me, yet I'm cold to the touch, so I pull the duvet up and hug it tight around my neck. There's nothing here: no gear. No coke. No spliff. And I haven't got any cash. More than anything, this sends my brain into overdrive. It lurches from thought to thought, panic to panic. I need something to stop this relentless ache that's ravaging me, shaking me and shooting at me.

'What's up, bruv?' Trevor says when he opens up the door.

'Sorry, man.' I apologise for hammering on his door so early, but he can see I'm in a bad way. All I know is I've run out of my own supply and I need to call in a favour. Maria's not long given birth to her baby, Matt, and I look after him sometimes if she ever has to score. I don't say anything, but I can't stand to watch him crawling around their living room floor surrounded by strangers, playing with needles and his nappy heavy. So I take him upstairs and Maria lets me babysit. His big round eyes look up at me and he reminds me of Huggy when he was a baby. For a brief moment, he lets me forget who I am.

'You got any gear?' I ask Trevor, and he goes to fetch Maria, but Maria doesn't have any powder left. She's already heated her last few bags on a spoon and soaked up the liquid in a cigarette filter, ready to draw it up into the syringe. There's nothing worse than a dirty hit, so this filters out the impurities.

'Stan, your clucking!' she says. 'That's what's wrong, you've got a habit! I knew you would, I warned you, didn't I?! It's ok, I'll give you a fix. It'll sort you out.' She is looking concerned, like she understands how I'm feeling and wants to take away the pain. I want anything to take away the pain, too. More than I want to admit. But I can't fix up. I can't. No way, man!

'Nah,' I say, shaking my head. I can't be the kid who sells gear to junkies in Maria's flat and be that junkie myself. It's a line I can't cross. I'm not a nasty, dirty, filthy-arsed junkie, I tell myself.

'Nah,' I repeat.

'Stan. You're clucking. You're in pain. You need to straighten yourself out...' My brain furiously skips between channels and before I know it, I've found a clear frequency. I'm holding out my arm.

'Don't tell anyone,' I beg Maria.

'Don't worry, Stan, your secret is safe with me,' she says and smiles.

'I mean it, Maria. Not anyone.'

I can't look as Maria wraps Trevor's belt around my upper arm, but my eyes follow her as she holds up the syringe, flicking it like a nurse. The gear is coffee-coloured and, as it's my first time, she squirts some back out onto the spoon. She wants to be careful, so I don't overdose.

'Fucking hell Stan!' she says. 'You've got massive veins. Trevor! Come and look at his veins.'

'Fucking Ada! Stevie Wonder could get a fix in them, mate,' he comments, as Maria's fingertips stroke my arm. They're big, visible, ready to receive. I turn away as the needle pricks my skin and only glance back when she draws up the barrel, filling it with an amount of my crimson blood. I'm scared, but more than that, I'm disgusted. When she loosens the tourniquet and slowly plunges the barrel in, the fix is instant. Boom! My face has no muscles. It's dropped, like Mum's. Saliva fills my mouth. I lift my hand to scratch the itches that vex every part of my body, but my arm is lead heavy and tips me forward, as a fire wraps itself around my veins. I'm overheating, flushing, sweat pours off me.

'You okay, Stan?' Maria's voice sounds far away.

'The pain's gone.' I don't know if I say this because my thoughts and words are scrambled. The pain's gone, but I'm not high. Instead, I feel crumpled, like rubbish, nodding out and sliding further down.

'Don't OD on me Stan,' I can hear Maria call again, her voice still faint.

'You've given him too much, Maria!' Now Trevor's shouting at her but I'm bent over, head almost touching my knees.

'Give him a snowball for fucks sake! he's overdosing!' Trevor's yelling at Maria, furiously.

'Stan! Stan! Maria's going to give you a snowball,' Trevor speaks to me, as if I'm a baby.

'Come on Maria! Move your arse!' he hurries her. They are both panicking now trying to bring me around, taking it in turns, slapping my face and talking to me while they prepare the concoction.

A snowball is a bit of gear mixed with cocaine which Maria prepares and injects into the same springy vein. Whooooosh! What the fuck? Now I'm wide awake, eyes popping, brain firing like a pinball machine. Now I'm high. Now, I'm moving. Now, this is fucking fantastic. Now I'm fucking loving it.

'Thank fuck for that!' Maria and Trevor keep repeating, staring at me as if I've just been resurrected.

'Don't tell anyone I banged up,' I remind her when I leave and head back to Mum's. She bats her eyes at me and smiles like there's something she knows that I don't.

***

Before I robbed to smoke gear and serve up junkies. Now I rob because I am a junkie. Skanker won't take my calls anymore. I called him over one night to serve me up but I didn't tell him I had no money. He saw the state I was in: washed out, stripped of everything. Most of all, he was pissed off I had nothing to pay him with.

Even Nicky calls me a skag head. I am a skag head. Whereas Maria sorted me out at first, now I inject myself. The first time I did it, I cried, but now doing it, it's become routine whenever I've run out of gear to smoke. I sit on the floor with the junkies downstairs at Maria's and gouch and dribble and talk shit just like them. I don't want the hit—I need the hit. I won't use today. Not now. Not ever again. Fuck it. Before I know it, against my will, I'm sitting back in the squat. When I don't have money to score, I collect the left-over filters lying in the spoons and syringe up the remaining gear. The hit is never as intense, but it's enough to straighten me out.

It's the shape of each day that gets to me the most. Injecting always means a better hit and using less gear than if I smoke it, but what used to get me high, now barely gets me up and functioning enough to score before evening. Steal, juggle, haggle, get money, find a phone box, call a dealer, wait, wait in alleyways at the bottom of shitty flats, wait for Maria who knows places to score, hold out a scrunched up £10 note, huddle up with the rest of the junkies, peeking out the squat window in anticipation every time a car pulls up, hoping that it's her returning with some gear A never-ending cycle. I cluck a lot of the time. And the only way to stop clucking is to find another hit. As soon as I have it, I feel normal again, whatever that means these days. I press pause for a few hours until the shivering starts again, then it's time to rewind and repeat. I'm tired and feel trapped. I've had enough of being a skag head, and enough of the street life, but I have no way out.

I'm clucking now, again. I'm sat on the edge of my bed. To take my mind off the pain, I smash my fists into my thighs to give myself a dead leg, then do the same on my arms and chest and lay back on the bed, feeling it subside for a brief moment. I'm imagining myself running. I imagine this when I lie awake for hours, which is often. I think about being back in Nottingham running cross-country, and all those times at school when I broke free from the pack and pushed out in front, outpacing everyone. Running to forget. Running from my past and into my future. Running like Kunta Kinte trying to find my way home. I felt at peace: just me and the power of my muscles flexing, and the rhythm of my breath. I know why Mum walks, and why she keeps going. The breeze and the trees and the pulse elevates her from her grinding routine—the illness that controls her. Like me, she finds that silent space where nothing matters.

I shuffle outside into the morning air still wearing the same clothes I've slept in. I am waging a war inside, fighting need. I need to score. I need to score badly, but inside, somewhere unreachable, I know I need to stop. I can't do this alone, though. What I really want is for someone to rescue me and pluck me from Alkham Road, tell me that they're gonna help me, that they're here to straighten me out. I promise to surrender to whoever steps up.

Like a wounded animal, I walk at a snail's pace to the junction of Cazenove Road and Stoke Newington High Street and cross the zebra crossing. Ahead, there's a three-storey Victorian house painted black that's been split into flats. I ring the doorbell of the ground-floor flat, and when there's no answer, with my back to the door, I use all my strength and hammer my heel against the side. The wood cracks first and then the lock gives way. I do it loudly, clumsily. I want to wake people. I want a car to stop, a stranger on their way to work to notice me. To see me. I want to get nicked.

Once inside, I work on autopilot. I unplug the TV and the video and pile them in the middle of the floor. Then, I collapse into the sofa. I'm sneezing and my nose won't stop running, which I continually wipe on my cuff. I'm burning up and my bones ache with numbness. I'm agitated, shifting around unable to get comfortable. Then I sit still and surrender to being here alone, just me and the rattle of withdrawal, and the quietness of the empty flat. But I want to be found and I'm ready to wait it out. I'll wait here for as long as it takes before the anguish becomes unbearable. I sit. I listen. I wait.

The front door is still wide open, flapping on its hinges, and the traffic on the main road outside is speeding north and south. Someone will be here soon. Someone must have seen me, done their civic duty and reported the Black guy with the ripped-up clothes and the sunken face breaking into a house. In the distance I hear sirens. Finally, I can have some peace again.

Chapter 29

Skag Head

On the day after I broke into the flat, I appeared at Highbury Corner Magistrates' Court charged with burglary. No one did find me on the sofa. The sirens I heard whizzed straight pass the house on another call. In the end, I walked home in broad daylight cupping the TV and video in my arms which I stashed in my bedroom. Two uniformed police officers arrived at the moment I was heading out to get a cab to offload the goods. Apparently, a cyclist had seen me and followed me home into Alkham Road and when I confessed everything, the officers looked at me as if they couldn't believe their luck. Bail wasn't even considered. Instead, Mum would be notified that I was being sent to Feltham Young Offenders Prison to wait on remand until my case was heard. I was sent to Osprey Wing. I never knew whether it was a sick joke on behalf of the authorities, but all the wings at Feltham were named after birds. We were all doing bird, but our wings had already been clipped.

By the time I reached Feltham, I couldn't stop shaking. Two days without gear opened up a chasm in my soul that needed to be filled. I was 16 years old, ill-equipped to face anything, but most of all, unable to deal with the guilt of leaving Mini and Huggy with Mum for a second time. Heroin had become the stitch that held me together yet tore me apart. If a single thread got pulled, my whole being could unravel.

'Oi, wake up, I need to throw a line.' It was all I could hear other boys shouting as I sat in my cell off the main prison gallery, eight by six feet with a toilet, bunk, desk, wooden chair and one tiny window. As I listened closer, I heard a familiar voice. And when I climbed on my chair and called out under the open window, it was like I'd struck gold.

'Ron, is that you?' I recognised Ronnie's voice instantly, but I had no idea he was banged up. We'd lost touch for months.

'Who's that?'

'It's me, man. Stanley!'

'Fucking 'ell. Stan?'

'Ron, you got anything?'

Ronnie said he'd throw me a line later, and that thought kept me going all day. A line was made from unpicking the thread on the green prison issue blanket. As soon as there was enough thread to make a ball, you could attach a weight on the end: a piece of soap, or a pen. Once this got thrown out the window, a neighbour threw his line over it and they would entwine, then gear was tied onto one end before it got reeled back in.

Later that evening after dinner, Ronnie kept good on his promise and threw me a line that had a foil parcel with a small blob of gear on it. Not enough to straighten me out, but enough to take the edge off my shivering. Using a biro pen with its ink chamber removed and a borrowed lighter, I chased the bead around like it was my last ever hit. For the rest of the night, Ronnie and I talked through the prison telephone system: our toilet bowls.

'Just keep plunging with the toilet brush until the water disappears,' he instructed me. If the guy in the cell in between us did the same, then our voices could travel. I used the prison soap to clean around the rim first, so the stench of stale piss didn't hit my nostrils when I leaned in.

'Oi! Next door? Empty your bowl, man, I need to have a

convo with my mate,' I shouted to my neighbour when I heard the toilet flush in the night. For hours, Ronnie and I caught up on who was doing bird for what; who'd got shot, stabbed or 'nutted off' in the prison hospital wing nicknamed 'Fraggle Rock', and who was faking losing their mind to get a lesser sentence. There was one famous case talked about amongst the inmates, where a guy went to court pleading insanity after putting his hand down the back of his trousers and pulling out a big glob of brown gooey stuff and licking his hands and fingers clean in front of the judge. It turned out to be peanut butter, but he got his time reduced and worked the system.

By morning, I was rattling so badly I needed out of my cell. It was as if the four walls had collapsed in on me. Sleeplessness and nausea gripped me. After some hesitation, I pressed the red emergency button and called for a screw.

'I need to move around,' I said. The last thing I wanted was to end up on Fraggle Rock, so I said nothing about my withdrawal. Yet what I was about to do broke all prisoner codes: never ask the screws for favours. 'Fuck it,' I thought. Heroin took my dignity months ago.

'I'll do anything to get out of here,' I told the screw who was eye-balling me through the toughened glass.

'*Anything?*' he asked.

When I eventually got led out, I was handed a big broom and a cloth and a bucket and was shown the outside prison yard flanked on all sides by cell windows, like a gladiator's arena, a vast empty rectangle.

'Sweep it, and when you're done, you can come back in and clean the tiles on the security box,' he said. My muscles ached like hell as I shuffled around, but with each flex came a nanosecond of relief, and the air a respite from the claustrophobia of being banged up. Focusing on the task became a diversion from the mental craving gnawing at my brain—the worst of all agonies. I kept my head down and swept, even when an orchestra of inmates threw out a symphony of disappointment from their windows.

'Oi, put the fucking broom down, you muppet! Don't let them do that to ya!' I couldn't admit that it was me who'd asked the screws. I felt shamed, as though I was sweeping the arena for the *real* gladiators to enter when everyone later filed out to the exercise yard.

'Want a job?' said the screw, interrupting my detox therapy. I did and I didn't. My worse job at Hollesley Bay was cleaning the toilets and my toothbrush marathon on the M1. Could anything be as bad?

'What's the job?' I asked.

'It's yes or no,' he replied.

Quickly, I weighed my options. If I had to, I could defend myself against anyone who gave me any beef for sucking up to the screws. And a job would get me out of my cell…

'Yeah,' I confirmed.

'Okay, you're on Servery, pack your kit' he announced. The Servery? What the fuck, I'd come up smelling of roses.

That afternoon, I was moved into a dorm of four beds, spacious and super clean. A roommate, Asif, was sent to show me the ropes, looking bright like a beacon: white chef's hat, white overalls, and a sparkling white smile.

'Best job in here, mate,' he said, and he was right. Even the other inmates who'd catcalled me from their windows later congratulated me on what they saw in their eyes as a stunt I'd pulled to my advantage. Now they could put in their orders. One perk of working on the Servery was that, unlike the other boys getting banged up at 6 PM, we only got locked in after our bang-up at 8 PM. The rest of the time we were free to walk around. In the narrow window between 7 PM and 8 PM, when many of the screws went off-duty and all the cells were locked for the night, we transformed from chefs to post men. Leftover food got taken back to our dormitory, but it was our job to collect the trays from each cell door. By special request, we moved drugs from neighbour to neighbour at the same time, for a slice of the pie of course, and we never knew when that favour was going to come in handy.

Although my time at Feltham was short, I felt closer to my roommates than I'd ever done at Hollesley Bay. On my first night one ex-army guy, John, told me he was in for helping a mate dispose of a body after a fight. It made my burglary seem small-fry, so I exchanged my most mortifying confession: I was a junkie, withdrawing from heroin.

'If I get up in the night and move around a lot, I'm sorry,' I apologised. At that, the room laughed. Then, John lifted up the frame of his bed, undid the cap at the base of one foot and shook out a tiny parcel.

'Gear?' I asked. I wanted so badly for him to say yes. Instead, the room erupted again while Asif brought out a chopping board stolen from the Servery. Around five-or-so pills got crushed in folded white paper before being finely chopped with a razor blade on the board.

'Charlie?' I asked again.

'Nah, sleeping pills,' they said. Now positioned into eight neat lines of powder. When they offered me the first line, I hung back. Did I trust them? Sleeping pills were new territory for me, but I was desperate. I bent over and snorted. Whooaa! It was like snorting bleach. The burn was endless. Eyes watering, brain flipping. I was jumping around on fire trying to put out the flames, and then I manned up for the other nostril and watched the other guys do the same dance of fire after they did their lines, all of us pissing ourselves with laughter at each other's reaction. Yet, when I eventually lay down on my bunk I was out for the count. By the time

I got shaken awake, I was still dressed, I'd been asleep for 12 solid hours, straight, and couldn't remember a thing. For the next four nights, this was a part of my detox.

After three months on remand, I was sentenced for burglary. Also rolled into my sentence was a robbery and two more counts of burglary after police matched my footprints to other drums I had done. I was handed an 18-month sentence to be served at Warren Hill Young Offenders Prison. Having already served 3 months, I had 15 remaining. On good behaviour, I could be out on parole in seven.

Being a stone's throw away from Hollesley Bay, the journey to Warren Hill was as familiar as the Suffolk countryside surrounding it. The prison itself was larger, with landings and railings overlooking a large atrium, like something out of the TV sitcom *Porridge*, but the real difference was me. I never wanted to be a junkie. No junkie ever does. But at home, I never had space to break the cycle. Recovery needs space: space to think, space to understand yourself, space to heal and space to flourish. At Warren Hill, I was determined to carve out a space, however small.

Chapter 30

VO: Visiting Order

The emergency siren is sounding. It's piercing every corner of the prison. It won't be long before boots hit the corridors and the guards swarm in and peel me off. The guy had it coming. Calls himself Sergeant, and I know why. He's a 'Sergeant' because he acts tough. But a real soldier can endure, achieve, overcome defeat and still keep going. This guy to me is a weak-arsed motherfucker, yet another brother fallen victim to the system of Black-on-Black violence, no matter how much love I tried to put his way.

I don't know why Sergeant has chosen to have beef with me. It's like that in here. All it takes is one look and you're marked. Besides, I'm from East London, he's from South. It was never going to be love at first sight. It's been building for months: stare-outs in the canteen, lip curled up at me in the gym, snide comments under his breath. But now I have a reason. Sergeant's going to help me and he doesn't even know it. There's method to my madness when I attack him in the gym changing rooms.

Months from now I'll be released from Warren Hill, but I have no intention of leaving. Not yet. Not until I'm done. I've worked hard at this, and I can't go back. I can't go back to Alkham Road, to the surreal environment where I barely exist, walking on eggshells around Mum, feeling the weight of her schizophrenia and negotiating the chaos of our lives. I can't go back to the street that will suck me in and spit me out like phlegm on a pavement or leave me for dead. I can't go back to heroin which will twist me up like a Rubik's Cube, or to Maria's squat to wade through the bodies moaning and slipping down the walls.

Here, I've created a tiny window of space. There's a few guys from the streets who I recognise and one or two that I know from detention centre. Des's younger brother Neil is here too, but he's on another vibe so I let him be. I need to sort myself out and put my head down, so I stay away from the riff-raff. Richard's helped me. I met him not long after I arrived. He's the gym orderly and lives in that place. Of all the brothers here, I gravitated towards him. Richard's thickset with a puffed-out chest and biceps ripped like a pit bull, but he's soft spoken and thoughtful and keeps himself to himself. We have conversations about life and spirituality. He brings out all the parts of me that I've buried deep behind my anger and the walls I've built and the numbness of drugs. I'm nine-and-a-half again, sat with Rasta Mark above the health food shop, or cross-legged with Simeon on Hackney Downs, alive to the world. I refuse to wear a watch in here. Counting down the minutes and the hours has no appeal for me and makes no sense, especially when an inmate ask what time it is like he's got somewhere to go. Why would I want to know the time when I'm banged up doing time? All I want to do is lose myself in this time machine and forget about it.

Richard's nearly halfway through a ten-year stretch for shooting a brother. He's been here since the age of 14 and when he turns 18, which isn't far off, he'll graduate to adult prison. At Warren Hill, even though he works as the gym orderly, he mainly spends his time in the education wing, the room above the visiting hall with its tables and chairs and easels and a small library of donated books. We don't talk, we discuss. We don't want to be slaves to the system, we say. The system has trapped us and has been designed for us to fail. We're not victims. We can shape our own destinies. We can be who we want to be. Discuss.

Richard has dreadlocks but he's not a Rastafarian, though he's interested in Rastafari and Black power, which I teach him. And I'm interested that he studies. He's completing his O levels, and he says that learning is the key to him living a better life. At first, I didn't believe him. Learning's too much like school. Besides, I'm unteachable. Why would I be teachable here? But with his encouragement, I've thrown myself into it. And I'm enjoying it. It's like I had all this bursting inside of me and I didn't know it, no way to express it.

In books I've found a whole new world over the prison walls that I can escape to at night. I have three or four on the go in my cell at any one time: the former slave and American abolitionist Frederick Douglass; the works of 19th-century sociologist and civil rights campaigner W.E.B. Du Bois; and trashy page-turners by Harold Robbins, packed with sex and intrigue, just to balance things out. I've taken a course in computer studies and English, and I've chosen Black history as the subject for my O level Art thesis. All my drawings are based around the books I'm reading. I've sketched African stone heads found in South America before Columbus, and the faces of Arawak Indians—Jamaica's first inhabitants. My teacher, Mr Owen, is my greatest champion. 'You have so much potential, Stanley,' he says. I don't know if I believe him.

Poetry is my new weapon. I've won first prize in a competition for the prisoner's poetry book *Inside Writes* with a poem called 'King Henry vs You',and my design was used for the front cover. King Henry being slang for heroin. We slug it out over 12 gruelling rounds in a boxing ring. King Henry draws me in like a love affair when I'm fit and energised before it pins me against the ropes. I jab left then right before I gather all my mental and physical strength to knock it clean out for the count. I haven't used gear once since the last time in Feltham, when Ronnie threw me that line with the parcel.

It's why I can't leave, even though I'm almost free. It's why Sergeant's going to help me. When I sat in front of the governors at my review, they smiled at me. 'You're doing really well inmate Browne,' they assured me. 'If you keep this up, you'll be out on your EDR—earliest date of release.' I smiled back. But behind it, I was slowly boiling up inside. However much they try, they'll never understand me, just like Alan Mackie. I've passed all my exams other than O level Art. I need to pass it. I want to pass it. I need to stay to finish what I started. There is no way I can complete this outside. No way.

After the panel, I took Mr Wilson aside. He's a Geordie screw who works on my unit, with a thin black moustache, an ex-marine, tough as boots, who looks like Blakey, an old-time character from the hit TV show *On the Buses*. Of all the screws, he's probably the one I have an understanding with the most.

'I need to see out my sentence,' I told him. 'I need to pass my O level.' He stood in the door of my cell, shock breaking across his face.

'Do you mind, son?' he said, moving into my cell and perching on the edge of my bed, glancing at me like I was his real son—the first time I've seen him looking vulnerable. He removed his hat and twiddled it around in his hands as if he had some bad news to tell me and finding the right words.

'Son, you don't have to stay here, man. You can finish your studies on the outside. Life's out there, man, not behind these bloody walls. Not here man!' He said this while tutting and shaking his head, trying his best to make sense of my nonsense. I could see I had put him on the spot and he was in a right conundrum as much as he was trying to help, I realised he didn't get it, and never would. As he launched into a monologue, his words faded into the background. I knew he couldn't really understand, and I was on my own again.

'Ok, thanks for the chat,' I mumbled. How could I begin to explain what 'out there' is for me?

It's why I've got Sergeant pinned up against the shower room wall. All my weight is against him with my fingers and thumb of one hand pushing into his eyeballs, the other around his throat. I'm squeezing his neck hard, then muzzling him while he spits and thrashes like a rabid dog. I'm wired like lightning. All my rage is spewing out over him: my rage and my fear and my loneliness.

I wrote to my dad a couple of months ago. I thought about what he'd said about taking me to America, and how I wanted to go. I told him how sorry I was that I couldn't stay out of trouble, but that I was studying hard and how he would be proud to see what I have achieved with my time. Then, I waited for weeks. Eventually, when his reply got delivered to my cell, I recognised the handwriting immediately, slanted and curly. In here, a letter is as good as a visit—a reminder that someone cares. And I always read a letter slowly. I never wanted it to end. Or I re-read it over and over, squeezing out every last drop from it, like the sweetest fruit. Anthony's letter was handwritten on a single piece of paper: short and to the point.

> *Dear Stanley,*
>
> *Please do not contact me anymore. I need to get on with my life. I will not be living in England anymore and when you get out I will be living in the States. You bring shame on me. You are not my son. Do not contact me again. Leave me alone to get on with my life.*
>
> *Anthony.*

That afternoon I sat on my bed with hot, silent tears pouring down my cheeks. Then, I destroyed and smashed up all of my belongings in my cell: my books, the ornaments I'd made out of matchsticks, my paints and my drawings on the wall. As I did, I let out a deep, primal scream. It rose from the pit of my stomach, like an exorcism. And when the adrenaline stopped pulsing, I took a paper and pen and wrote down my rage in a letter back to him. Then, I trained harder, studied harder, and ran faster than I've ever done before. He'll have received it by now, but I'll never know, until 14 years later.

Anthony!

Don't ever let me bump into you on the streets! If I ever see you again, I will stab you up! My mum is schizophrenic, mentally ill, yet she sends me soap, toothpaste, a flannel, shampoo and food! You are supposed to be the sane person in my life! You're a weak man Anthony! One day you will get what you deserve! Don't ever let me bump into you man!

Yes, you better go to America! You better run!

Stanley

I didn't lie. Mum did send me a package. Opening it was like Christmas. She's sick, but she remembered me. But my own so called father abandoned me in my time of need. At Warren Hill, I've wanted my family to visit. I've missed them, but most of all I want Mum to know how well I'm doing, even though I know she's too sick to really understand what I've been going through. Instead, I posted visiting orders, to Mini who wrote back to tell me she and Angie were coming. That wasn't long after my 17th birthday when they sent me a card and a Tracy Chapman cassette.

I love listening to Tracy, and am inspired by her to buy a guitar when I get out and write my own songs. I put on my headphones, press play on my Walkman and take her for a run with me, in my cell. I change into my gym shorts and vest and jog on the spot, looking at my reflection in the gloss painted door until I am dripping with sweat. I can go for hours and do some serious miles around the streets of Hackney in my head. In here, you don't tell anyone it's your birthday. Instead, you protect your heart from the pain of not being home.

On the day of their visit, I dressed up in my Sunday best. I put on my shirt, tie and prison jean jacket, and my smart trousers and shoes. These clothes are mainly for church and to wear on visits. Sometimes I go just to break up the routine and have a catch-up with guys who are on different wings. I waited in my cell for my name to be called, but it never was. I waited all afternoon, watching other inmates through my window being marched up the path towards the hall for their visits. I felt gutted. Broken. Nothing worse than getting all dressed up and the other inmates knowing you are expecting a visit, and the shame of it not happening. Some guys lose it when this happens and you can hear the screams of rage and frustration, and their cell being smashed into little pieces. Most of the time the screws leave them to it until they have calmed down and got it out of their system. It's like an unspoken empathy when a man doesn't get his visit.

Apparently, they missed the first train and had to get the next one. Then, by the time they'd travelled the three hours here, they were too late. A second time, Mini couldn't find the visiting order. 'No VO. No visit'. I'm being punished for having a family that can barely function. A crime we didn't commit. Sometimes it's hard not to, but I really can't blame them. I know they have had their own fair share of trauma in their lives too, and I try not to put any unnecessary pressure on them. I try to protect them, still trying to be the man of the house. I've stop sending VOs. I can't face the disappointment. It cuts too deep to the bone. And I do my sentence without seeing anyone from the outside.

In the changing room, I'm on top of Sergeant who I've slammed against the wooden bench and he's slithering on his back in an attempt to get away from me. His eyes are bulging out of their sockets, fighting for breath. With one hand locked around his throat, I use the other to reach for anything to use as a weapon. A soap dish slammed into his face; a shampoo bottle smashed against his head until I draw blood. My head is bleeding, too. Unbeknownst to me, Sergeant's got a metal spanner from the weights in the gym and he was stabbing it into the back of my scalp when I had him braced to the wall, but I'm so fired up I can't feel any pain.

The guards are here now, bending my wrists into a lock-hold and lifting me off my feet, carrying me in this position all the way down to the block, solitary confinement, just like my first night in Hollensey Bay. The pain is excruciating. There are no words to describe the torture of being lifted by your writs. And Sergeant's in the cell next door like a volcano, mouthing off, spewing out what he's going to do to me. I'm silent. Resolute. With a half-smile on my face. I know my O level is in the bag now. In nine months' time, after my release, I'll call Mr Owen to check what score I got. 'Stanley!' he'll say. 'You got 98%! Do you know how good that is?' Then he'll tell me that my paintings were included in the prison's annual art exhibition and that I had an offer on two of them. But I'm not selling. I poured my soul into them. Too much blood, sweat and tears for any amount of money.

Chapter 31

The Oscars

Before she knew I was there, I watched Mum in the kitchen of Alkham Road, moving and talking to herself. Her head was wrapped in a scarf and she wore a long black cloak which skimmed the floor. Most shocking were her fingers, knotted up in string, like macramé gloves.

'Mum?' I called, but for the first time, this didn't feel like my home.

'Hey Mum?' I repeated, unsure she would even recognise me. It had been almost two years. On my release from Warren Hill, my dreadlocks had grown long just above my shoulders and I looked fit and healthy and my skin was glowing from the Ital diet I ate banged up; no dairy, no meat, no chicken, no fish, no salt and no sugar. I looked as if I'd been away on holiday in the Caribbean—a far cry from the ruin who had left the house flanked by two police officers.

'Oh! You're home. Good for you!' Mum looked up. In my absence, she'd re-hung the beads in the kitchen doorway, and they rattled again as she pushed past me and into her room. I felt heavy-hearted.

Before leaving Warren Hill, I thought about what I'd come home to. It made me anxious. As Angie had moved back to Mum's temporarily to help out with Huggy, I asked if I could stay at her place as a stop-gap. Angie's council flat in London Fields had been given to her when she turned 18 and could leave the independent

250

unit at Forest Road Children's Home. Besides, Mum's and the surrounding streets haunted me. Too many memories lingered.

Downstairs, Maria's squat was boarded up with corrugated iron and an imposing green, metal door replaced the old one and it was bolted to the frame. They had been evicted by the council. And many of my crew were in prison, including Nicky and Ronnie. I took it as a sign that it was the perfect time to continue going straight. I needed to earn money, legit. I needed a job, as I did almost ten years earlier when I went from shop to shop on Stoke Newington High Street. The health food shop was now a Turkish bazaar; Minerva's Greek shop transformed into an Indian news-agent; Woolworths still stood proud with its rotunda of candy pic 'n' mix. And just like then, there were no vacancies anywhere. Only luck saved me again. For some reason, I always seem to land on my feet. Must be Uncle Bob Marley still watching over me, I thought. When I got to Angie's place, she'd left a note saying a guy called Carlton from Nottingham had been searching for me at Mum's while I'd been inside. He'd left a number. *Carlton?*

'I'm in London!' Carlton talked giddily when he heard my voice on the other end of the line.

'How you find me, bro?' I'd forgotten, but apparently, I'd written down Mum's address during one of our late-night chats, when I longed to be home.

'London was always on your mind, bro, so I knew you'd go back one day,' he said, before cussing me out for not saying goodbye. Carlton was staying with his uncle who ran a bakery in Walthamstow, north of Stoke Newington. When we met the next day he arrived in the bakery van, with a massive spliff hanging from his lips and reggae music pumping from the driver's cabin.

'Your sis said you were doing some serious porridge, man!' he laughed before we hugged tightly. Carlton was now 21 but still as skinny, the only difference there was hair on his upper lip and chin.

'You disappeared Stan!'

'Story of my life,' I smiled. Man, it was good to see him.

'What you gonna do with yourself now?'

'I want out, bro,' I said, as Carlton slapped my prison chest and handed me the spliff. 'I need a job.'

'Come work for my uncle. He's a mean son of a bitch, but I can get you in. What you say?' I didn't need to be asked twice.

The bakery was a 4 AM start. Carlton picked me up in the van every morning, and when our shift began, we bobbed and weaved through the obstacle course of Carlton's uncle's abuse: 'What you doing?' 'Yu stupid?' 'Yu Deaf?' 'Yu dummy?' According to Carlton, he was a harmless Jesus-loving, short and grumpy old man. I wasn't sure how long I'd last. I was fresh from prison, and on edge from the chaos of being locked up. The only saving grace was the work itself. Folding in the flour and water and yeast and kneading the bread with my fist was therapy. It was a skill in itself to prevent my eyebrows from singeing as I loaded the loaves on a large spatula and into the oven, cavernous like a cremation furnace. Jamaican hard-dough bread, buns and bulla cake, my favourite, made with molasses and spiced with ginger and nutmeg. And when they were baked and bagged, Carlton and I made deliveries in the van, as small as a Mini with a box seat up front. By 2 PM we were done. I lasted two weeks.

One morning when Carlton was out on a delivery, his uncle cussed me out so badly it lit the touch-paper. Without skipping a beat, I smashed my mixing bowl and whatever else was on the table to the floor and put my face in his face.

'I WILL BREAK YOU INTO FUCKING PIECES! Don't you EVER speak to me like that again!' I yelled, with my fist clenched pointing at his head while he cowered, looking up at me. 'WHO THE FUCK DO YOU THINK YOU ARE!? You don't know me! You better thank fucking Jesus you're Carlton's uncle, old man, otherwise I would teach you a fucking lesson you will never forget!'

After I threw down my apron and left, I leaned against the bakery wall and waited for Carlton to drive me home. Carlton said his uncle was still shaking when he went inside, but that he apologised and said he was wrong for pushing me so far, but he still wanted me to work there. I kissed my teeth and said I couldn't have a man talk to me like that, and it was only because he was Carlton's flesh and blood that I didn't bruck him up.

'Well, even though he's my uncle, I can't say he didn't have it coming, next time he will think twice,' said Carlton, before breaking into hysterics. 'Man, you should see the look on his face! What yu do to him? I'm sure you mek di man wet-up himself! Lawd jeezus, Stanley, yu still noh easy, yu haven't changed one bit, still ah Tuff Gong.'

Not long after that, I landed a job on a building site but that didn't last either. 'Fuck this, man, I'm done,' I said, bumping fists with an African brother from the Congo before walking out. One of the jobs was chipping away at the sand and cement on a wall with a chisel and hammer so the bricks could be repointed. The job seemed insurmountable given the size of the wall and the tiny tool in my hand. Besides, my pay packet was a pittance compared to what I could earn on the streets. But I had to stay focused and not give in to temptation.

Next up was a job at Pizza Hut on Walthamstow Market which I got on the back of my bakery experience. There, I witnessed the manager harass staff, spitting out the same bullying torrent as Carlton's uncle. One night after he bawled me out in front of a packed restaurant, I slammed down two unbaked pizzas and pinned him against the cash register. *What do you know of my life?* I wanted to scream. He had no clue how hard it was for me to go straight, to stay away from drugs, crime, to stay away from everything I knew. But it was the abuse of power that vexed me the most. In the straight world, managers talked to workers like shit. If you're treated like shit, you become shit. Then, you rise through the ranks and become that same piece of shit. In the street world, there's no way you could talk to a man like that, you would have a knife in you before you could blink. At Warren Hill, I had a tiny taste of encouragement, and I wanted to keep going and not cave in. I was already skating on thin ice with my anger.

Soon after I quit my job at Pizza Hut, Angie wanted her flat back which forced me to return to Alkham Road. My room there tormented me. The damp seeped into me and there were still stains on the carpet where I'd vomited heroin sick. Then, there was Mum. Her violence towards us had receded over the years, but the world inside her head had given birth to new, more fantastical worlds. Her living creations multiplied; scribblings covered every wall; paintings were strewn everywhere. We found her outside, walking without shoes. At times, I wondered if she knew who we were.

I hustled for a short while selling black and white posters for a £1 on the streets, at underground tube stations, and outside Ridley Road Market, after I met a mixed-race brother from Liverpool doing the same and asked him to show me the ropes. It was decent money while it lasted, until the police confiscated all your stock which was money down the drain. Like the game of Snakes and Ladders, I had to keep starting over until I received a warning that next time, I would face court and be prosecuted. While I searched for work, I contacted Hackney Council again to see if more repairs could be done on Mum's house, the place was still falling apart. My brief holiday in Angie's clean, heated, Georgian flat made me recalibrate. Mum can't live like this anymore, neither can Mini or Huggy, who would be starting secondary school in a couple years. And I was defiantly fed up with the dilapidation and dealing with the council. Surprisingly, the council said it wouldn't schedule any further repairs: they needed to completely refurbish the house and remove the asbestos in it. Instead, they offered to rehouse Mum. Straight away I jumped at this opportunity to hustle the council and get a flat for myself. After much negotiation and putting lots of pressure on them, they said a three-bedroom property could be made available. Huggy and Mini could have their own rooms and the council would also consider giving me a one-bedroom flat, after I threatened we would refuse to move out unless Mum was offered 'like for like' and rehoused in another Victorian property, which was the council's policy. For the first time since my release, I dared to dream.

As fate would have it, round the back of Angie's flat I noticed new council housing being built: modern, red-brick palaces that were almost complete. One afternoon I wandered over and introduced myself to the site manager. I told him about the state of Alkham Road and mum's illness and how she wheezed because of the asbestos in the building's fabric, and how the council had offered her a new place, none of which had been finalised yet.

'Do you want to have a look at a three-bed here?' the short Indian man said, peering over his small, round Gandhi glasses. He showed me number 75. It wasn't grand like Alkham Road, but new, like a hotel. Double glazing; central heating; a toilet that actually flushed; a ceiling with no leaks. As I ran my hand across the kitchen worktop, I got ahead of myself.

'When can my mum move in?' I asked. He didn't dismiss me outright. Instead, he promised to call the council office to see what could be done. He must have sensed my desperation when I handed him the number of my contact there scrawled on a piece of paper. If it worked out, Mum would have papers to sign, he explained. I didn't show it, but my heart plummeted. Mum wasn't in a fit state of mind to sign anything.

I needed a plan. If there was one thing life taught me, it was how to act. Now it was Mini's turn. If and when it came time to sign, I didn't want any officialdom poking its nose in. She would have to pretend to be Mum.

'You're crazy, Stan,' Mini said when I put the idea to her, but all I could see was this moment being snatched from us, like everything else. 'Opportunities like this don't happen,' I told her. When I called the manager days later, he confirmed that Mum could move into number 75 and be rehoused in two weeks after she signed the paperwork.

For that performance, Mini should have won an Oscar.

'Mrs Brown? Would you like me to show you around?' The site manager couldn't have been more pleased to welcome us in with Mini disguised as Mum. Thick stockings and several over-coats hid her youthful frame. Scarves covered her head, and glasses perched on her nose. She had a walking stick, and shuffled slowly with her head bowed.

'Come on Mum, one step at a time.' I linked arms with her as we made our way upstairs. I explained that Mum's fragility meant she found strangers overwhelming.

'I'll leave you alone to look over the house,' he said kindly, and when we finally sat down with the papers, Mini feigned deafness and talked Mum's thick patois while I translated. It was only when she held the pen that I realised her hands were obviously a girl's. I should have given her gloves. I quickly started talking to the manger to distract him, asking him a barrage of questions about this, that, and the other, maintaining eye contact. If the manager did notice, he didn't ever say.

Mum, Mini and Huggy and I moved in the following week and Mum cussed us out forever for uprooting her from Alkham Road. We didn't care. Although it felt weird leaving the place I'd always called home, this felt like the home we'd been waiting for all our lives: a new beginning.

A month later, I was offered a one-bedroom Victorian flat on Middleton Road, a sought-after tree-lined residential street a five minutes' walk from Angie's flat and Mum's new place. It's small, and the homely kitchen was perfect. The bedroom looked out onto a massive, shared garden. When I was shown around I couldn't stop smiling. I'd feigned agoraphobia and came up with a doctor's letter to avoid being put in a tower block of flats. Having burgled a couple of houses on that road, I never thought I'd actually be living on it. In the upstairs flat, John, a chef, and his wife Victoria, a teacher, lived with their two children. It felt like a safe haven. A chance to reinvent myself.

Not long after I moved in, I got a job working for London Underground as a ticket collector. I can tell you how to get from any station, anywhere on the underground, and where to change trains. At Warren Street Station, Mr Barnsey became my manager. A Barbadian by birth, he worked his way up through the ranks. Now a proud warrior patrolling the Victoria Line, he held his braces out over his cascading belly whenever he delivered his fatherly sermons.

'Been here 42 years. Started off like you, bwoy. In fact, in dem days you had to clean the tiles of the platform. Look at me now, eh? Manager!'

Maybe Mr Barnsey meant well, but his tone was condescending. 'You have to play smart, Browneeee. Cut your hair, be clean shaven.' And four teeth were missing at the front, and only two teeth were left on his bottom row, which fitted neatly into the gap when he closed his mouth. Like a fish mouthing words, he spoke with a lisp, the air escaping through the gaps whenever he talked. From the start, I had him marked as an Uncle Tom—happily working for the white man, happy to be fed the scraps thrown to him. The sort that would cuss out his superiors behind their backs then straighten up quick-smart if they ever turned up for inspection: 'Yes sir, no sir, three bags full, sir.' Hardly a day went by when he didn't pull me up for something. As much as I tried, I couldn't fit into his system. But I couldn't go back to the life I'd known, littered with its never-ending human debris.

While I'd been in prison, the roll call of friends lost to the streets got longer and longer. Skanker died after an asthma attack, smoking gear. Ambulance crews tried to revive him, but he was gone at the scene. Ronnie's brother Keith had a heart attack while smoking a crack pipe—a mother left without a second son. Des overdosed and died, locked behind a toilet door, and his younger brother, Neil, got shot in the head during a drive-by at a traffic light on Murder Mile, in Clapton. And Jamie's decomposed body was found in his flat weeks after his death. He had survived being: shot, stabbed, beaten with baseball bats, and even run over, like a cat with nine lives. But this time his luck ran out, dying of suspicious circumstances and found curled up on his living-room chair. Apparently, he had allowed junkies to use his place to smoke and fix gear. They continued to stay at his flat and spent the money left in his account while he rotted.

They all fell, one by one. Some were doing life sentences for murder, some were nutted off and had lost their minds, while others became hardcore junkies on the streets. The list is far too long to name them all, but I can never forget who they were. I am constantly reminded that it could have been me, especially when I see someone who I think is someone else that has fallen victim to the system, buried, because of circumstance. The reality of these facts humbles me. I pay homage and show my respect through rememberance. I'm not going back to that, I promised myself, but the hinterland between my old world and my new life became impossible to navigate.

Chapter 32

"If Your Name's Not Down, You're Not Coming In."

The warehouse is filled with smoke curling and twisting through strobe lights. Ultraviolet glows lantern-like off corrugated walls and basement bricks. This vast space is filled with hundreds of bodies, wide-eyed and hazy, raising up their arms, finding salvation in the throb of the deep bass. The music is pulling me now, and I weave my way further in. In the distance the DJ hunches over spinning turntables, bringing the crowd to a state of ecstasy, keeping it there, longer... longer... longer still, before taking them down through a journey of sound.

On the makeshift dance floor, hair swings out from under bucket hats and bandanas and luminous T-shirts glow pink and orange. Shapeless figures in baggy shirts move like a pulsating jigsaw and trainers beat out a rhythm on the concrete floor. Mixed in with the smell of weed is the smell of sweat and excitement, and I take my place in the centre of this crowd, joined together as one large family, my new tribe.

The beat thumps out and the tune rises up before the drum 'n' bass beat lands. I'm jumping now. I close my eyes, feeling the beat vibrate through me. My movements are endless, hypnotic. I'm on one foot now, arms outstretched. I look up. A crowd is around me, smiling and floating their arms up. My body rises and drops as I move from foot to foot.

It's 1990 and I am 20 years old. On weekends I move from rave to rave, Friday through to Monday morning. Our cars snake out to industrial estates on the edge of the M25 to the Telepathy rave, or through lanes leading to open fields in the Kent countryside. I move with a new crew: Decker, Ricky. K, Mark, Demon, Jason, Leroy and his brother Terry, all of whom I know through Don. He and I got chatting on Ridley Road Market while I was juggling posters. He's tall, mixed-raced, with a goatee and wide-open eyes. Me and Don bonded straight away, with him also coming from a broken home and not growing up with his father. Don likes to drink too much and would lose himself and sometimes pick fights when we were out, so I or one of the crew would have to pull him away to calm him down.

This crew are weekenders—the happy hardcore, not the hard-core criminals I am used to hanging out with, but they also know how to look after themselves if shit went down. And Don knows DJ Reggie—a brother who started out DJing at the East London sound systems. We hang out in DJ Reggie's bedroom, at his mum's house three streets from me on Richmond Road, and drink beer, smoke weed and play cards, blackjack, the London way. Then he spins decks, mixes tracks, cutting and fading. So many of us fight for a place on his bed that his mum rations who's in and who's out, like security. And we head en masse to Buzby's, The Astoria, The Breakfast Club—all the venues we know will welcome us, because we know DJ Reggie and bowl in on his guest list. 'If your name's not down, you're not coming in', is the bouncers' motto. But we're special. During the week we hold down nine-to-five jobs but at weekends we dance. We dance till we drop, bathed in love and good vibes and washed down with champagne and bottled water.

I manage my job at London Underground, but I'm bored out of my brains. Same thing day in day out: smile, collect tickets, watch the world ebb and flow around me, hear the endless pipe dreams of the men I work with. They have wives and kids and mortgages but I juggle my work around raving. I swap shifts all the time so I can have my weekends off. And because the money's crap, I've been earning a bit on the side to do up my flat, selling small weights of hashish because I had a good connect for the supply. Nothing big—just dealing to selected people.

I laid some hash on to a brother I knew from the streets and he tried to skank me and went missing with my money and drugs. Then we bumped into each other and I went all Hackney on him, holding my knife to his face, threatening to whet him up. He begged and promised he would get my money and got his mum on the phone to stand surety. This grown-arse man running to his mummy to bail him out only vexed me more. We arranged for me to collect what he owed the next day and I was to come to the infamous Nightingale Estate, in Clapton, a hardcore place where fatalities were high from knife and gun attacks. I sensed this could go pear-shaped so I went prepared and put on my big boots and baggy jeans, tucking the leg bottoms into my socks for a military look. I put on three jackets to puff me out with a long coat on top and got my black metal baton and placed it in my waistband with the handle sticking out and put my longest kitchen knife on the other side for good measure, just in case. I'm at the block of flats, ready to take the lift to the 17th floor, but instead took it to the 15th and walked up the flights of stairs, while sending the lift up to the 17th. I peeped through the glass door on the landing and saw him and his two brothers armed to the teeth with baseball bats, knives and two pit bulls waiting to ambush me. I bided my time for the empty lift to open and leapt out on them and threatened to shoot, yelling at the top of my lungs that I would if they didn't drop their weapons and put the dogs away, holding on to the butt of the baton still lodged in my waistband, as if it were a gun. The noise was deafening from the echo's bouncing around in the tight space, the dogs barking, the men shouting, then their mum came out of the flat screaming and begged me not to draw the gun and told her sons to go inside, while she went to the post office to get me my money. Still bluffing, I demanded it came with interest for the stunt they tried to pull. Only God knows how I walked away unscathed. It must have been Uncle Bob again.

At the raves I serve up Ecstasy. Love Doves: bright white pills with the shape of a dove stamped on them, and Dennis the Menaces—red and black capsules of pure bliss. I'm making a killing. I love getting high like this, but this scene is different. It's kinder. Safer. I don't have a habit. I exist free of heroin. I'm in control. And when the party's over I head back to work and smoke weed for the rest of the week. It's not dark or seedy like the street life, that's hard, and having to watch my back all the time, ready to fight or flight. This is filled with bright colours and open spaces and endless beauty. The weekend rolls out its psychedelic carpet—a rainbow of love to lose myself in before Monday spins around.

I love my flat. I love my road. It gives me enough distance from my family to enjoy the space I crave. As Angie is just around the corner from Mum she's often there, looking after things. I visit, too, mainly to check up on Huggy, but I have this flat to return to. I shut the door and stop worrying about them. There are times when we think Mum should be sectioned, yet Dr Egbonwon says the same thing: so long as Mum is not a danger to herself or others around her, this won't happen. It's up to us to cope.

It's a Wednesday evening when I bump into Nicky on Queensbridge Road. I'm surprised to see him. We've missed each other so many times, like ships in the night. While I was at Warren Hill, he was out of prison, and by the time of my release, he was back in. I don't hesitate to invite him back to my new flat around the corner. He's family. Ours is a history stretching way back—an unbreakable bond.

At the same time, I'm cautious of Nicky. Our lives intersect, but I'm different now. Nicky looks clean because he's just been released, but I tell him I'm never going back to heroin. I drop E's on the weekends and smoke hash and weed, but that's all. I've turned a corner with my drug use. 'Good for you, Stan, but I'm not going to work like some mug,' he says. He's doesn't care whether he goes back to prison.

This night has the shape of the all-nighters we used to pull and, as we have news to catch up on, I fetch cans of Tennent's from the off-licence and we smoke spliffs into the early hours. We talk about how cut-up we are about the friends who are dead or lost to the streets. Subconsciously, we know it could be us, even if we never say it. My flat is the best thing that's happened to me, I tell him, and tonight it feels warm: like old times but without the darkness of heroin and the need to drum houses while neighbours sleep. I tell him about the couple upstairs whose two kids always shout out, 'Hey Stanley!' whenever they see me, faces beaming. And the water fights and the football I play with them in the back garden.

It's around 2 AM before Nicky finally makes his confession. He's brought a tiny bit of gear with him and he asks if I mind him smoking it. He's been sat here all this time, just waiting. Waiting for the moment when he can have his hit. I think it's strange that he hasn't mentioned it. Maybe he was getting me comfortable; maybe it's all he's thought about the whole time he's been here. I'll say no. I'm bulletproof, I tell myself.

'Sure, don't bother me one way or the other, bro!' I say. I'm two years clean of heroin. I don't want it. I don't need it. I'm strong now.

'Got some foil I can use?' he asks.

'Sure!' I head into the kitchen and reach for the roll in the cupboard. Then, the flashback. My stomach lurches. I feel the buzz of excitement. I stamp it down, but I can't shake it and saliva starts to fill my mouth. *I can do this*, I repeat. Back in the living room, I watch Nicky unfold the parcel and heat a glob of gear on the foil. Suddenly, I'm transported to the four walls of my attic room in Alkham Road.

'You want some?' Nicky asks after he chases. I stare at him and he stares back at me. Our eyes lock. Part of me wants to cuss him out for coming, asking me to be a friend to his misery. Part of me wants to test him to see if he would really give it to me after everything I shared with him about my life and staying clean. Another part of me wants it. But I'm strong. I can ask him to leave. I can do this.

As I reach for the foil our eyes meet. But, it's gone. Every sinew of willpower is gone. When I chase, I hold the smoke in my lungs and the warmth washes over me like it did for the very first time—an old unwelcome friend. I itch and gouch and talk. And when I look over at Nicky, I'm sure he's smirking, like he knew this would happen all along.

By the time I wake up late the next day from my heroin stupor, I'm sick with regret. *Once an addict, always an addict.* I torment myself with this. Then, I think of Richard serving his sentence, and studying and everything we spoke about inside. I think of my art teacher and my portfolio of work on the walls in Warren Hill. I even think of Mr Barnsey and the men at work and my new crew who have nothing to do with heroin. I feel the world on my shoulders already. I feel like a fraud and a total failure. What the fuck was I thinking? I know I am in trouble now and have awakened the beast within me. Most of all, I feel betrayed by Nicky. He was meant to be like my family, but he's a Judas. I won't ever have anything to do with him again.

I am standing in front of my bedroom mirror fixated on how gaunt my face has become. My eyes bulge like saucers and my locks hang like curtains on a window to a lost soul. It's 3 AM. Tonight, I rode my bike to Hackney frontline to score and came back on foot after trading it in for crack. I'm defeated. In my hand is a pair of scissors. I've been growing my locks since Warren Hill. They framed me, gave me context: locks are sacred in the eyes of the Rastafarian community, who refuse to call them 'dreads' because of the word 'dreadful', keeping positive vibrations in everything they say and do. Now I take each lock and cut them one by one. I'm outside my body looking in. The scissors are blunt and I have to hack several times before I sit staring at the matted pile on my bed. 'I don't deserve to wear these locks,' I tell myself.

I ask myself why I ever welcomed Nicky back into my life. But I know I have to take responsibility for my own actions and can't blame him, as much as I want to. I am drowning in heroin and crack. I'm a weak, powerless addict. For a short while I controlled it. The money from hash sales paid for the odd hit, reserved for weekends and I've stopped juggling E's and raving now after the scene turned ugly when 'jungle' music arrived. It brought all the hardcore street man with it. The lightness turned dark and all the love was gone. Instead of E's, the smell of cocaine rocks filled the air, which meant fear and paranoia. Decker got stabbed in the heart and died instantly after an altercation outside a club with someone he knew. Then on my last night out, Don was wasted and got himself into a fight with some brothers in Astoria. We pulled him off and tried to get him outside, but he wasn't having any of it and started to fight us instead. We ended up leaving him to it. The next day we heard Don was in intensive care, after being stabbed multiple times and sliced in the face, from the top of his head to his jawbone. The guys he had beef with waited for him outside the club. We all felt guilty for leaving him and went looking for revenge. But what was done was done. There was no way of turning back the hands of time. Everyman has to walk his own path I suppose and face up to the consequences that we all have to answer to, in the end.

It's like I have these antennae, always alert, always wanting more. One is too many, a thousand is never enough. Once I start, I can't stop. And I've connected with a brother to start dealing crack. Godwin got introduced to me by an acquaintance when I was on the rave scene. He's wiry, with short, cropped hair, and Coolie, a term now considered derogatory, commonly used by Caribbean folk describing mixed-race Black people who have Indian heritage in them. But he's as soft as pie. Too soft for this game, so he's a target to be robbed by other dealers. He asks me to juggle with him, as way of protection.

A few months ago he turned up at my flat with parcels of crack cocaine he needed to shift, said he was trying his luck selling stones and he knew I could handle myself.

'Stan, can you juggle this with a few of your clientele?' he asked, laying out a small cellophane bag full of £20 rocks, then showing me the other five bags he had stuffed down his underpants.

'Sure,' I agreed. The streets are flooded with crack right now— it's become the virus of the '90s, choking the life from the already dead. And it's going for silly money so there's lots of takers. And when Godwin lit up a pipe for me to sample, it took me right back into the bosom of Skanker's White Lady; the hit was like a punch, the mind-fucking explosion, the crazy, superhero power and the need for more to stave off the heart-thumping paranoia of the crack comedown—the prang. When I was out of the room, I'm sure I heard Godwin open one of my kitchen cupboards and the teacups rattle.

As soon as he left, I went on one. 'I'll find a way to pay him back,' I thought, before I worked my way through the bag of rocks, like a crack-guzzling monster. And when the whole lot melted like candle wax on the pipe, and there was nothing left for my lungs to catch, I sat still, thinking what money I had in the flat to go buy some more. I felt something wasn't right about the way Godwin left, he seemed anxious and didgy, he kept averting his eyes and couldn't look at me. I started recalling the noise I'd heard from the kitchen. Then it hit me, that sly motherfucker has hidden his stash in my cupboard. I went straight in there and re-played the sound in my head and started opening cupboards and moving cups to reproduce the same effect. Bingo! I stood frozen in a Mexican standoff between me and the five bags of rocks hidden underneath three of my cups. I stared for a good while, not moving a muscle.

I stayed awake for two whole days, smoking, riding the peaks and troughs of my insatiable addiction, working my way through his stash. I've been off work for almost two months after pulling a skank during a night shift. It happened not long after I was purposely moved from Warren Street and up to Tottenham Hale station: the graveyard shift of the Victoria Line. No man's land. Mr Barnsey had reported me on countless occasions, but I always found a way out by getting in touch with the union. He says I'm a troublemaker, never wearing the correct uniform or wanting to toe the line. But this was a sneaky move. His way of getting back at me and having the final word. Tottenham Hale feels like being sent down the block. I wasn't in the mood to play games or to be treated like a prisoner and devised my plan to escape. Working lates is the highest paying shift, because of the inconvenience of trains no longer running after hours and staff having to take taxis home. And whatever shift you go off sick on, you received that allowance for the duration until you returned to work.

Once I had flagged the last train out of the platform. I then quickly used the pin from my work badge to prick the tips of my fingers to draw blood, then used toilet paper to soak it up, bloating it all over, before wrapping it around my hand. Then I ran up to the ticket collection cubicle at the barriers and smashed the glass with my elbow, and began screaming in pain, calling for help. The station manager came running out of the main office half dressed, panic stricken. Obviously, I woke him up from his siesta.

'Browne, what happened, what happened to you!' he shouted frantically.

'Two white skinheads try to go pass without showing me their tickets and smashed the glass which cut my hand' I said in agony. The manager got straight on the radio.

'Let me call an ambulance to take you to the hospital?' he pleaded.

'No! I don't like hospitals, just call me a taxi so I can go home,' I said wimpishly.

Godwin came back the next day, early, and has been here several times, but I don't answer, even though I've promised I'll meet him. I locked the black iron gate that covers my front door and closed all the doors inside so he couldn't peep through my windows to try and see me, while I stood in my bedroom, alert to every sound. He didn't stop knocking. Then, I heard talking. Someone was with him. Then my letterbox flap being pushed open. I heard them mumbling, plotting to get me. Or maybe those were other voices? My head's full of voices. But it's being trapped in my own flat and so pranged that I can't handle—the mad ruckus in my brain, paranoia beyond my wildest imagination. I felt exposed, so

I crawled underneath my bed with the crack pipe and pulled the duvet down over the foot of the frame to make a den and smoked. My heart jumped out of my mouth when he knocked again. His voice outside my window, then my neighbour's voice. I lay still for hours in the darkness before I eventually find the courage to crawl out and tiptoe to the toilet.

I'm taking voluntary redundancy at work on the advice of the union. It's a polite way of them sacking me after being absent for the past four months. Besides, I can't face 40 years of moving up the ranks like Mr Barnsey. Sick pay is still dropping into my Barclays account, which I empty on Kingsland High Road every week on Friday and have smoked by the crack of dawn on Saturday. I've sold all my gold, my TV, my video recorder and my stereo on the frontline. The high street's littered with war-torn soldiers now: ragged, hair-matted, bodies wasted in shop-door fronts in the early hours, scattering like rats as daylight breaks. When I walk past them, all I see is me.

Josie says I should apply for a summer job in the States. She's a girl I know from way back, from my college days. She's stunning and works as an airline stewardess, but I've never had the bottle to ask her out. If she's home in the UK, occasionally Josie drops by to see me, brings a drink, and sometimes we smoke together, too. She's as straight as a die, so I hide my drug use from her, even though she knows I've been in prison and I'm trying to sort my life out. She's hopeful, bringing an application round, she says, to help me find a job. According to her, I'd make a great counsellor at Camp America, working with inner city kids who get sent to their camps over the summer to be taught life-skills.

'They come from broken homes Stanley, like you, so you can understand them and can guide them,' she says with such sincerity and care that it's hard for me to say no to her. Josie has no idea how much I'm struggling just to understand myself.

'The interviews are in Ealing, I'll come with you if you like,' she offers. The camp starts in three months and lasts for 12 weeks. If I'm successful I can be posted anywhere in America. 'I'll apply,' I tell her. I have nothing to lose.

Chapter 33

Flesh and Blood

It's June 1991 when I arrive at JFK airport in New York. The city is a stopover where I'll have my induction for Camp America before I'm posted to Michigan for the summer. I pulled out all the stops for my interview, digging out the shirt and trousers of my London Underground uniform and cleaning myself up. Then, I spent the whole hour smiling politely and asking questions and secretly obsessing about scoring. When the guy said I'd be perfect and offered me the position, I was speechless. I've never travelled abroad before. Until now, I've never even had a passport.

The minute I received my acceptance letter I stopped smoking crack. Instead, I've used heroin to tide me over—not injecting, just smoking. I was scared I wouldn't stay out of prison long enough to get there, so I've begged and borrowed money and sold the rest of my possessions to avoid drumming houses. I even knocked on my neighbours' doors saying I had run out of gas or electric to squeeze a tenner here and there, but they soon caught on that something wasn't right.

I've brought no luggage. Just my tickets, passport and the clothes on my back. I was clucking so badly on the flight over, I drank myself to sleep on the free alcohol after I was bumped up to first class. I chased my last bit of gear before I left home, knocking on a dealer's door early hours of the morning with no money and got it on tick, credit. I took a cab to Finsbury Park station and told the driver straight up, I'm broke and couldn't pay him. We had a moment of a stare-off, until he told me to just get out of his car. I jumped the barrier of the Underground and got on the Piccadilly line all the way to Heathrow. Getting out the other side was going to be harder. Approaching the exit, I saw two inspectors checking tickets. Just my luck. A big group of Muslim women wearing hijabs, speaking loudly in Swahili to each other, sauntered towards the inspectors and I ducked behind them as they got closer. When my moment came, I slipped past and ran like the wind with one of the inspectors yelling after me.

I'm shaking like a leaf and totally discombobulated in this massive, vast open space. The airport is full of signs and chaotic; it's both imposing and intimidating. I'm stopping anyone that I can, asking for directions, showing them my ticket so I can keep moving to get on the flight in case the inspectors are looking for me. But I don't realise I have to check-in first and then go through security before I can even get on the plane. I am paranoid beyond belief, thinking they are going to arrest me for not paying my tube fare, or because I have an outstanding court case for theft and have jumped bail. My nerves are on end as I pass by all the uniforms after getting my boarding pass, but nobody stops me. I make my way to the gate and finally try to relax, thinking it's all over. Then I hear my name being called over the tannoy: 'MR STANLEY JAMES BROWNE, please report to the front desk...' It's repeated over and over and other passengers start to get involved asking each other if they are Mr Browne. I join in and do the same, thinking if I go up to the desk I will get nicked. Eventually, I surrender, and walk with my head down to the crew at the front and hand myself in. 'So close, but yet so far,' I thought to myself. America will have to wait for another time.

'Are you Mr Browne?' one of them asks.

'Yes.'

'I'm really sorry sir, but economy is full so we will have to move you to first class.'

'Sorry, what?' I say, thinking they are trying to trick me so I won't cause a scene and the undercover police can arrest me and put me in the van waiting outside the airport.

'We will have to move you sir, to first class,' she says this slowly and deliberately, looking at the confusion on my face.

'Ok,' I say, playing their game. I still didn't clock on to what she meant by that, having not flown before.

'Please take a seat and we will call you when the flight is ready to board.'

'Ok', I say, and sit back down scouting around for any sign of plainclothes officers.

Billboards and Marlboro cowboys; neon lights; flyovers; six-lane freeways; yellow taxis. The New York cityscape blows my mind. I feel like Starsky and Hutch weaving my way from the airport to the suburb of Queens. I was supposed to book a hotel, but I have no money. Instead, I've an address for Mum's real mother, Grandma Greta, that I got through a cousin. I have no recollection of having met Greta before she left London for the US in 1977, but if the address is correct, Greta lives in Queens.

When I get there, there is no answer from the front of the house—a replica Victorian red-brick with an apple-pie veranda. I walk to the side entrance and knock on the door there. After a few minutes an old woman shuffles to the door. She has a round face and glasses and she looks the spitting image of my sister, Mini. A warmth surges through me and I have a natural urge to hug her. My flesh and blood. My family. But I stop myself. It's obvious Grandma Greta doesn't know who I am. She thinks I'm a friend of Mum's brother, Melvin.

'Who you looking for? Melvin not 'ere, 'him gawn out and 'him will be back later. Who should I say call?'

'I'm Stanley. Joy's son?'

I watch Grandma Greta as my words sink in. She softens, then the tone of her body shifts and she straightens up her back.

'Stanley? Joy's son? From H'ngland? Ohhhhh, so you come fi cuss mi!'

I'm confused. I haven't come to cuss out Grandma Greta. Why would I? I've come to find her. I've come to piece together my crazy, dysfunctional life. I follow Greta as she invites me into her kitchen.

'Let me fix yu sumting to eat. What you want? Me have likkle rice and curry inah di pot meck mi heat it up for you?'

As she prepares food, we talk. I'm sweating and my muscles ache from the withdrawals, but I desperately try to hold it together enough for her not to notice.

'So what happened wid your sisters dem? Angie? Minerva? And wah di likkle baby name? Mi ear say she ave another one?'

'His name is Huggy.'

'Huggy? Huggy Bear in ah the TV wah it call? Like *Starsky and Hutch*?'

'Yes, that's the one, like *Starsky and Hutch*. It's short for Hogarth.'

'Hogarth? Mmm. You have a uncle in Jamaica wid dat dere name. She must ah name him after she great Uncle Hogarth. Ah bwoy. So what yu mudder doing wid herself? She working? What job she do?'

'Mum is mentally ill. Mum suffers from schizophrenia. I thought you knew?'

'Mi did 'ear seh she sick but mi never know is real mental illness she ave, mi tink ah di weed she was smoking dat send her funny. So she really sick for true?'

'Mum has been suffering from schizophrenia since I was five years old. Me and my sisters and my brother have been in and out of children's homes and foster care most of our lives. Didn't you know?'

'Lawd jeezus. Mi sorry fi h'ear dat son, aaahhh bwoy. Mi so sorry fi h'ear dats what you guys went true. Whaappen to Joy now? She getting help from di doctors dem?'

'She's on medication but she won't take it a lot of the time.'

'Oh God. Ohh, lawd have mercy! What ah ting, what ah ting.'

I start to tell Grandma Greta everything, but then I remembered the taxi driver waiting outside to be paid. I tentatively asked Greta for a loan, telling her I've been waiting for my first paycheque to show in my account, but when I checked the cash machine at the airport, there was nothing there.

'What! Him outside now? All this time? Why you never say sumting? How much is di fare?' We both stepped outside after she found her purse. The driver speaks with a strong Indian accent and keeps apologising and says I owe $90.

'NO WAY man, uh, uh, no way,' shouts my grandmother. 'It's no $90 from di airport, are you crazy? Have you lost yur mind? No sireeee.' At that point my Uncle Melvin, dark skinned, dressed head to toe in black, swaggers over to join us out of the blue.

'What's sup, ma?'

'Dis crazy mudderfucker trying to charge him $90 from the airport!'

'Who dis, ma?'

'It's yu nephew, Joy's son, h'im just come from H'ngland.'

'Who, Stanley?!'

'Yes, mi dere,' she says.

'Word up dawg,' he says, embracing me, before leaning into the taxi window and talking to the driver.

'Listen up homie, yu trying to rip my nephew off man? Lemmie tell yu how dis is gonna play out, awright? I'm gonna give yu $30, awright, so that yu can get the fuck on outta here before I put a cap in yur ass, awright? We clear?'

'Please, please, I waiting very long time, mister, please, please,' the driver begs.

'Awright, so yu know what? Now yu can get the fuck outta here with nothing! Go on now, yu better get the fuck outta here, don't make me smoke ya!' Melvin then reached behind his back. The driver hit the gas and drove away at speed. I had definitely found my family. When we go back inside and Uncle Melvin stops drooling all over me, he finally leaves me and Greta to catch up, telling me to come downstairs when I'm finished talking. I tell Greta about the homes, my foster care, the police and the social services. She listens intently and we form a bond between us. In the end, I stay with Grandma Greta for two weeks, and every day when I get home from my induction, I try to drip feed her with what I really want to ask. I've come armed with the story Uncle Winston told me about Grandma Greta's husband, Mr Simpson. I also want to know who my real grandfather is. Mum has never spoken about him. All I know is that compared to her siblings, who are almost blue-black and dark-skinned, Mum looks different with freckles on her face, almond-shaped eyes and caramel skin. I've come to find the missing pieces of our past, the missing pieces of Mum.

'What happened between you and Mum?'

'Eh? What yu say? What happened wid mi and yu mudder? Dats what yu asking mi? What yu h'ear?'

'Well I heard different things. I heard Mum was the black sheep of the family... that something happened... that something happened between Mum and... Mr Simpson...'

'So dats what yu h'ear? Well since as yu know so much, yu tell me what happen?' Grandma Greta hardens with an acid sarcasm.

'Fi tell yu di truth. Tings did happened yes! Between yu mudder and dat rass of a man, dats why mi divorce him! Mi had to.' She says this firmly, fluttering around the kitchen doing nothing in particular.

'Did he mess with Mum? Is that the truth?'

'If him did mess with yu mudder? Is dat what yu h'ear?'

'Is that true?'

'Well dat depends how you look pon it, lovey.'

'Are you saying it never happened?'

'I'm telling you tings happened but not like what you tink. Yu h'ear?'

'You're saying things happened between my mum and Mr Simpson, right?'

'Yes sirrrryyy.'

'And that Mum was a kid? A teenager?'

'She wasn't no kid! A teenager, yes, but no kid! Mi noh remember! Maybe she did 13 or 14. Onc a dem age dere.'

'Was Mum molested by him?'

'If yu say so mi lovey, if you—say—soo. But I was there and I see with my own eyes. I come home from work an see them both with mi own eyes. Dats what happen. So don't listen to what people say 'bout molestation.'

'Come on, she was only 13 or 14. She was just a kid, right? I don't want to upset you Grandma Greta, but I need to know.'

Grandma Greta turns silent. I tell her that we've never had any contact with Mum's side of the family. That I've never known grandparents. It feels strange even calling her Grandma. I tell her we've suffered for all the secrets of Mum's life and that Mum has suffered too.

'It's okay lovey, yu never upset mi. It's been a long time since mi have to tink about any of dat. Di pas is di pass.'

'Who's Mum's dad?'

A large grin spreads over Grandma Greta's face and she laughs from the pit of her belly. 'Bwoy, yu noh easy! You really come to interrogate mi. Ahh bwoy. Yu come to trouble mi soul. He is one China man.'

'A China man?'

'Yes, ah one China man. Mi noh remember him name, it happen a long time ago and when I was a likkle girl. Dats all mi remember.'

'It would have been nice to meet my grandfather, that's all?'

'Well, yu can go look fi him, him inah Jamaica somewhere, yu might find him.'

'How will I do that if I don't have a name?'

'Mi can't help yu wid dat mi lovey. Mi—can't—help—yu—wid dat…'

Chapter 34

Brotherman

In the Autumn of 1990, when I arrived back in the UK after a summer in the States, Huggy came to live with me in my flat in Middleton Road. Finally, the authorities sectioned Mum and she was due to spend months back in the psychiatric ward. Andrea and social services wanted Huggy to return to Forest Road Children's Home and there was also talk of fostering him out. My brother lost to the system once again. I couldn't let it happen.

'You won't qualify for your mum's child allowance,' Andrea pleaded with me. 'He's better off in care.' She was concerned I wouldn't cope or have enough money to feed and clothe him.

'I'll cope fine. He's not going back into care. Period,' I said before hanging up the phone.

In truth, Andrea wasn't wrong. In my heart, I knew I would go back to drugs. I was an addict managing a habit, and in the States I managed it well. Now, I was plunged straight back into my old life.

Being a camp counsellor had given me time out, and an unexpected focus. The camp itself was set in acres of rich woodland surrounding a large boating lake. The great expanse of the American landscape overwhelmed me. I lost myself in the freedom of it all. A chance to reinvent myself once again, even though I spent the 18-hour journey from New York to Michigan tormented about if or where I'd be able to score.

Immediately on arrival at the camp I noticed the division. Like me, all the counsellors employed to babysit the kids were Black, while the specialists who taught arts and crafts or sports and got paid more were white, and well-to-do from different parts of the world, doing their bit for mankind. The camp hierarchy vexed anyone wanting to graduate to a better position and I got educated early on by two counsellors, Biggie and OG who quickly became my friends.

Biggie, a huge 17-year-old from Chicago, had attended the camps as a boy and returned as a counsellor. Baseball cap turned back to front, black baggy jeans and baggy sweater: he looked one hundred percent hip hop, like the band NWA. OG was an ex-gang banger, a street kid straight from the projects on Chicago's East Side, staying out long enough to stay alive. Average life expectancy for a Black kid there: 20. Both of them smoked weed like it was going out of fashion.

Then, when coach loads of kids turned up to begin their two-week vacations which rolled back-to-back throughout the summer, I was faced with so many versions of myself, four thousand miles from home. Kids arrived from broken homes and halfway houses, where one or both parents were heroin or crack addicts. When summer camp was over, they probably didn't return to the same beds that they'd left. This holiday might be the only stable time they ever had among the churn of their existence.

As counsellors, our job was to take care of around 20 kids aged between five and ten. We lived and moved with them all day, every day. At first, they found me strange—a Black man with an English accent.

'Is you perpetrating?' one kid asked on my first day. I had never heard that word before and had no idea of its meaning.

Biggie had to explain that meant faking it. And they nicknamed me Brotherman on account of me calling everyone 'brother' and 'man'.

Just as London was divvied up into gang territories, so were the Chicago streets these kids inhabited. At camp, rival gangs were expected to mix together, but violence simmered below the surface. Against camp rules, kids continued 'gang-banging', throwing up the letter of the gang they belonged to with their fingers to taunt others. Some wore their bandanas or gang colours and were from the Gangster Disciples or Vice Lords, the two most notorious gangs in Chicago. Then, there were the 'violations' which mostly involved beating up a kid from a rival gang or initiating kids, which involved the same.

Immediately, I saw a way to create a ceasefire, however temporary. After talking with Biggie, OG and the other camp counsellors, I suggested that we gather the boys together to stop the gang-banging. I sat with the kids and taught them everything I knew about Black ancestry and Black history. I talked to them about Uncle Bob Marley and I played them 'Redemption Song'. I discussed slavery and the Black struggle. Biggie and OG came armed with statistics on mortality rates of Black kids in cities all around the world. We discussed integrity and self-worth. I was talking to them but, in truth, I was talking to myself. After that, the only symbol they were allowed to throw up was a fist held high above their heads: the Black Panther emblem of unity.

'Who wants to be in my gang?' I shouted to them at the close of the meeting. 'To be part of my tribe, they would have to undergo a different kind of initiation,' I told them. I don't know where it came from inside of me, but when one of the youngest kids said yes, I signalled for him to step up.

'Spread your arms out wide like a cross,' I instructed him. His eyes closed and I noticed his body wince as if he only expected me to hurt him. Instead, I moved towards him, wrapped my arms around him, lifting him off his feet and gave him the biggest bear hug on the planet.

'That's your initiation. Who else wants to join?' I said, and I watched as a hesitant queue formed. Even the toughest kids seemed to bring out my soft centre—it was as if they gave me licence to let down my guard.

At first, one kid called T-Bone sneered at my alternative cere-mony, and I challenged him. He continued to challenge my every word, and I had to come down hard on him for the duration of his stay. Yet when it came time for his group to gather for their closing ceremony before heading home, he shocked me. Each kid had an opportunity to give honest feedback on their experience and I expected him to cuss me out. Instead, he said the one person he would miss the most from camp… was Brotherman. When he broke down, burying his face in his cap with embarrassment, I realised I'd touched someone. I ran forward to hug him, and I've never forgotten the strength in his arms. I still get goosebumps when I remember the urgency in the way he clung on to me with all his might. I cradled him in my arms, knowing we may never see each other again. Home for him was life or death, and I was the big brother he'd only ever dreamed of.

All those boys were in my mind when I insisted that Huggy live with me. However unable I was to care for him, I convinced myself it would be okay. I couldn't leave him to fend for himself. Just as the kids at Camp America had unlocked something positive in me, I thought taking care of Huggy full time would too. Anyone could see he was the brightest of kids, bursting with creativity. He went on to become the first in our family to go to university and obtain a degree. He showed enormous talent in painting, like Mum. As I escaped in drugs and crime, Huggy escaped in books, reading mythology and non-fiction. Even when I look at him now, there is always a child in me wishing that I had been championed the way we championed Huggy. He even spoke differently than us. In Alkham Road, Mum smashed up the TV after she became irritated he was watching too many cartoons. From then on he heard only Radio 4, which he tuned into daily, listening to all the broadcasts, unwittingly adopting the BBC middle-class accent.

As Huggy would be starting secondary school soon, I took him to Sir William Collins School in Camden to discuss whether he could move there from Trinity Road primary, even though it was outside the catchment area. I didn't want him to set foot in Homerton House where I had gone, knowing full well how hardcore it was there. After a frank discussion and a little persuasion, the headmaster secured a place for him. Although Mum was hospitalised for only a few weeks in the end, Huggy stayed with me for the best part of nine months.

'Make a list of everything you want to do,' I told him after he moved in.

'Anything?' he said.

'Anything.' Huggy wrote a list of gymnastics, bike riding, swimming, tennis and cadets, and I enrolled him into all of them to see what stuck. He became an amazing tennis player and won lots of trophies, but chose to pursue art.

But the longer Huggy stayed, the more difficult it became for me. The responsibility of juggling the role of parent and liaising with social services over Mum suffocated me once again. The monkey on my back that laid dormant never went away. I worked a succession of driving jobs to keep us going, but before I could stop it, I was using vans to score, hiding in the bathroom to smoke gear, or using after I'd taken Huggy to school. When everything started to close in on me, I engineered another spell in prison— the safest place I thought I could be.

While I was doing a job for a company that erected 'For Sale' signs for estate agents, the manager pulled me aside to complain about my work. I had only been with them for two weeks. He wanted rid of me with any excuse, even though I had done no wrong. I later learned that the manager had lied and only employed me to cover for another employee who was on holiday leave, and that he had done this before with other guys, employing and then sacking them instead of telling them it was a temporary position. That day I vowed to cause him as much inconvenience as he caused me, without committing the more serious crime of GBH, grievous bodily harm. I parked the van outside the yard and marched upstairs into his office to get him, then I marched him down to the room where the rest of the staff worked and held them hostage, pulling the phones from their sockets and robbing the secretary who had been rude and disrespectful to me when I first started. Even worse, I smashed up all the machines the company used to print the signs, along with any other machine they had, before starting on the windows and anything else that was breakable. Then I gathered up sets of van keys and dropped them in various drains along the road outside.

I served six months from a 12-month sentence in Brixton and Pentonville prisons for criminal damage and robbery. This was after a hearing at Wood Green Magistrate's Court, and writing a letter to the judge, explaining why I had done what I did. The judge looked up at me over his spectacles when he'd finished reading my letter, then shouted out across to my solicitor: 'Is there a psychiatric report for this man?' I couldn't bring myself to tell Huggy that he was going back to Mum's. I'd let him down again, unable to break the cycle of crime and addiction.

I got gate arrested at Pentonville after serving my time, which means I don't get to walk free but instead I was taken by two detectives, who were waiting for me to be released, straight to City Road police station. I was charged for another burglary where they found my fingerprints and went back to court. I got given community service and bound over to keep the peace for 18 months. I was grateful to be bound over on this occasion, but my main concern at the time was my first ever oil painting I had finished during the art classes, it hadn't properly dried yet when they put me in the back of the car. The Detectives helped by covering it with a sheet for me in the open boot, after I explained how delicate it was, and I held on to it for dear life with one hand as we sped off, my other hand cuffed to the door handle.

Chapter 35

Denial Is Not A River in Egypt

My life has been negotiated around a variety of wooden tables: social worker's; head teacher's; solicitor's; probation officer's; council worker's. Why should this table be any different? All these people round this table are white. These people look clean. They're not my family. I should never have come here.

Clinton brought me. He's a brother I knew from Hoxton frontline who I used gear with; and he talks with a thick cockney accent. I bumped into him on Kingsland High Road he ripped me off once when he sold me brick dust instead of heroin, before I did time at Warren Hill. It's the first time I've seen him since. I buried my head, and tried to walk past him, but he called out my name. Clinton's looking clean, and he took me to McDonald's and offered me anything I wanted on the menu. He then watched me eat.

'There's a place you can go, if you want to stop using,' he said, while I gulped down burger and chips with a milk shake and an apple pie.

I've spent six months in prison smoking gear and clucking. I'm sick and tired of being sick and tired, but I can't stop. On the day of my release, I went straight out and scored with my £46 discharge money, then signed on at the Jobcentre. I'm a 'signing on' addict, waiting for my next paycheque.

I've stayed away from Mum's. I only visit if I need money. I let myself in and rummage through her purse. I steal money from Mini's room. Huggy's so wise to it now he sleeps with his pocket money under his pillow, but if he's asleep I gently prise him off and slip my hand underneath. Whenever I leave, I feel worthless. Sometimes I run into Mum walking on the street, cussing out people and things that are not there. Both of us criss-crossing familiar streets, lost to the system. She with her mental illness, me with mine. Occasionally, if I meet her on the high road, I bum a roll-up if she's lucid. And one time, I came home to find a plastic bag hanging off my iron security gate: bread, milk, tea, butter, eggs and a tin of corned beef. Mum must have sensed I was in trouble and still had the maternal instinct to feed me, even when she wouldn't feed herself.

Everybody around this wooden table shares their stories, but I sit silently drinking tea and eating biscuits. And I've shoved some into my pockets for later. I only came because Clinton bought me food and I felt obliged somehow, but also curious. At first, I thought he'd joined the 'God Squad' and now we're here at St Leonard's Hospital in Hoxton at a meeting of Narcotics Anonymous. We're the only Black guys there, but I've positioned myself nearest the door, so I can duss-out when I've had enough.

I won't share my story. It's not necessarily that I don't want to. I don't have the words for it. Where would I start? Who would understand? Who would care? Who would care that I've wanted to kill myself? Who would care that I smoked a last bit of gear, sat on my kitchen floor, and laid back with my head in the gas oven. Relief swept over me and I cried at my hopelessness when I realised there was no credit left on the gas meter. I couldn't even top myself properly.

The voices sharing fuzz and crackle, like an untuned radio. I don't want to be here, so my mind isn't in the room. It's busy working out where my next hit is coming from. There's no space for reflection. I'm only here, now, in the moment, in the grip of anxiety and need that barely hold me together. I nod to Clinton, quietly lift myself up and head out towards the foyer. Outside, I exhale with relief, before someone taps my shoulder.

'Take these, mate,' a guy says. It's one of the group members who's followed me out. He shoves leaflets into my hand and a helpline number to call. And he moves to hug me before I'm lost to the streets. My insides squirm. I don't know what to do with his hug. It's genuine and painful. It hurts like hell.

Months go by and I don't see Clinton, and I don't go back to St Leonard's either. I'm supplementing my dole money with burglary and I lucked out when I found a haul of tom and expensive camera equipment in a flat on Kingsland High Road. New trainers. New jeans. Enough to keep me in gear for a while. And on a good day, I met a woman I started seeing on and off.

Charmaine lives in Bristol, but I bumped into her on the overground train to Dalston Kingsland. She's ebony-skinned and works as an IT trainer for a bank. She took my breath away.

'If this woman gets off at my stop, I'm going to talk to her,' I said confidently to myself when we both reached the top of the escalator.

'Sorry, you talking to me?' she replied, cautiously, as I followed her through the ticket hall.

'So, let me guess, you happily married?'

'Nah,' she laughed. She had the most stunning smile. We talked and I wrote down my address and asked her, if she wanted, to write to me with her number. I was trying to be a gentleman, not wanting to pressure her to give me her digits, like some other brothers would. My phone wasn't working because the bill hadn't been paid, but Charmaine didn't know this. She doesn't know anything about me. To my surprise, she does write. I call her from the phone box and we meet in London for a date. She's older than me by three years but the youngest in a large Jamaican family who go to church every Sunday. I make sure I dress smartly whenever I see her to hide my truth.

With Charmaine, I can be whoever I want to be, until the time when, of course, I can't. Part of me knows this will happen, but I deceive myself that it won't. I always want to be the Romeo with the starry-eyed smile at the top of the escalator. Whenever I visit her in Bristol, I smoke gear before I get on the coach. I borrow her car and pretend I'm going to the garage to buy beers, when actually I'm scouring the streets, working out where to score in this alien city. I steal money from her purse. A double life is so much worse with a girlfriend. I'm scared she'll find out who I really am. That she'll see me.

One night she catches me smoking crack in her bathroom. She's angry and tearful that I'm taking drugs and she asks me what's in the pipe. I don't want to tell her. Like my family, she doesn't deserve my chaos.

'I know you take drugs,' she says, tears streaming down her face. 'And I know you've stolen from me.' She wants me to smoke in front of her, so she can understand what it is that makes me leave her bed and go out in her car in the early hours of the morning.

'What's more important than what we have?' she asks. I have no answer. 'Nothing,' I want to say, but it's not true. The truth? She's beautiful and pure and I want everything she has. I want to siphon off all her goodness and inject it into me. She wants to try the pipe, to experience what I experience. I erupt with anger and rage. 'You stupid fucking woman,' I think.

'No fucking way! What, you think this is a fucking game, do you think I really want to be doing this fucking shit!?' And when the argument and her tears subside we both collapse on her sofa, spent, and I let her in and tell her about the children's homes and the foster parents and the prisons. She throws her arms around me and says she wants to support me and be there for me. I am shocked and overwhelmed that this human being still wants me in her life after all I've shared and after all I've done. I bury my head on her shoulder and let myself go. Later that evening, I borrow money from her to get a coach back to London the next day. After I arrive in London, I stayed away from her for a few months ashamed of myself. I didn't realise at the time it would lead to my first long-term relationship. But sadly, it wasn't meant to be.

When I finally call the Narcotics Anonymous helpline number, suicidal thoughts are flooding my brain. I see death everywhere. I think about overdosing all the time and whether this might be an easier death. These thoughts aren't fleeting. They stick, like limpets, stubbornly working out a way.

I still have their literature shoved in a corner of my flat where I don't have to see it. When I stumble across it, I don't know exactly what it is that I want. Maybe I only want to hear someone's voice. And when the voice persuades me to attend another meeting at St Leonard's, I go, but I don't want to be hugged. I want to sit and eat biscuits and slip out when it gets too much.

At Narcotics Anonymous everyone there is a recovering addict and different people volunteer to host the meeting while others share their stories.

'Why Are We Here? Who is an Addict? How Does It Work?' The members sit in a circle and begin the session by reading from a set of cards with various headings.

'Denial is not a river in Egypt.' This is a phrase that gets thrown around and members laugh and nod in recognition. All I know is that if I don't surrender, I'll die.

One man shares his story, the main event of the meeting. He's been clean for three years. I can't imagine being clean for three days. But when I listen, it's as if the room goes dark and I'm bathed in a spotlight. The schizophrenic mother; his care for his siblings; the children's homes; the foster parents; the violence; the drug abuse. His inventory of cause and effect is my inventory. I'm ticking off the collateral damage as he speaks.

'The meeting is open, who wants to share?'

'I do,' I say, before I can stop myself. 'My name is Stanley and I'm an addict. I want to stop but I don't know how.' I'm falling apart now, bumbling, blethering, with my face soaked, but I don't care. I keep on talking. Up until now every part of me has been pushed down and locked up. I've held it together for 23 years but now I've nothing left to lose. These strangers are witnessing my breakdown. I'm like a broken fire hydrant, pouring out water. I talk and talk, and sob and sob and nobody stops me.

'I couldn't even top myself properly,' I say, and the room laughs when I tell them what I did with the oven. 'Is this my family?' I wonder when I leave that evening. 'Are these people my tribe?' The weight of the world fell from my shoulders and I felt lighter just by admitting I was an addict and had a problem.

I continued to attend NA meetings and I continued to listen and share. The policy at NA is total abstinence from all drugs, including alcohol. I relapsed three times in the first three months, first with weed, then alcohol, then crack. But I kept going back. Mostly, I went to meetings daily and I got a sponsor, someone in the programme I could look up to and who could guide me with the written work I needed to do through the programme's 12 Steps, which challenged me to examine all areas of my life. And I began to understand the powerlessness of addiction, the unmanageability of my existence, the insanity. I challenged my belief system and faced my fears and my wrongdoings. I examined my defects and shortcomings; I explored how damaged I was and how I damaged other people and the amends I owed them and that I was willing to make. I continued to take personal inventory of myself and promptly admitted whenever I was wrong and asked for guidance from a power greater than myself, whatever that was. And I carried the message of hope to the addicts that still suffered. Many people need recovery, but only a few want it. I wanted it and I needed it. I committed to facing my truth.

Those early days in recovery were priceless. Bumming from meeting to meeting, hanging out with other recovering addicts, growing together and being there for each other no matter what, ready to hit the streets to find an addict who had relapsed and bring them back into the rooms. 'I alone can do it, but I cannot do it alone.' I learnt that it was a 'we' programme and not a 'me' programme. I learnt that, 'If nothing changes, then nothing changes.' And I chose to stick with the folks who worked the Steps to change their insides and not their outsides. I had come way too far to turn back and not use this opportunity to change and take this seriously. I poured my heart and my soul into my written work, and I vowed to finish the whole 12 Steps no matter how long it took me.

As well as NA, I begin counselling through a charitable organisation called the Redcliffe Project, based in Earl's Court. The therapy is free and I attend while signing on. Immediately, I am connected to Marion who becomes my counsellor periodically over 12 years. A calm, no-nonsense Caribbean woman, she allows me to open up in ways I could never imagine doing with a man or a person from a different culture. One of the first things she encourages me to do is to stay away from my family while I'm in early recovery. She helps me to see Stanley: the hero child, the caretaker, the fixer, the co-dependant. The child who picked up the pieces but never looked after himself. She helps me explore what I love in life, what I have the potential to do, and how I might move forward. I remember back to when our life was happy: Mum's blues parties and how I entertained guests; and how in Alkham

Road, Mum and Angie and Mini used to roll around on the bed giggling at me putting on shows and mimicking family members, dressing up in Mum's wigs and Uncle Ashley's hats. And how, when I was in Nottingham, one teacher said that I'd make a good actor. The truth is, I realise, I've been acting all my life.

While in recovery, I enrol in night classes at the famous Anna Scher Theatre in Islington. Anna is friendly, fair but strict. There's no lateness or mucking around in class and each week I turn up religiously to learn how to act in scenes and sketches and how to improvise. She teaches me how to inhabit every character. 'Make it believable,' she says. Most of all, I explore what it feels like to really let go of my inhibitions and I start to understand the person that I truly want to be. Free, in every sense of the word.

Chapter 36

Thespian

I wish Mum could see me. I wish she could see me now in front of the cameras and the lights and on TV. Angie and Mini and Huggy are watching and friends are too. But I wish I could reach into Mum and find her and say: 'Look at me. Your son. Look what I did.'

I have to pinch myself. I'm on the set of *EastEnders* in Elstree Studios in north London. Albert Square looks like Fassett Square in Hackney, where the programme's first pilot series was filmed ten years ago—a five-minute walk from my flat on Middleton Road. Terrace houses just like here, and the small, central patch of green. And the market stalls that look like the market on Ridley Road. It mirrors the walls and frontages and railway lines of my life. I blend in immediately.

There's crew with headphones and boom mics and cameras and clipboards, scurrying like ants to construct this make-believe world. In this episode, I have my first speaking part. It's not the first acting part I've had since I graduated from the Anna Scher Theatre, but it's 30 seconds of me playing a part that I want to play.

It's 1994 and *EastEnders* is the soap opera to appear on. The nation is glued to the storyline. Frank Butcher, who runs the second-hand car lot is in debt and asks Phil Mitchell, played by Steve McFadden, to torch it in an insurance scam. I'm to play Phil's solicitor in the police interview room after his arrest. The camera will pan to the officer, who will interview Phil under caution, and then to me. 'My client doesn't have to answer that,' I'll say. Then I'll turn to Phil. 'You have the right to say no comment.' The cameras will roll and we'll retake the scene until it's perfect. I'm a Black solicitor, representing a white man who's been arrested for a crime. Lights. Camera. Action.

My agent, Sue Hammond, has phoned me with all kinds of roles. I found her after I left Anna Scher Theatre by working my way through the Spotlight contacts directory—the mecca for actors wanting to break through to the industry. I travelled to Leicester Square in the West End to buy it, and had my headshot taken at a photographer's at the end of Dalston Lane. I leafed through each page, underlining the names of agents I liked the look of and, at Hackney Library, I typed out a letter I'd handwritten, using the computer skills I learned in prison. Then, I photocopied it and sent it out to 30 agents. No one said yes other than Sue.

In her cottage in Surrey, packed with ornaments, like an antique shop, she interviewed me over her spectacles. I sat among cups and saucers, teapots and statues and glass cabinets filled with curios.

'Where do you see yourself going in this business?' she asked.

'On the stage and on TV playing top roles,' I replied.

Her kindly face smiled, encouragingly. 'You have to start at the bottom and work up. Are you prepared for that?'

'I'll do it,' I said. I've told Sue nothing of my recovery or my criminal past or that I've been to prison a few times. I don't tell anyone in the industry or any of the new friends I make outside of the meetings either. I'm fearful that someone will use it against me. I'm scared that a producer or a casting director won't see a man desperate to escape his past, a man who's pulled himself out from the abyss to be clean enough to start again.

The first job Sue got me was also at Elstree—my debut TV role. It was a 'featured role' which meant no speaking, more like being an extra than an actor. It was on the set of the BBC One comedy Birds of a Feather. Actor Pauline Quirke's character, Sharon, has a husband in prison, and I played one of the inmates, chatting in the visiting hall opposite my make-believe family. The irony wasn't lost on me—of all the experiences I had in prison, a family visit wasn't one of them. But I watched Pauline Quirke with awe—how relaxed she appeared delivering her lines, how confident she seemed on set, how alive she looked. She inspired me. 'How can I get there?' I thought.

'Crimewatch needs a robber for a crime reconstruction,' Sue said when she offered me my next role. It was an appeal for witnesses to a street snatch-and-grab. Black hoodie up, legging it down the high street, arm outstretched, a scuffle, and the hand-bag's mine.

'Beggars can't be choosers,' I said through gritted teeth.

'You never know what it might lead to,' said Sue.

Since then, I've played a thief, drumming houses while people sleep, stealing tom and electrical goods. I've played a hospital porter on the ITV series, The Bill. And I've played a dealer. For a crazy moment, I imagined myself in a white shirt and a bow tie with a perfect waistcoat laying out cards across the blue baize of a casino for blackjack and craps games. But when Sue sent me the brief, it wasn't that dealer. Instead, they wanted me to stand outside the casino in the shadows, leaned up against the wall, while men in tuxedos brushed past me, palms touching palms, notes slipping into my hands and cocaine into theirs. I auditioned and got the part. The whole thing felt wrong to me but, as Sue said, you never know what it might lead to.

But now, I'm a solicitor. For me, sitting beside Steve McFadden feels like sitting next to De Niro. *EastEnders* is a soap I watched in Alkham Road, in prison, and gouching on heroin in front of my small portable TV, balanced on a chair in Middleton Road. And now I'm on it. In this small scene, I'm in charge. I'm not the street kid with the torn clothes dragged in for questioning, or the kid made an example of in front of a judge. I'm suited and booted. I speak with authority. I'm in command. And when the episode airs people will stop me on Kingsland High Street.

'Oh my God, Stan! Was that you? We recognised you straight away!'

'Yeah, man!' I will feel like a million dollars. This could be the start of something good, I'll think.

Calls will come in to Sue for my next role. I'll play the part of Alex Joseph on a feature-length *Crimewatch* episode called 'Crimewatch File: A Stolen Life'. Joseph is the Black boyfriend of the mother of nine-year-old Daniel Handley, abducted from a street in East London and never seen again. I'll feature briefly with a speaking role in reconstructed scenes on the night of Daniel's disappearance. In reality, Joseph is wrongly suspected of the crime. The real killers—two white men—won't be convicted until 1996.

'Are there more roles like the solicitor, less derogatory?' I'll ask Sue when we next speak. This world of make-believe is too real for me, and I'm struggling. I'm struggling to play the parts I've been playing all my life. I'm struggling to control my anger. I want to play a proper hero's part, the part of the man with so much potential, the part of someone who's done something good with his life, the part of me that's buried inside. Maybe this dream of mine is just a dream. Yet, my fellow Black actors will endure these roles. They'll play the long game, and in years to come they'll break through and be rewarded for their patience and tolerance and resilience in the face of racism and exclusion. At this moment, it's not a journey I can take. My recovery and my life depend on it.

Chapter 37

Ashes to Ashes

It is June 2000 and I am 29 years old. I am on the southern-most tip of India, in the coastal town of Kanyakumari. It is a little after 5 AM and the sun will rise soon like a ball of fire on the horizon. This is the point where three seas meet: where the Bay of Bengal touches the Arabian Sea and the Indian Ocean, and a place where, if you stay long enough, you can see sunrise and sunset. With me, I have my Canon camera, my CD Walkman and two CDs of Uncle Bob Marley. Mum is with me, too. She's been beside me since London. Already, her ashes have travelled more than 6,000 miles in a plastic container, smuggled through security at Heathrow and Mumbai in my backpack. A risk, but I took it. No more red tape, no more interference from the authorities, no more courts telling me what I could and could not do: just Mum and me.

I've been clean for six years. Whilst I was getting tired of being offered acting parts in the roles I'd been playing all my life, I was doing voluntary work by going into prisons to talk with guys who were struggling with drugs and alcohol. A friend I knew from recovery had become the manager of the drug treatment wing in Pentonville, a prison I had been in myself, and it felt surreal to be on the other side, to be addressed as 'sir' by the officers, and

298

to be given a belt with a chain and keys attached, allowing me to open the internal gates to move from wing to wing to see clients. And when he saw me appear on *EastEnders,* my friend asked me to join him in helping other men turn their lives around. Not long after, I decided to train full time as an addiction counsellor, and got offered a scholarship to become a qualified therapist, which I worked at before embarking on this round-the-world trip.

I've begun back in the place I started when Mum died: Mumbai. And from there I've taken the overnight train south to Kanyakumari. Twenty-seven hours of watching another world pass by.

Wherever I am, as I have done all my life, I seek out a family, if only for a fleeting moment. Among the traffic of chaiwallahs and train vendors selling chapatis and samosas, I found myself surrounded by Indian people who treated me with curiosity. I talked with them as the train trundled from station to station. An endless supply of food appeared from their steel tiffin boxes and they insisted that I eat with them. Outside, a flow of travellers jumped on and off while the train was still in motion, some hauling others up with hands outstretched to save them from being left behind.

I paid extra for a sleeper—a bunk that folded down from the carriage wall so I could sleep in comfort. Yet when my new-found family huddled up on the floor, unfolded their blankets and leaned on each other's shoulders for pillows, I pushed the bed up, closed the latch and squeezed in among them. I couldn't bring myself to lie above while they slept below, simply by virtue of the poverty they'd been born into.

We'd reached Kanyakumari only hours ago in the dead of night. The streets were deathly quiet, but now, as I head towards the sea it's teeming with people of all ages and shapes, colours and sizes. I had imagined I'd be here on my own, taking Mum out into the vast expanse of the ocean, but it's hard to even find a spot on the beach among the hundreds of people preparing to meditate and pray, by brushing their teeth, washing their bodies, and squatting to relive themselves before the sun comes up. This is a holy place: a spiritual mecca to salvation. I look up into the open sky, smile and chuckle to myself. Maybe the reality is better than my dream. It's beautiful. This wide and vast universe with its power greater than us, is busy carrying out humble duties for all of mankind.

Among the crowd, I've found the perfect place to make a small mountain from the sand and I perch my camera on it. I want to record this moment for Angie and Mini and Huggy. Soon, I will sit cross-legged and watch a new day break. I'll press play on my Walkman and smile as Uncle Bob Marley drifts out. Then, I'll wade out into the warm ocean. And, when I release Mum to the breeze, I'll watch mesmerised as the specs of dust dance on the surface of the waves until they disappear from view.

You go travel, you hear me. You're free now Mummy.

See you on the other side.

Epilogue

After leaving acting frustrated by the lack of positive roles for Black actors, I returned to the stage. At age 38, I was accepted to study classical acting at the prestigious Mountview Academy, then based in Wood Green. At my audition, I recited Edmund's speech from Shakespeare's *King Lear*:

'Thou, Nature, art my goddess; to thy law
My services are bound. Wherefore should I
Stand in the plague of custom, and permit
The curiosity of nations to deprive me?
For that I am some twelve or fourteen moonshines
Lag of a brother? Why bastard? Wherefore base?
When my dimensions are as well compact,
My mind as generous, and my shape as true
As honest madam's issue? Why brand they us
With base? With baseness, bastardy? Base, base?'

I won the only male scholarship for that year. When I asked the tutors why they picked me, they said I had a natural aptitude for Shakespeare and will make a great Shakespearean actor. I had no affiliation with Shakespeare growing up whatsoever and didn't take this comment seriously at the time.

Since then, I have appeared in various Shakespeare productions as well as in films, TV and contemporary theatre. I'm not a star, or a celebrity, but I get by doing what I enjoy and what I believe I was born to do, and I nurture this gift bestowed on me.

At the time of writing this memoir, I am 28 years clean of drugs and alcohol and still engage in the odd therapy session from time to time, when I feel the need. I have found the therapeutic way of life a great tool to champion the mind and nourish the soul. I see it as a gym for my mental health and well-being that keeps me honest. It can be easy to get lost in this world full of complications and complexities, but it's a relief to know there is a safe place I am able to access to get back to basics. Although it can be challenging and difficult to face oneself at times, it requires a different kind of courage; the rewards are far greater than the sacrifices. I continue to practise the 12 Steps I learned at Narcotics Anonymous and I continue to be a productive member of society.

Through my recovery process, I have been fortunate to have lived a life far beyond my wildest dreams; I have backpacked around the world, over four years, which is another book in itself! I have taught myself how to play the guitar and have performed at various gigs and have written and recorded an album of my own songs which are circling around on the big wide web. I have enrolled at the City Lit college, a centre for adult education, and re-sat all the GCSE exams that I missed after leaving school with no qualifications. I have been honoured to have saved the life of my close friend Tom, who suffered a cardiac arrest one evening at the age of 29, by administering CPR and keeping him alive until the paramedics arrived with the correct equipment. A call I had never thought I would ever have to answer. The surgeon told his parents that had it not been for what his friend did in the spur of the moment, their son would have died. To be held up in the eyes of his loved ones and seen as a true hero, I found myself shying away, not wanting the role of the rescuer or the hero child anymore. Yet, at the same time, in a strange way, there is an element of me that feels as if I had been placed in that situation to redress the balance for some of the bad karma and the hurt I've caused others, by giving him back his life. And then being invited as a guest on the BBC Breakfast morning news to share our story.

I have been privileged to have worked at a primary school in Hackney, as a family support worker, after witnessing knife-crime rates sky-rocket amongst young inner city teenagers and wanting to do something about it. I thought I could maybe have an influence in their lives, and worked with behavioural kids who were on the same path of self-destruction as I was by using my own life experiences to help them and their families navigate some of the pitfalls that lay ahead. Like starfish washed up on the sand, not all of them can be saved, but for the ones I could put back in the sea, hopefully I have made some small difference and given them a chance for survival.

And to write this memoir and share my story, in the hope of helping others who are on their own journeys of self-discovery and recovery, whatever shape or form this takes. That by reading this, I can be of some service, to move, touch, and inspire the humility of change that is within us all, regardless of what adversities we have faced in our lives.

I wish I had a fairy tale ending I could share with you: the wife, the four kids, the house with the white picket fence, the Volvo, the rocking chair and the family pet Labrador, but this is real life and shit happens. As Uncle Bob Marley said: 'When it rains, everybody's roof top gets wet.' So I try to remind myself I am not alone. You are not alone.

There is another quote that rings true for me. It's by the Greek philosopher Aristotle: 'Give me a child until he is seven and I will show you the man.' My siblings and I have all suffered from our early childhood trauma, and we are all coping with the impact it has had on our adult life; we are dealing with this in our own ways. We give each other support by just being there for one another, more so in our older years.

Although I have decades in recovery, I am not completely out of the woods just yet, and that's fair. There are days when I still must make peace with my past and there are days when I am still learning how to accept myself for whom I am, and not who I used to be, and that's fair. It's fair that there are days when I battle with depression, anger, fear and anxiety from the wreckage of my early years, when I fall short and my shortcomings get the better of me, and that's fair. And then there are days when I have to pinch myself, when I feel humbled by life and have an attitude of gratitude, surrendering to the moment as if my past never existed, bathing in an abundance of self-love, and parenting little Stanley. When I feel like the luckiest man alive, and that's fair. I try to take my life one day at a time. It takes time to heal, and I am still healing, and that's fair.

My son Malakai, born in 2013, has had the most impact on my life. Sometimes when I look into his eyes, or when he playfully ambushes me and says, 'My papa', loud and proud, I can't help but well-up inside and have to turn my face to hide the tears of love. I've always desired to be a father, yet, at the same time, I have also feared what that would be like and how I would cope with this huge responsibility that I am all too aware of. Being a father to him is the biggest role I will ever play. The unconditional love between us makes me more determined to be the father that I never had: a role model and his hero. Sometimes, I envy his child-like spirit when I think of who I was forced to be at his age. Like most parents, I can struggle at times to find the balance of healthy parenting, trying not be too firm, yet not being too soft, either.

Coming from a place where I had to raise myself without the love and support I craved, and without having had parents to guide me, I have no blueprint to turn to, so I improvise. I watch and observe, and try to learn from others, giving my son everything that I would have wanted as a child: love, support, time, and lots and lots of hugs. I have endured and survived as a soldier so that he can live a life safe and free from fear. Most of all, I see my mother in his face and her character in his soul: the happy-go-lucky, funny, and imaginative person she always was but never had the chance to be:

'Joy' in every sense of the word.

Acknowledgments

A special thanks to a special person, my editor and chief, the amazing, wonderful, Valerie Brandes for believing in me and giving me this platform to share my story. A massive thank you to the entire team at Jacaranda books for all their hard work and due diligence. I am forever grateful.

To my close friends who have become my family and have been there for me through thick and thin; Adam, a brother from another mother and his wife Liv, the marathon conversations over the phone betwcen us bro just never end! My beautiful Brazilian family, Venancio and Carolina, you held me up many a time when I could not hold myself, thank you. My lovely vegan family, Jo, Mahaliaha, and Dayan, my dear friend Karine, a sister from another mister, we have both come a mighty long way, it has been priceless to share this journey with you. And my old primary school friend from way back in the dayz, Fela, thank you for having my back. I am humbled by you all for your continued support and encouragement in writing this memoir.

A very special acknowledgement to my friends and old neighbours Karen and Tim, although Karen is no longer with us, I have not forgotten you. Thank you both for those early days of reading my first draft, marking my work with your suggestions and comments, I still have it! You gave me hope that I could write this book and share my story.

And to all those friends who have been with me on my journey in one form or another over the years, including my Scottish friends up in Inverness, there is far too many to name, you know who you are. I thank you for your friendships and for being there for me.

Above all else, a huge thank you to my beloved siblings Angela, Minerva and Hogarth. Thank you for your input and being there for me throughout this process, words are not enough to express my love and gratitude. I couldn't have written this memoir without your love and support. My story is your story. This is our story. Against all the odds we survived and lived to tell the tale. Mum would be proud of who her children and her grandchildren have become.

'Fall down seven times, get up eight.'
Denzel Washington, Acceptance Speech at the 48th NAACP Image Awards

'It's a funny old life.'
Stanley J. Browne

About the Author

Stanley James Browne was born in Hackney, East London, UK in 1970 and is of Jamaican and Antiguan parentage. He is the second child of four and grew up in the care system from the age of five. He is an artist, singer-songwriter and an award-winning actor. He trained at the Anna Scher Theatre School in North London and was awarded the sole scholarship for men at the Mountview Acting Academy in classical theatre. Throughout his career, he has appeared in both television and film, and has performed at venues such as the Globe Theatre, the National Theatre Studios and the Edinburgh Fringe Festival. His notable stage performances include, *Titus Andronicus* (2013), *Chigger Foot Boys* (2017), *Romeo and Juliet* (2019), and *One Under* (2019). He won the best actor in a lead role award for his work in *Bethlehem Lights* (2017) and garnered rave reviews for his performance of Shakespeare's *Othello* (2011). *Little Big Man* is his first book.